Philosophy and Psychoanalysis

PHILOSOPHICAL TOPICS

PAUL EDWARDS, GENERAL EDITOR

Philosophy
and
Psychoanalysis

Edited, with an Introduction and Bibliography by

BRIAN A. FARRELL

CORPUS CHRISTI COLLEGE,
OXFORD UNIVERSITY

Macmillan College Publishing Company
New York
Maxwell Macmillan Canada
Toronto
Maxwell Macmillan International
New York Oxford Singapore Sydney

Editor: Maggie Barbieri
Production Supervisor: Bert Yaeger
Production Manager: Nicholas Sklitsis
Text Designer: Angela Foote
Cover Designer: Angela Foote

This book was set in Caledonia by Compset, Inc.
and was printed and bound by Arcata Graphics-Fairfield.
The cover was printed by New England Book Components.

Macmillan College Publishing Company
866 Third Avenue, New York, New York 10022

Macmillan College Publishing Company is part of
the Maxwell Communication Group of Companies.

Maxwell Macmillan Canada, Inc.
1200 Eglinton Avenue East
Suite 200
Don Mills, Ontario M3C 3N1

Library of Congress Cataloging-in-Publication Data
Philosophy and psychoanalysis / edited, with an introduction and
  bibliography, by Brian A. Farrell.
    p.   cm. — (Philosophical topics)
  Includes bibliographical references.
  ISBN 0-02-336361-4 (pbk.)
  1. Psychoanalysis and philosophy.   2. Psychoanalysis —Philosophy.
  I. Farrell, B.A. (Brian Anthony)   II. Series: Philosophical topics
  (New York, N.Y.)
  BF175.4.P45P485   1994
  150.19′5—dc20   93-27223
                                                  CIP

Printing: 1   2   3   4   5   6   7   Year: 4   5   6   7   8   9   0

ACKNOWLEDGMENTS

My chief debt in preparing this volume has been to the series editor, Paul Edwards. I have benefited greatly from the stream of critical and constructive comments which flew across the Atlantic to guide and help me.

I have also been helped by Donald Levy and the late Eveline Farrell as well as by Ewen Bowie and Christopher Taylor on a small matter about Freud's use of Greek.

CONTENTS

INTRODUCTION

I

The word 'psychoanalysis' is generally used to refer to the family of psychol-
ogies and therapies which have their origin in the work of Sigmund Freud,
and which fall within the tradition that centers around this work.

It is a commonplace to say that psychoanalysis has been the center of great
interest and controversy throughout the twentieth century and has generated
all manner of problems. One large group of these are philosophical in character. For example, can Freud's theory be established? If the Unconscious is a
part of our minds, what sort of part is it? Is psychoanalysis compatible with
our conviction that we are free agents? The chief purpose of this book is to introduce the reader to some of these problems and to the attempts by some
philosophers to deal with them.

It is important to note that the book is an introduction. It does not dive into
the minutiae of the text of Freud's writings; nor into the theoretical niceties
that some philosophers delight in exploring; and it barely touches the surface
of empirical studies in this large field. In short, it does not take the reader at
all deeply into the technicalities of this wide-ranging subject. What the contributions from philosophers in this volume do is to clarify the nature of the
conceptual problems to which psychoanalysis gives rise. It is important, however, to note that what our contributors themselves say (as well as what I myself say in this introduction) is also open to criticism and is far from being the
last word on any topic. For one thing, we are apt to disagree among ourselves
about the nature of psychoanalysis. This helps to explain why it is that this
subject is so interesting and challenging to philosophers and why it has been a

center of controversy during this century. The contributors in this book take the reader through some first and, I think, essential steps towards a grasp of the conceptual issues in this field.

II

The book starts with an early paper by Freud himself: "A Note on the Unconscious in Psycho-analysis" (1912, *Standard Edition* (from now on abbreviated as *S.E.*), Vol. XII). This paper was written in English, at the request of the Society for Psychical Research for a symposium on what was a troublesome topic at the time—namely, multiple personality, and related states of consciousness. The symposium was published in a special Medical Supplement of the *Proceedings of the Society* (Part lxvi, Vol. XXVI, 1912). In this brief paper, Freud introduces some of his central notions. These include unconscious conceptions, the unconscious, preconscious ideas, dynamic and therefore active unconscious ideas, unconscious tendencies present since childhood, repression, resistance, latent and manifest thoughts in dreams, and indirect cogent proofs of the presence of an unconscious idea.

What Freud was particularly concerned to establish in this essay was that his notion of an unconscious conception was a legitimate one. It is plainly not the case that my conception of, say, Oxford is in my consciousness all the time. Yet, Freud maintains, we cannot say that, when I am not actually thinking of Oxford, the conception ceases to exist as a psychological object, and only exists "as a physical disposition for the recurrence" in my mind of the same thought, namely of Oxford. We cannot say this because to do so is to identify, in a way which begs the question, the mental life of a person with his conscious life, and to deny to "psychology the right to account for its most common facts, such as memory, by its own means." In other words, Freud claims that he is justified in postulating the existence of unconscious states and processes which are psychological in nature, so as to order and explain the psychological phenomena which he draws to our attention—phenomena such as post-hypnotic suggestion and those exhibited by patients with neurotic problems.

Now, though Freud introduces us here with commendable clarity to the central notions of psychoanalysis, the case he makes out for them is not particularly persuasive, if only because he does not show us how they actually work. The obvious way to do this is to put these notions to work to describe and explain a particular case, say, some patient of his. But it is difficult for him to do this in the space of a very brief paper. What he does is merely to assert that "the mind of the hysterical patient is full of active yet unconscious ideas; all her symptoms proceed from them." Thus, the hysterical woman who vomits "may do so from the idea of being pregnant." I shall now try to unpack and explain these cryptic remarks by looking into an actual example of a very well-known sort of case to which Freud is referring. I shall choose an example from my own clinical experience, and one which, in contrast to that of the woman who vomits, is easier for our introductory purposes. I shall also rely on what Freud says about this sort of case elsewhere, especially in his paper on "Repression" (1915, *S.E.* XIV), and in *Inhibitions, Symptoms and Anxiety* (1926, *S.E.* XX).

Consider Mrs. K., a woman in her late twenties, slim, of medium height, good-looking, and recently married to a professional man, who was described by the psychiatrist in charge as a large, bull-like sort of person. Mrs. K. was referred from the dermatology clinic of the local hospital, to which her doctor had sent her, on account of painful inflammation and swelling around the inner thighs, vulva area, and buttocks. Otherwise she was quite healthy, and at the case conference presented a well-groomed appearance and a bland, slightly amused, unruffled impression.

Given this information about Mrs. K., Freud could apply his account to her as follows. It is likely that she has a certain unconscious conception, which is the chief active idea at work in her, namely, a wish to avoid sexual intercourse with her husband. But this conception is repressed and excluded from Mrs. K.'s conscious life by a barrier, which keeps it apart from the latter. The reason for this is—to use Freud's explanation, which he has elaborated elsewhere—that sexual intercourse, and the prospect of it, arouses anxiety which she cannot tolerate. This is due, in turn, to the fact that she suffered some upsetting, traumatic sexual experience in her early years, which was repressed and which left her with unconscious tendencies connected with this experience. Sexual intercourse with her husband now threatens to revive the anxiety of this early experience. She copes with the threat by completely excluding all anxiety about it from consciousness. Hence her bland and unfussed appearance—well known as *la belle indifférence* of the hysteric. But the repressed emotion returns, and comes out in a disguised and distorted form. It is "converted" into bodily form as an inflammation of the skin. This inflammation occurs on parts of the body which give Mrs. K. a further, or "secondary," gain. It gives her an acceptable reason for refusing to have sexual intercourse with her husband, which is what she unconsciously wishes to avoid.

This account of Mrs. K. diagnoses her condition as that of conversion hysteria; and Freud would have claimed that it is open to "indirect proofs of a most cogent kind." He would have been confident that, if Mrs. K. were to be given psychoanalytic treatment, these proofs would be forthcoming in the course of it. And he claims, in effect, that the same is true, not only of conversion hysteria, but also of neurotic phenomena as a whole.

III

On any showing, this is an extraordinary story and set of claims. It is no wonder that they have aroused such widespread, fundamental, and persistent criticism.

Perhaps the most fundamental criticism comes from Jean-Paul Sartre. The gist of this is to be found in Selection 2—"Bad Faith." Sartre argues that

Freud's notion of the unconscious is simply incoherent, and cannot therefore be used to explain Mrs. K.'s difficulties or those of anyone else. Its fundamental incoherence is this. In order for Mrs. K.'s wish (to avoid sexual intercourse) to be repressed and so be unconscious, it is necessary for the barrier, or censor, to know what it is repressing. It has to be aware of what it is doing. This means that the barrier, or censor, must itself be conscious of the wish that is to be repressed, and of its own activity as a barrier or censor, in order to make the wish unconscious. Likewise, it must be conscious of the disguised form in which the wish reveals itself, namely Mrs. K.'s inflammation of the skin. The same objection arises about the resistance which Mrs. K. may show in an exploration of her problem. But Mrs. K.'s self cannot be split into two. Hence she must first be conscious of the wish, in order to make it unconscious. Hence Freud's account is incoherent. It does not, and cannot, explain what has happened in the past and what is happening now.

Sartre offers a very different explanation. Mrs. K. is lying to herself. She is in the state he refers to as "bad faith," and is the victim of her own self-deception. Mrs. K. intentionally sets about escaping her husband's sexual attentions and hits upon her symptoms as a way of doing so. Her whole illness is a project on her part; and, in what Sartre calls "existential psychoanalysis," Mrs. K. can make known to herself the choice which makes her what she is, and which proves to herself that sexual intercourse is painful and something to be avoided (see *Being and Nothingness*, Part Four, chapter 2).

I do not think that Sartre's fundamental criticism of Freud holds much water. It is clear, no doubt, that Freud does not explain, in a generally acceptable way, how repression works. He never comes to grips with the details of its operation; Sartre's criticism is of value in drawing our attention to this. But from this defect in Freud's account, it does not follow that the account is incoherent and should be jettisoned in toto. Sartre only makes it appear to follow that it is incoherent and absurd, because he uses the ordinary concepts of, in particular, self and consciousness to describe what Freud is speaking about; and because he assumes that no other way of speaking about it is possible. This is a mistake. It is quite open to us to speak about Mrs. K., and to explain repression, in other ways—ways which will allow us to try to make good the defect in Freud's own account of repression. Sartre seems to be a prisoner here of his own Cartesian-derived psychology.

Let us bear in mind that large aspects of our mental functioning take place without our being conscious or aware of what has been, and is, going on. For instance, when I notice an apple lying on the table in front of me, I have only the very minimal awareness of what my embodied mind, or psychological system, or whatever we call it, has done to enable me to arrive at this cognitive achievement—noticing an apple on the table in front of me. Likewise, when I understand your remark, "I am afraid it is going to rain very soon." Now, if this can be true in the large and important fields of visual perception, auditory perception, and language comprehension, why can it not also be true in the field of our conative and sexual behavior? Is it logically absurd to suggest—as

Sartre would have us believe—that because of past experience as a child, Mrs. K.'s psychological system is now sensitized to avoid sexual approaches and to take defensive evasion from them, without Mrs. K. being aware of what has happened and is happening to herself? This suggestion may or may not be true. But it cannot be dismissed as incoherent, as Sartre does, just because Cartesian psychology disallows us from speaking in this way. On the contrary, we have some very *hard* evidence that an account of Freud's sort may indeed be true. For example, it has been shown experimentally under strictly controlled conditions that a person can take defensive action to avoid seeing sexually disturbing words, without having the slightest idea that this is what he is doing, and of what is really going on in the laboratory.[1]

So Sartre's argument fails to demolish Freud's account. Still, it is of value in that it points to an important defect in the account: It fails to describe how repression works. Sartre's argument is also of value in another important way. His own positive view of the matter centers around people whom it is natural to describe as victims of self-deception, and for such people his account has some force. But it is very doubtful whether his account can be applied to the usual run of seriously disordered cases. It is with these cases, however, that Freud was primarily concerned, and at which his own story was directed. Sartre's argument forces us to ask the essential question: "Can Freud's account be applied to cover the everyday cases of self-deception?" If we adopt Freud's stand as expressed in Selection 1, we seem to have to say that a conception is either conscious or it is not; there is no gray or shady area here. On this stand, the answer to our question seems to be: "No, Freud's account cannot be applied to cover the ordinary cases of self-deception." But if we reject this stand, and accept that in the gray area a conception may be conscious in some way or to some greater or lesser degree, then we may be able to extend Freud's story to cover self-deception. But even then, it looks very much as though we would have to go beyond Freud's own story and rely on later developments in psychoanalytic theory to do this job. All this takes us away into very technical matters; and it is doubtful whether analysts have managed even today to deal with the problem Sartre has forced upon our attention.

IV

Whereas Sartre argued that Freud's account is incoherent, philosophers and others who have been influenced by the tradition of analytic philosophy have argued that Freud's account is vacuous. Miles outlines a case for this view of Freud in Selection 3.

It is quite misleading to suppose, Miles argues, that the expression "the unconscious" refers to anything real at all. What it refers to is unobservable in principle; and the only evidence we can find for its existence is the very conduct and so on of people and patients that the notion of the unconscious is introduced to explain. If, therefore, we postulate the unconscious, we cannot deduce any observable consequences by the aid of this postulate which will give us independent grounds to support it. According to Miles, when Freud uses the concept, what he is really concerned to refer to are items such as un-conscious wishes, purposes, and so on. But now he is referring to conduct which is evidence of a person having a wish, a purpose, and so on, *except* that the person is unable to grasp and so acknowledge that he has this wish or pur-pose. When Freud emphasizes the important role of past experience—of, for example, "unconscious tendencies present since childhood"—what he is say-ing is that, when a person has certain experiences in childhood, she is liable to have certain adult tendencies with related wishes and purposes, which she is unable to grasp and acknowledge, in the present.

When, therefore, we explain Mrs. K.'s difficulties in Freud's way, we are saying, according to Miles, that she had certain early experiences as a child; and that these set up certain dispositions such that she is now disposed strongly to avoid sexual intercourse with her husband. This disposition mani-fests itself in the related, unacknowledgeable, and verbally inexpressible wish to avoid sexual intercourse. This wish has been repressed, that is, she is un-able to acknowledge it because it is painful or upsetting (see T. R. Miles, *Eliminating the Unconscious* [1966],—our Selection 3). Apparently, the only way in which she can express her wish is through her body. She develops a skin disorder which reveals that she wants to avoid sexual intercourse and which, at the same time, helps her to satisfy her wish.

I think Miles's objection has force and importance. He emphasizes, quite rightly, that he is not criticizing anything that Freud, or any other analyst, ac-tually does. He is objecting solely to the way in which Freud describes and accounts for what he does. Likewise for psychoanalytic discourse in general. On the other hand, this objection from Miles does present to psychoanalysts an important and disturbing challenge, which can be put in the following way: Most analysts are apt to believe that their wide-ranging, grand-sounding, the-oretical talk is really as informative and illuminating as it seems, and that they could not live and work without it. On Miles's challenge this belief is false. In their dealings with patients they can get along without it, and can use ordi-nary common speech instead, which is what they do for the most part anyway. In short, their theoretical talk can be eliminated without loss. This can be done, because the account Freud gives us in Selection 1 and elsewhere in his writings makes use of a theory which does not logically generate any ob-servable consequences, by reference to which its truth, or adequacy, can be judged. If Freud's theory *were* confirmable in this way, and some of its prop-ositions were actually confirmed on inquiry, we would then have a good rea-son to accept them. But nothing of the sort holds for Freud's theory. Moreover, according to Miles, analysts *ought* to dispense with Freud's theo-retical talk. For it just confuses them, and everyone else, into inflating the sta-tus and claims of psychoanalysis, and imagining that, by means of it, Freud has told us something much more important about human functioning than he really has.

Miles's objection is arresting, but I do not think it is conclusive. Even if he is right in asserting that the notion of the unconscious, and Freud's related theory, can be eliminated without loss in the way he points out, it does not follow that it can be eliminated without any loss at all. For it should be plain that Miles's argument applies to a fairly advanced stage of empirical and scientific inquiry, when we are already either in possession of competing theories with deducible empirical consequences, or in a position to develop theories of this sort. It is then reasonable to demand that a proposed theory should have such empirical consequences, and reasonable to dispense with it if it has none. But during the early groping, bumbling, foggy stages of empirical and scientific inquiry, it may be very useful and advisable to develop theories from which no confirmable consequences can be deduced. These can then serve to describe, order, and crudely explain to some degree or in some way the observable material of the field under study. In so doing, theories keep their inquirers oriented, and may be of service as heuristic guides. Now Freud's account is plainly one of this type. So also, for example, is the story offered by Lucretius about the constituents of matter in Books I and II of *De Rerum Natura*; and so are the views of atomists in the seventeenth and eighteenth centuries. It is plainly inappropriate to make Miles-like demands of Freud's theory, and then dismiss it because it fails to satisfy them.

Furthermore, the objection from Miles omits to recognize an important merit in Freud's account, a merit which inclines us to use it in spite of its limitations. If we suppose that Mrs. K. has a unconscious wish to avoid sexual intercourse with her husband, in what sense does she "have" it? In Miles's view, only in the sense that *when* her husband approached her sexually, she came to react with an aversive skin response; that *if* she were to be asked whether she wished to avoid intercourse, she would reject the idea with bland firmness, and so on. But all this tells us nothing about the sense in which Mrs. K. has the wish now, and has had it for some time. Nor does Miles's account tell us how supposed traumatic incidents in her past bridge the years to dispose her to wish to avoid sexual intercourse in the present. In short, it tells us nothing about what it is in virtue of which she is now disposed to behave as she does. It is evident, in other words, that his account is built around hypothetical statements about Mrs. K.; and these fail to unpack what we are saying is actually the case now about her. In contrast, Freud's account does try to fill in the categorical import of his claim about patients with unconscious wishes, and the like. This is a merit in his account that moves us to use it.

With hindsight, it is clear that Freud anticipated a practice very familiar to contemporary psychologists. He gave us a theory in a form which suggested a certain model of our psychological functioning. But he did not spell out any connections between the psychological elements of his model, on the one hand, and the neuro- cum physiological constituents and components of the body and nervous system on the other. In short, he suggested a model which is uninterpreted neurophysiologically. He contended, in effect, that he was quite entitled to do so; and this is a contention that would be widely accepted by contemporary psychologists.

V

Though Freud did not try to relate his psychological theory to neuro-anatomy and physiology in any work published during his lifetime, it is well known that he did try to do this very thing in a work written in 1895 and published posthumously as *Project for a Scientific Psychology*.[2] "The intention," Freud tells us in the first sentence, "is to furnish a psychology that shall be a natural science: that is, to represent psychological processes as quantitatively determinate states of specifiable material particles, thus making those processes perspicuous and free from contradiction." What Freud went on to do was to use the available knowledge at the time of neuroanatomy and physiology to describe how the ways in which the human body worked neurophysiologically enabled us to function in the ways set out in his own psychoanalytic psychology. In other words, he tried to show how neurophysiology could form the 'organic foundation' of the psychology of psychoanalysis, and thereby 'subserve' it, to use our contemporary word.

It is widely accepted that the *Project* is a remarkable piece of theory construction. It is not only worked out with great power and precision; it also anticipates in some striking ways later developments and thought in research on the brain. However, it is manifestly an exercise in speculation which ran far beyond the then-current knowledge in neurophysiology, and was not open to confirmation or disconfirmation at the time. Freud very quickly lost interest in it. This was quite understandable, since it was of no real help to him in ordering and understanding the clinical material—in all its richness and complexity—with which he was actually concerned.

Since the 1890s there has been a quite prodigious growth in our knowledge of the nervous system as a whole, and especially in our knowledge of the brain and brain function. Our knowledge has grown in ways that have far transcended the imagination of the 1890s, and by means of techniques of investigation which could not be anticipated at that time. This great progress raises a natural question. If we were to try today to realize Freud's aim in the *Project*, either for the whole or some important part of his theory, would we be more successful than he was in the 1890s?

I fear the answer is no, that our efforts in this direction are unlikely to be any more successful than Freud's. The reason is not difficult to find. In spite of the prodigious and continuing advances in our knowledge of brain function, we are still very ignorant indeed about the fundamentals that are relevant to the central themes of psychoanalytic psychology. Thus we are only just beginning to understand the mechanism in certain animals that subserves what appears to be a simple form of learning, namely Pavlovian conditioning. We are only just beginning to understand how the neural networks do this job for long-term memory in humans. In spite of the immense amount we know about the organic basis of visual perception, we still have a very incomplete idea about how the brain functions so as to enable me to see a tennis ball in front of me, rather than an orange. All this means that we cannot begin to say what goes to serve anything as complex as the experience of the infant and child. Even if we assume that the central concept of psychoanalysis, namely repression, is a valid one and is subserved by the interplay of certain excitatory and inhibitory synapses, we have no idea how it is subserved by them and in what networks. Nor do we know how the brain subserves conscious functioning in general, or the psychic homeostasis which was so important for Freud.

If, therefore, we try to connect psychoanalysis with present-day knowledge of brain states and processes, we will not be able to say much of value for psychoanalysis or for the brain sciences. The reason for this is that the two subjects barely touch each other, if they can be said to touch each other at all. When we consider the central core of psychoanalytic theory, it seems clear that our current knowledge in neurophysiology does not conflict with this theory. What is more, it is difficult to find any place where it is evident that our current knowledge *can* conflict with psychoanalytic theory.[3] But, if it cannot conflict with, and therefore, upset, psychoanalytic theory, then it cannot support the theory either. No doubt we can quite easily try to bring the two subjects together by constructing pictures of the brain showing pathways of neural connections between different parts of it—pathways and related processes which, we can claim, subserve the psychological activity described in psychoanalytic theory. But such pictures make us take flight into a world of vague speculation, which is at present beyond the bounds of fruitful empirical inquiry. If, therefore, we try in this way to connect neurophysiology and psychoanalysis, we will hardly do much better than Freud himself in the 1890s. I think we may still have to wait some time before we are able to determine what neurophysiological states and processes subserve the unconscious states and processes which are central to psychoanalytic theory. Furthermore, we may have to wait even longer before our neurophysiological knowledge and techniques will enable us to examine a patient such as Mrs. K., and to determine—independently of her conduct—whether or not she has an unconscious wish to avoid sexual intercourse with her husband.

VI

The last section helps to explain why Miles's objection to Freud's account is unpersuasive. However, Freud's theory and model have a further feature which works the other way, and continues to make Miles's criticism valuable. It is all too obvious that Freud has given us a poorly developed model. In his other and later writings, he improves on it, but not by very much. Because of this, the skeptical outsider and the hard-headed psychologist and biologist are liable to suggest that, if psychoanalysts cannot do any better theorizing and modeling than this, then they had better not try at all! It is this feeble character of Freud's model which also serves to attract us to a hypothetical view of the unconscious, and to its elimination as a real entity.

But, of course, the analyst *can* do better than this, and thereby reduce the temptation to throw Freud's account into the dustbin. He can go to the psychologist for help. For the fact of the matter is that in recent decades some theoretical psychologists have produced better models of the core of psychoanalytic theory than Freud did. In Selection 4 Erdelyi outlines and discusses two such models. The one is that produced by Dollard and Miller, under the overall inspiration of Clark Hull (at Yale) and the learning theories he developed. It is a powerful model. For it is close to the observable data of experimental work; it uses a limited set of concepts to order and explain a considerable range of phenomena; and it thereby shows how it is possible to bring analytic notions inside a scientifically controllable theory of learning and behavior. (See figure 4.1, p. 34.) But this model has very serious limitations, some of which Erdelyi points out; and he then goes on to set out a very different type of model—one constructed by the use of the fashionable concepts of information processing. As Erdelyi presents it, it is an application of a development in mathematics which has been extensively used in psychology under the name of Signal Detection Theory. With the aid of this theory he constructs a flow diagram to exhibit Freud's account of repression. (See figure 4.2, p. 39.) It should be clear that his model, just like the one by Dollard and Miller, is far from being the whole story either. A human being is not just like a flowchart of a computer. He or she is a near-holistic system with a very subtle, continuing, interrelated play of constituents—a feature to which Erdelyi does, in effect, draw our attention. The model also underemphasizes the past history of the individual and his acquired dispositions, merely putting these in the boxes of long-term memory; contrary to what the model suggests the items to which a person reacts are not all perceptual inputs in any ordinary sense; to speak of 'signals' and 'information' is to use metaphors, which need to be unpacked to avoid possible confusion; and the place of language function in all this is left almost entirely blank.

Still, however thin the model may be, it serves to bring out how wide of the mark is Sartre's main objection to Freud (that he is incoherent). It also brings out, as does the model from Dollard and Miller, that Freud's account may be defective in emphasizing the divide between what is unconscious and what is not, since both models make the distinction a shady one of degree. It also seems clear, and this is implicit in Erdelyi's discussion, that what we should work towards are better and more comprehensive models than those we have at present. Indeed, it seems reasonable to suggest that we shall need the contributions from all the respectable models we can think of before we arrive at a reasonably adequate account of human functioning. This will obviously be one which incorporates what has been found by scientific inquiry to be veridical in the theories that Freud and other analysts have given us.

However, though the two models Erdelyi discusses are better than Freud's in the ways indicated, they suffer from some further important limitations:

1. They still do not appear to help us to derive empirical, and hence testable, consequences. In this regard, therefore, they both fail to meet Miles's challenge. In this regard, also, they do differ from the typical model suggested by experimental psychologists, which is testable. When confronted in their work by an untestable one, they do not give it much weight, and are apt to regard it as merely propaedeutic, and of possible, but unproven, heuristic value. It is plain that, if psychologists wish to meet Miles's challenge, what they must do is to extract from Freud's theory a respectable psychological model, from which testable consequences can be derived, and which, therefore, is open to empirical confirmation and disconfirmation. This is not an easy task, given the largely holistic character of Freud's theory—that is to say, one in which our various psychological functions (of cognition, conation, and affection) are so interlocking that it is difficult to abstract any one function for testing, and hence difficult to test the theory at all.

2. It is obvious that the two models do little to fill in the categorical import of what Freud is saying i his account of Mrs. K. When we say that, for example, Mrs. K. is an unconscious wish to avoid sexual intercourse, the two models tell us little about the state of Mrs. K.'s personality or mind, or psychic system, or whatever we call it, which we are referring to in the expression "have an unconscious wish." It seems plausible to suggest that what we need, in order to help Freud, is a model of a psychologically homeostatic control system that contains a particular internal state, which helps to give rise causally to a certain pattern of conduct. This pattern has to be such as to provide us with grounds for asserting that Mrs. K. has an unconscious wish to avoid sexual intercourse. To date, psychologists have not come up with a model of this internal state, or of any others of the same sort.

3. Miles objects to Freud's theory on the grounds that it commits us to a dualist view of body and mind. I think that many people, including doctors and scientific workers of all sorts, will be inclined to agree with Miles about this. Now Freud may or may not have accepted dualism.[4] But the sad fact is that, if a theory does commit us logically to dualism, then it plunges us into a morass of further difficulties. The case of Mrs. K. exhibits the most important of these. How can Mrs. K.'s psychological state—having an unconscious wish to avoid sexual intercourse—possibly produce her skin rash? How, in Freud's language, ca the psychic energy of the mental state (the unconscious wish) be converted" into the bodily symptoms? What possible sort of mysterious causal relation can this be?

This is hardly the place to try to resolve the problems which dualism produces. All I can do is to point to considerations which go to show that (a) Freud's theory does *not* entail dualism, but is philosophically neutral between various views of the body–mind relation; and (b) though the causation of Mrs. K.'s skin rash is quite unknown, there is nothing inherently mysterious about it.

Let me draw attention to a presupposition which is very widely accepted in the scientific world of neuroanatomy, physiology, and brain research. Any psychological state and process is subserved by some state and process in the person's neurophysiological machinery and activity (for short, an NP state and process, or just an NP). That is to say, crudely and vaguely, the occurrence of an NP is, in fact, a necessary condition at a "lower level" for the occurrence of a psychological state and process at a "higher level." Hence, when Mrs. K. entertains a wish at some time, this psychological occurrence is subserved by some NP at a lower level. If Mrs. K.'s past experience as a child with erotic tension and excitement has led to anxiety that now produces a wish, as an adult, to avoid sexual excitement and intercourse, then again this whole psychological history is subserved by NP states in long-term memory. If we accept a Freudian account of Mrs. K., namely, that acknowledging this wish would produce more distress than she can bear, then the wish is an unconscious one. Again, this latter psychological state, involving the unconscious wish, is subserved at a lower level by some NP state. Now there is nothing mysterious in supposing that this NP state can give rise at its *own* level to other bodily states, such as skin inflammation around the parts of the body the sexual use of which has become aversive. Of course, we have no idea yet of the way in which the causal change operates at this level to produce this bodily outcome. But if Mrs. K. comes to acknowledge the unconscious wish, then this acknowledgment is a psychological and specifically cognitive achievement, which is also subserved by some further NP state—just as are all the cognitive achievements involved in our utterances and stream of thought.

It is very unfortunate that Freud was in a conceptual muddle when he came to describe and account for cases of Mrs. K.'s sort. For he imagined that her psychic energy has to be converted somehow into the somatic form of the skin rash. Hence he saddled psychiatry with the category-confusing, diagnostic box of "conversion hysteria."[5] It may be right to maintain that Mrs. K.'s unacknowledged anxieties, as well as her felt anxieties, if any, can contribute to producing her skin disorder. But if they do, then they do so via the NP which subserves her anxieties. We are not obliged to speak of "converting" psychic energy into bodily forms.

Next, we must remember that Freud's model is uninterpreted. When we do interpret it, we specify the NP states which we think do subserve the constituents of the model, and their functioning for conscious and unconscious activity. But this interpretation leaves quite open the traditional body–mind questions. All that the vague presupposition about subserving asserts is that some NP is in fact necessary for the occurrence of psychological states and processes, such as Mrs. K.'s unconscious wish and her later acknowledgment of it. It leaves unanswered just what the precise relation is between Mrs. K.'s acknowledgment and awareness of her wish, and the NP which subserves this cognitive achievement. Is it one of identity? or parallelism? or reducibility? or interaction?—and if the last, how does this take place? It is plain that Freud's theory does not explore and answer these questions for us. It is philosophically neutral. Hence there is no logical incompatibility between a Freudian account of Mrs. K.'s difficulties and an NP account of them. If at some future date we are able to offer an account of the latter sort, and if Freud's theory is still acceptable at that time, it seems clear that the two accounts will then complement each other in critically important ways. Jointly, they will give us what we are striving to reach at the present time.

VII

The contributions in this book by Sartre, Miles, and Erdelyi center around what philosophers call the ontology of Freud's theory. Just what is he referring to when he speaks of an unconscious conception, of repression, and so on? But why should we be troubled by this question if Freud and psychoanalysts have no grounds, or very feeble grounds, to believe that we have any unconscious conceptions at all? In Selection 1 Freud claims that "the presence of such an idea in the mind admits of indirect proofs of the most cogent kind." Is Freud's claim correct? How good are the grounds for asserting that, for example, Mrs. K. has the unconscious wish we ascribe to her? These questions take us into the maze of epistemological issues that surround Freud and psychoanalysts.

In considering Freud's contribution we have concentrated so far on the parts of the theory which contain his fundamental explanatory notions. But there are two other related features of Freud's position and contribution which should be noted. The theory also contains a large number of generalizations—about human development and character, how conflicts arise, how we deal with them, and about the origin and character of neurotic disorders. Freud also gave us case studies, in which (typically) he used his theory, in conjunction with his generalizations, to give us a coherent description and an explanation of the patients' difficulties. It is generally agreed that the chief support for the theory, and the generalizations in it, is to be found in the case studies which analysts report. Hence the key question is: "How good or weak is the support offered by these reports?" It is generally agreed that they are built upon interpretations which have been put by the analyst to the patient and which are true. The problem then becomes: "What grounds have we for asserting that an interpretation is true or false?" In discussing this question we will find ourselves asking at some stage: "Does the patient accept the interpretation or not? And does not his or her acceptance have some bearing on the matter?"

Now Habermas (Selection 5) is concerned to deal with the place of acceptance and acknowledgment by the patient. I think he faces the immediate objection that he exaggerates and misconstrues their place. Grünbaum (Selection 6) brings out incisively the central difficulties in the view offered by Habermas. The patient does not have a privileged access to the truth about herself. She does not enjoy, as Grünbaum puts it, "a cognitive monopoly of appraisal of interpretations as to their validity vis-à-vis the analyst." In my own view and words, acceptance by a patient is neither sufficient nor necessary to show that an interpretation is true. It is not sufficient, since acceptance may be an artifact of the pressure from the analyst in the analytic situation. It is not necessary, because it may be possible to obtain independent evidence for or against the interpretation—evidence which is enough to justify our claiming that it is true or false, for example, evidence from other people and sources that the patient did or did not suffer some traumatic episode(s) as a small child. Acceptance is not logically necessary for another related reason. Suppose, for example, that the interpretation involves the application of Freud's Oedipal generalizations. Since these purport to be generalizations about matters of psychological fact, it is logically possible for us to obtain evidence which is independent of the psychoanalytic process, and which is strong enough to justify us in claiming that the generalizations are correct. Then it is quite possible that the clinical material from the patient may be enough at some stage to warrant our applying these well-attested generalizations to her case, without waiting for an acceptance from her.

But to say this, and this alone, is to overlook something very important in Habermas's argument about the patient and her acceptance of interpretations. It is characteristic of an analysis that, as it continues, a great deal of material is accumulated. This contains evidence that the patient has assimilated and adopted a point of view about the nature of his or her personality, and problems, which the material supports. If the patient did not assimilate and adopt this view, if he or she continued to give evidence of rejecting or opposing it, then the view would be in doubt. Indeed, the analyst, and the outsider studying the material, would not be able to frame a view of the patient with much confidence. Thus, they would not be able to tell with confidence whether the patient was just persistently resisting the analyst, or whether the analyst's view of him or her was mistaken. This, then, is the important role which acceptance by the patient plays in the story. Acceptance, in the sense of assimilation, is necessary in practice in the typical case, if we are to develop an account of the patient which we can claim is well supported by the case material of the analytic process. I think it is the practical necessity of assimilation that Habermas is getting at, in an obscure way, when he writes: "He [the analyst] makes interpretative suggestions for a story that the patient cannot tell. Yet they can be verified in fact only if the patient adopts them and tells his own story with their aid. The interpretation of the case is corroborated only by the success or continuation of an interrupted self-formative process" (see p. xx in this volume). But the patient's acceptance is not conclusive, since, as we have noted, it may to some degree be an artifact of the analysis. Like-wise, it is also not conclusive for the material as a whole. Hence, until we can sort out the problem posed by the presence of (possibly) artifactual and contam-inated material, we must remain unsure how much weight to give acceptance by the patient, and to the material as a whole. This, in my judgment, is a criti-cal, empirical problem in the epistemology of psychoanalysis. Hence, accep-tance cannot give us the "indirect proofs of the most cogent kind," which Freud claims he offers us in the psychoanalysis of neurotic phenomena.[6]

So far, however, we have been assuming that, whatever the grounds may be to support Freud's theory, they are sufficiently good to make it worthwhile to look carefully into the nature of the theory. But is this assumption true? If we accept Wittgenstein's criticisms of Freud in Selection 8, then our assumption would seem to be false. It would then hardly be worthwhile bothering seri-ously about psychoanalysis.

Now it is always interesting and advisable to see what a philosopher of ge-nius, such as Wittgenstein, has to say on any topic. But it does not follow that what a genius tells us is always right—far from it. Indeed, I am forced to re-mark that much of what Wittgenstein says in his "Remarks on Freud" and psychoanalysis is wrong and occasionally fatuous.

Wittgenstein is wrong in saying that, to Freud, all anxiety is a repetition of the birth trauma;[7] and he is misleading about Freud's view of the role of the primal scene.[8] Freud does not accept the subconscious—this is a Jungian con-cept;[9] and it is a misreading of Freud to say he holds that the hallucinatory character of our dreams stems from the deep wishes of early childhood.[10] Wittgenstein claims that, if a patient is led by analysis to say what his or her real motive or thought was, this is not a discovery about the patient, but the result of persuasion by the analyst. This claim about fact may be true in some particular case, in most cases, or in all of them. But how does he know this? Wittgenstein's presentation of this claim is an example of fatuous armchair psychology. He also claims that "there is no way of showing that the whole re-sult of analysis may not be a delusion." Perhaps so, for it is a truism that prov-ing a negative is a difficult or impossible task. But this overlooks the obvious riposte that we may have good reasons to believe that psychoanalysis does sometimes arrive at part of the truth about our patient. The validity of analysis as a tool of discovery is itself a matter of empirical research, not a matter for decision by a philosopher. Wittgenstein attempts to explain the attractiveness of psychoanalytic explanations and interpretations by saying: "Many of these explanations are adopted because they have a peculiar charm." I find this sug-gestion very inept. It may be that, to the theorist and the philosopher, a psy-choanalytic explanation has charm, in virtue no doubt of its power to order and unify the data. But to the distressed, unhappy patient, the thought that an interpretation has charm simply does not occur. More often than not, it is dis-turbing and upsetting. To say to a patient that he accepted it because it has charm would almost always be callous and unfeeling, and quite wrong. The conditions which lead a patient to accept an interpretation are, in a typical instance, likely to be very complex indeed, as an examination of the psychoanalytic process makes abundantly clear. And, to the working analyst, what matters primarily is not "the charm" of an interpretation, but whether it helps him, or her, to keep things moving in the analysis in what the analyst senses is a fruitful way.

Wittgenstein also declares roundly that analysis is likely to do harm, on the grounds that one is liable to be taken in by, and not "see through the mythology" of, psychoanalysis. This is a feeble argument. If Mrs. K. is offered analysis and happens to improve, largely or completely, Wittgenstein would have to say that her analysis was harmful to her *unless* she also came to reject psychoanalysis as a myth. I doubt whether any workers in the field of mental health would go along with this. Still, Wittgenstein is quite emphatic that Freud has offered us "a powerful mythology." In this context Wittgenstein can only mean, I take it, that Freud's theory is very persuasive but false. Well, Wittgenstein may be right here—Freud's theory may be false. But how does he know? Where are his reasons to justify this big claim about Freud's wide-ranging story? Wittgenstein does not begin to give us adequate answers.

Why is Wittgenstein so far off the target? What has gone wrong? I suspect he was seriously misled by Freud himself into supposing that psychoanalytic work, and interpretation in general, are very like what Freud did with his own dreams in *The Interpretation of Dreams*. The truth is that they are very unlike Freud's own self-analysis in *The Interpretation of Dreams*, something which a little study of psychoanalytic work and interpretation will reveal. Wittgenstein is plainly handicapped by being out of touch with the clinical material which bears on the truth or falsehood of Freud's theory, and of psychoanalytic theory in general. However, we must remember that, according to the editor of the small volume from which Wittgenstein's piece is taken, Wittgenstein did not write or check it, consisting as it does of notes taken down by students. The editor also tells us that "it is even doubtful if [Wittgenstein] would have approved of their publication, at least in their present form."

Nevertheless, in spite of the handicaps under which Wittgenstein labored, he does point to some matters of great importance. He challenges Freud's methods of dream interpretation by asking, in effect, how Freud knew where to stop in interpreting an item. How do we know when the interpretation is complete? Is it ever? These are questions that analysts have not yet dealt with to their own satisfaction or to that of their critics. He also points to the persuasive character of psychoanalytic method, and this raises the large questions we have already met: How far is the patient persuaded by analysis into the psychoanalytic view she adopts of herself? How far can we say that this view is imposed on her? Wittgenstein's contribution is manifestly pervaded by an attitude of fundamental skepticism about psychoanalytic method. Just what can it discover about human beings? Since Freud and analysts have traditionally regarded analysis as a method of research, it is very necessary that we should be alive to its possible limitations and should try to determine its validity. These are problems which surround psychoanalysis, and Wittgenstein does us all a service by drawing our attention to them.

VIII

The contributions from Habermas and from Wittgenstein give me the impression that both of these philosophers are remote from the clinical material of psychoanalysis. I think that they would give the same impression, not only to psychoanalysts, but also to most psychotherapists using insight therapy. How can philosophers and students generally overcome this limitation and get closer to the material?

There is no easy answer to this question. It is no good saying, "They should all be analyzed." For, if Wittgenstein is right and analysis involves persuasion and imposition, then it may be difficult or impossible for the analyzed philosopher to examine psychoanalysis with the detachment required. Nor is it much use saying, "Publish some case material, so that we can study it." For this material is very bulky, and difficult or impossible to present within the confines of a small volume such as this one. The solution I have chosen here is to try to exhibit how some of the central notions of psychoanalysis actually work by showing how they can be applied to describe and explain human activity and conduct.

This is what Malan offers us in Selection 8. He gives us some short "stories"; and, if we include Aesop's fables about the fox and the grapes and the snake and the wasp (which Malan mentions) as being about people, then he offers us ten stories in all of people who are in difficulties of various sorts. He sets about explaining their difficulties by the use of psychoanalytic notions. The central ones which Malan concentrates on for this purpose are those of unconscious defenses and feelings, repression, and disguised expressions of feelings. Malan uses the word "mechanism" in a way which is standard in contemporary psychotherapy. On this use the word is a shorthand for the ways in which, on a psychoanalytic and psychodynamic view, we can and do deal with disturbing thoughts, feelings, impulses, and our potential and actual conflicts. It is important to note that, to Malan, the difference is a shady one of degree between a feeling which the patient is totally unaware of and one which he is unwilling to acknowledge. Hence he differs from Freud in rejecting a sharp line between items which are unconscious and those which are not.

Quite obviously, Malan's explanatory accounts cannot take the place of a full explanation of the way psychoanalytic concepts work. Still, they are of value in making Freud's notions come alive by showing how they can be put to work. In giving us his accounts, Malan does not provide what Freud described as "indirect proofs" of his notions. He does not provide such proofs either for Freud's model of the mind, or for any of his generalizations about it. What Malan does do is to give the theory some weight and plausibility by showing how the notions in it can make intelligible sense out of the data.

However, in doing this, he does not offer us sufficient grounds to justify the claim that any of his explanatory accounts is true. For his interpretations of the data, which are presented in his stories, may be false, or inadequate, or misleading in some way or to some degree. The logical gap still remains between an intelligible story and a true one. Hence in his contribution Malan does not succeed in meeting the skeptical challenge which has been leveled at psychoanalysis. Nor does it look as if the challenge can be met satisfactorily by any explanatory accounts of this type about people and patients, no matter how plausibly they are constructed and presented.

Can we do any better than this to meet this skeptical challenge to Freud's theory and psychoanalytic theories generally?

Freud maintained (Selection 1) that unconscious items belong to "a system of mental activity" which he designated "the unconscious." From these remarks it is clear that he does not attempt "to prove" the existence of the unconscious. What he seems to be saying is that the notion of the unconscious is forced upon us, if we are to explain the existence and nature of unconscious ideas. That is, we are obliged to postulate that there is "a system of mental activity" that he designates as the unconscious. It is a part, therefore, of a theory of mental functioning. As such, it should be open to confirmation, disconfirmation, and refutation in the same sort of ways as any other theory that claims to order and explain empirical fact. To date, however, as Miles and Habermas point out, we have not been able to support the theory by deriving any empirical consequences from it, which we could then, perhaps, confirm. But this does not mean that it is impossible in principle for us to find any empirical considerations at all, which can go to confirm or disconfirm or refute the theory (for such considerations, see Selection 10).

What about "proving the existence of an unconscious idea" and other unconscious items—for example, Mrs. K.'s alleged unconscious wish to avoid sexual intercourse with her husband? Do these items admit of "indirect proof" of the most cogent kind as Freud claims in Selection 1? Indeed, do they admit of any proofs at all? It can be maintained that Freud does offer an indirect proof of one such item, which takes the following form (Freud, *Introductory Lectures on Psychoanalysis* (S.E. 16): If a patient is to improve or be cured, it is necessary that she should achieve correct insights about herself. Therefore, when a patient does improve, or is cured, it follows that the insights she has achieved are correct. They correspond or tally with what is really the case about herself. Therefore, if Mrs. K. comes to recognize that she has an unconscious wish to avoid sexual intercourse, and she then improves or is cured, it follows that her insight is correct: she really did or does have this unconscious wish.

Unfortunately, this simple argument is very weak indeed. Assuming that Freud did actually make use of it, the immediate question is this: How does he know that only if an insight is correct will the patient improve? His criterion of correctness cannot be that improvement follows on insight, because in

the context of insight therapy (which alone we are considering here), it is then
an uninteresting tautology to say that the achievement of a correct insight is a
necessary condition for improvement. He must give us a criterion of correctness, which is independent of improvement or cure. It is doubtful if Freud
does this. But if he were to offer one, he would then have to tell us how he
knows that an (independently determined) correct insight is a necessary condition of improvement. This is not a captious demand; for, after Freud's early
work, it became very clear that the conditions necessary for, and contributing
towards, improvement are very complex and not yet fully known and established. For example, it has been widely argued that improvement is primarily
dependent on what is *common* to all types of insight therapy. If so, improvement as such provides little evidence to support the *specific* insights achieved
by any one brand of psychoanalysis and insight therapy. Such insights may
not be necessary for improvement. But, in any event, this whole argument is
passé. For psychoanalysts have given up stressing any close tie between insight achievement and improvement or cure. They have done so in the light of
the difficulties (a) of establishing in general any close links between many (or
most) insight achievements and improvement; and, what is worse, (b) of establishing that any improvement or cure has taken place at all and as the result of
the analysis. It is well known that in his later years Freud seemed to give up
the claim that in psychoanalysis one necessarily discovers the truth, and must
do so in order to arrive at improvement or cure. It was sufficient, he said later,
to produce in the patient "an assured conviction" of the truth of the account
the analyst was building up and offering about her, the patient. To say this is
to concede that no "proofs" need be offered for the existence of any unconscious idea or item involved in these accounts.[11]

The fact is that, in general, analysts have not tried "to prove" the existence
of unconscious items. They have gone about trying to establish their existence
in a very different way. In the course of treatment, they are constantly offering the patient interpretations of her remarks, conduct, and so on. Not infrequently, an interpretation is about a (supposed) unconscious item. Thus, for
example, the analyst might say to Mrs. K. at some suitable stage and point:
"You give me the impression of being nervous about sexual intercourse, and
more particularly perhaps about having intercourse with your husband." Analysts have argued that such an interpretation is true or correct if it satisfies
some criterion or criteria. They have suggested various criteria over the years,
and in the course of doing so they have shown us how difficult the whole
problem is.

In Selection 9, "Testing a Psycho-analytic Interpretation," Wisdom faces
up squarely to the problem and explores it courageously. If an interpretation
is to be taken seriously as a hypothesis about the patient, then, Wisdom maintains, it must be open to testing. Testing can be done by reference to the responses of the patient when she is offered the interpretation in analysis.
Wisdom then gives us a certain complex criterion to distinguish between the

responses which confirm and those which refute an interpretation. However, Wisdom points out that if psychoanalysis acts by suggestion, this criterion will not work; and he goes on to argue that analysis does not in fact act in this way.

This bold answer to the problem faces serious difficulties. When one inspects what actually happens in analysis, one is apt to be faced by an overwhelming mass of confused and confusing material. It is far from obvious, therefore, that Wisdom's complex criterion can be easily and reliably applied, with any confidence, to much of the analytic material. To make his case, Wisdom seems to be relying on an artificial, highly simplified picture of the analytic process. I doubt, therefore, whether he succeeds in helping analysts with their central problem: How are they to distinguish between a patient's responses which are evidence of resistance or of negative transference, and those which are evidence that the interpretation is false? When he examines the possible role of suggestion in analysis, he offers a psychological account of it which, I believe, psychologists generally would regard as inadequate; the problem of suggestion is much more complicated and serious than he supposes. On the other hand, even if suggestion does play a role in analysis, this does not ipso facto make the clinical material evidentially worthless. Here, I think, Wisdom concedes too much to the skeptic. Even if the psychoanalyst does influence the patient so as to produce material which is artifact-infected and therefore contaminated, the chief source of the material obviously remains with the patient herself. Hence it is still open to us to assess the weight which the infected material lends to the hypotheses making up the psychoanalytic account of her difficulties. Wisdom's contribution has the great virtue of making us all aware of some of the difficulties involved in securing a firm foundation for psychoanalytic interpretations and theory on the base of the clinical material of patients.

On top of all this, however, there is a further fundamental difficulty which Wisdom does not deal with. The clinical material is to be found typically in the reports of individual analysts. But the analyst is a participant and very involved observer whose selective recall and note taking cannot be trusted to present us with "data" that satisfy the criteria of acceptability used in the scientific world. To put it differently, his reports do not contain the "observation sentences" that we need to secure a firm foundation for psychoanalysis. The only way out of this quagmire seems to be to use the lifeline of audio and video recordings. These can then also be examined by third parties to try to determine the evidential weight which the case material in these recordings lends to psychoanalytic and psychodynamic orientations. In my view, this is the fundamental epistemological problem that faces analysts and insight therapists generally at the present time—how to provide us with scientifically acceptable data. Their subject will not, and cannot, be brought into the body of established knowledge until we begin to master this problem.[12]

Some philosophers, psychiatrists, and psychologists may be inclined to maintain that this view and the stand I have been taking about psychoanalysis are quite mistaken. Analysts are not really faced by the epistemological problems I have mentioned above, for the simple reason that Freud's theory is not open logically to refutation at all, whether by clinical or any other evidence. Freud's account has no more claim to be taken seriously than any other occult or mystical account of the mind. Likewise for other versions of psychoanalytic theory. I examine this question in Selection 10, "Can Psychoanalysis Be Refuted?"

Now this is a very big and alarming-looking question—one that is apt to stun us. I examine it by trying to make it less frightening and more manageable. I do this by pointing out that psychoanalytic theory is not a unified affair, and that its parts are related to empirical fact in different ways. The fact to which I refer ranges from the "hard" findings of scientific inquiry to the "soft" data of projective tests. The upshot is to suggest that the big question is not really worth asking; and I hope that the chapter does something to remove our temptation to ask it.

IX

Whatever may be the validity of psychoanalysis as a psychology, and as a method of inquiry and therapy, it has undoubtedly had enormous influence in Western culture. There is no need to spell this out. It has come to be widely believed that psychoanalysis, in exerting this influence, has a bearing on various aspects of our lives and culture and that it raises a number of questions about them.

Ginsberg concentrates on two such aspects in his contribution on "Psychoanalysis and Ethics." What contribution has it made to our understanding of the conditions that produce our moral attitudes and the moral rules, which an individual and a group accept? Does, and can, psychoanalysis justify any set of principles by which a moral code can be evaluated? Ginsberg's stance on psychoanalysis is a sympathetic one, and he points out what he considers to be its contribution in this area. However, he argues that this contribution is much more limited than some analysts may suppose; and he claims that psychoanalysis fails to explain our sense of moral obligation, our respect for rationally accepted principles of conduct, and our sense of justice.

Two concepts which are closely involved in ethical issues are those of freedom and responsibility. Psychoanalysis appears to raise important questions about them. Thus, it has been popularly supposed that, if Freud is right, our thoughts and actions are the outcome of conditions of which we are unconscious, and hence are determined for us. We are, to put it crudely, puppets of our unconscious. From this it would seem to follow that we are not free agents, and therefore are not responsible for what we do. These (supposed) consequences of psychoanalysis fly in the face of our commonsense convictions. Naturally, therefore, psychoanalysis is apt to disturb us.

Is the popular view right that on psychoanalytic theory we are puppets of our unconscious? This is patently a very large topic; and Hospers and Glover examine it in Selections 12 and 13. These make it only too clear at once that the topic is far from being a simple one, but embodies a nest of issues with a network of ramifications. Glover argues—and most of us who have explored the subject would agree—that psychoanalysis does not have the disturbing consequences it is popularly supposed to bring with it. In spite of Freud's own commitment to determinism, we are not puppets of our unconscious; we can and do choose to do this or that in the light of rational considerations; our freedom to act is a matter of degree, not an all-or-nothing matter. We can still speak of being responsible for our actions. But the critical question becomes that of deciding how to distinguish between actions for which we are responsible and those for which we are not. What Freud and psychoanalysis have done is to make us aware of some of the further difficulties that drawing this distinction entails. Psychoanalysis also suggests that the scope of actions for which we can properly be held responsible is not as great as we normally assume.

We end this volume by looking at two other issues raised by psychoanalysis and its influence. What is the relation between psychoanalysis and religious belief? In what way, if at all, does psychoanalysis offer us a general outlook on life and the world—a Weltanschauung?

At the beginning of 1909 a Protestant clergyman in Switzerland called Oskar Pfister wrote to Freud, and this was the beginning of a lifelong correspondence and friendship. In their correspondence Freud and Pfister discussed their views about the nature of religion and its relation to psychoanalysis. Freud set out his views on this matter in several places, notably in *The Future of an Illusion* (S.E. 21). Now, according to Freud, a belief in a delusion is one which is necessarily false. In contrast, a belief in an illusion, though it may be true, is one "in which wish fulfilment is a prominent factor in its motivation, and in which its relation to reality is disregarded." Take the example (and this is Freud's own) of the poor girl's belief that her prince will come. Freud uses his theory to explain how wishes lead a person, on becoming an adult, to believe in a substitute superhuman father, God, who will give the adult the protection and security that he or she longs for. So Freud offers a naturalistic account, which, in his view, is quite sufficient to explain the belief in God. Hence belief in God is an illusion.

In their correspondence, Pfister and Freud reveal much that is admirable about themselves. Pfister shows us throughout how much he admires Freud as a person and values his work as a therapist. Freud confesses that "it never occurred to me how extraordinarily helpful the psychoanalytic method might be in pastoral work" such as Pfister practiced; and he speaks of his fear that the public profession of his "completely negative attitude to religion" (in *The Future of an Illusion*) will be painful to Pfister. However, it is very clear from their correspondence that neither of them get near the roots of the philosophical problem which divides them. Pfister is plainly quite at sea about it. Freud is handicapped by his use of the word "illusion." Leaving aside its vagueness, it is logically possible, according to his use, for a belief in God to be true, just as it is possible for the poor girl's belief in her prince to turn out to be true.

But in the latter case, what shows the belief to be true are certain matters of fact, since the poor girl's belief is one about fact, and the prince may actually turn up. But the belief in God is quite obviously not of this sort. What, then, can show it to be true? Freud is not interested in telling us—naturally, because he really wants to say that psychoanalysis is incompatible with a belief in God and rules it out. But it is widely accepted that to give the origins of a belief (say, in a person's wishes) does not establish the falsity or invalidity or delusiveness of the belief.

In what way then is psychoanalysis incompatible with a belief in God? Freud is not clear about the matter. Yet his writings do reveal him groping toward an answer. What he is pointing to, I think, is the impact of empirical common sense, scientific discovery, and his own work in psychoanalysis on the way in which we categorize the furniture of our experience. As our knowledge of nature expanded in the West, most of us have ceased to believe in the existence and efficacy of beings like leprechauns, fairies, and witches. Furthermore, most of us have now also categorized these beings in a way that rules out the finding of any possible evidence, or grounds, to show that they exist. Freud is making a similar claim for his psychoanalytic explanation of the belief in God. His explanation is sufficient, he implies, to make us categorize God as an entity of the same kind as witches, fairies, and the like; and hence there can logically be no grounds to show that God exists. It is in this way that psychoanalysis excludes a belief in God and religious belief in general, and so is incompatible with them.

It is evident that Freud's argument presupposes that his explanation for the belief in God—and other religious beliefs and practices—is true. It is very far from certain that this is the case. For the truth of his explanation of the belief in God depends on the truth of his psychoanalytic account of mental development, and indirectly of his theory as a whole. But we have seen that this account and whole story is open to very serious challenge and doubt. To the extent that his explanation of the belief in God is open to challenge and doubt, to that extent is the pressure from psychoanalysis diminished—the pressure on us to put God among the fairies. Moreover, Freud accepted a nineteenth-century view that it is possible to explain social institutions—for example, taboos and religion—as manifestations of the psychology of the individuals involved. But this view overlooks the social conditions that help to produce and sustain these institutions. When we look at the social function that religious beliefs and practices seem to serve, for example among the black population in the American South, or among sections of the white Afrikaans-speaking population in South Africa, it is very implausible to imagine that Freud's Oedipal story is sufficient to account for the religious beliefs and practices of these people. Sociologists are well aware that we have to look further afield to explain these complex and variegated phenomena.

As for psychoanalysis offering us a Weltanschauung, Freud argued that it does not give us one in the sense of offering us a general view of existence in which all questions are answered. All it does is to expand the scientific way of looking at the world. That Freud should say this is quite understandable, since he regarded psychoanalysis as a science and his work as part of the scientific enterprise. But whether Freud was wise to regard his work in this way is quite another matter. For it plunges him and his fellow analysts into controversy—a controversy explored from various angles in the present volume.[13]

NOTES

1. N. F. Dixon, "Apparent changes in the visual threshold as a function of subliminal stimulation," *Quart. J. Exp. Psychol.* 10 (1958): 211–15.
   N. F. Dixon, *Subliminal Perception: The Nature of a Controversy* (London: McGraw-Hill, 1971).
2. S. Freud, "Project for a Scientific Psychology," *Standard Edition* 1 (hereafter *S.E.*), 1966, 281–397.
3. Cf. J. Alan Hobson, *The Dreaming Brain* (New York: Basic Books, 1988). Hobson argues that findings about the neurophysiology of the brain stem refute the psychoanalytic theory of dreams. For a criticism of this view, *see*:
   Brian Farrell, "What Dreams Are Made Of," *New York Review of Books* 36, no. 10 (June 15, 1989).
4. My own impression is that Freud was too wise a man to allow himself to be sidetracked by the topic. But if I am wrong, I am sure that scholars of Freud's life and corpus will be quick to put me right.
5. American Psychiatric Association, *Diagnostic and Statistical Manual of Mental Disorders*, 3rd ed. (Washington, D.C., 1980).
6. On the problem of contamination, which the psychoanalytic process may, or does, produce, *see*:
   N. M. Cheshire, *The Nature of Psychodynamic Interpretation* (New York: Wiley, 1975).
   B. A. Farrell, *The Standing of Psychoanalysis* (Oxford: Oxford University Press, 1981).
   A. Grünbaum, *The Foundations of Psychoanalysis* (Berkeley: University of California Press, 1984).
7. Freud agrees that a certain preparedness for anxiety is undoubtedly present in the infant but he does not accept the view that the child's manifestations of anxiety stem from the trauma of birth. "Inhibitions, Symptoms and Anxiety," ch. 8 (1926), *S.E.* 20 (1959).
8. Wittgenstein sketches a romantic picture of the pattern of tragedy which is determined by the primal scene; and this is quite alien to Freud's view of it. "Three Essays on the Theory of Sexuality" (1905), *S.E.* 7 (1953).
9. S. Freud, "The Question of Lay Analysis," ch. 2 (1926), *S.E.* 20 (1959).
   C. G. Jung, "The Relations between the Ego and the Unconscious," in *Two Essays on Analytical Psychology, Collected Works*, vol. 6, edited by H. Read, M. Fordham, and G. Adler (London: Routledge, 1957–1983).
   See also vols. 7 and 8 for further references.
   E. Glover, *Freud or Jung* (London: Allen and Unwin, 1950).
   J. Jacobi, *The Psychology of C. G. Jung* (London: Kegan Paul, 1946).
10. Freud wrote that "in point of fact *all* dreams are children's dreams, that they work with the same infantile material, with the mental impulses and mechanisms of childhood." "Introductory Lectures on Psycho-analysis," lecture 14, *S.E.* 15 (1963). But he also held the view that the hallucinatory character of the dream in adults is the outcome of the activity of the Ego on the infantile material. "On Dreams" (1901), *S.E.* 5 (1953); and "Outline of Psychoanalysis" (1940), *S.E.* (1964).
11. S. Freud, "Constructions in Analysis" (1937), *S.E.* 23 (1964).

12. On this large matter, *see*, for example:

R. S. Wallerstein, *Psychotherapy and Psychoanalysis*, ch. 11 (New York: International Universities Press, 1975).

Farrell, *The Standing of Psychoanalysis*.

K. M. Colby, and R. J. Stoller, *Cognitive Science and Psychoanalysis* (Hillsdale, N.J.: Lawrence Erlbaum, 1988).

L. Luborsky, *Principles of Psychoanalytic Psychotherapy* (New York: Basic Books, 1984) for examples of a way of objectively examining the material of psychotherapeutic sessions.

L. Luborsky, and P. Crits-Christoph, *Understanding Transference: The CCRT Method* (New York: Basic Books, 1990).

13. Cf. also J. Malcolm, *Psychoanalysis: The Impossible Profession* (London: Picador, 1982).

SELECTIONS

1

SIGMUND FREUD

A Note on the Unconscious
in Psycho-Analysis

I WISH TO to expound in a few words and as plainly as possible what the term 'unconscious' has come to mean in Psycho-analysis and in Psycho-analysis alone.

A conception—or any other psychical[1] element—which is now *present* to my consciousness may become *absent* the next moment, and may become *present again*, after an interval, unchanged, and, as we say, from memory, not as a result of a fresh perception by our senses. It is this fact which we are accustomed to account for by the supposition that during the interval the conception has been present in our mind, although *latent* in consciousness. In what shape it may have existed while present in the mind and latent in consciousness we have no means of guessing.

At this very point we may be prepared to meet with the philosophical objection that the latent conception did not exist as an object of psychology, but as a physical disposition for the recurrence of the same psychical phenomenon, i.e., of the said conception. But we may reply that this is a theory far overstepping the domain of psychology proper; that it simply begs the ques-

---

[1][In the 1925 English version, throughout the paper, 'psychical' was altered to 'mental'.]

From *The Standard Edition of the Complete Psychological Works of Sigmund Freud*, Vol. XII, edited and translated by James Strachey. Reprinted by permission of Sigmund Freud Copyrights Ltd., The Institute of Psycho-Analysis, and The Hogarth Press. From *Collected Papers*, Vol. 4, pp. 22–30, by Sigmund Freud. Authorized Translation under the supervision of Joan Rivière. Published by Basic Books, Inc. by arrangement with The Hogarth Press Ltd. and The Institute of Psycho-Analysis, London. Reprinted by permission.

The footnotes in brackets are by the editor of *The Standard Edition.*—B. A. F.

tion by asserting 'conscious' to be an identical term with 'psychical', and that it is clearly at fault in denying psychology the right to account for its most common facts, such as memory, by its own means.

Now let us call 'conscious' the conception which is present to our consciousness and of which we are aware, and let this be the only meaning of the term 'conscious'. As for latent conceptions, if we have any reason to suppose that they exist in the mind—as we had in the case of memory—let them be denoted by the term 'unconscious'.

Thus an unconscious conception is one of which we are not aware, but the existence of which we are nevertheless ready to admit on account of other proofs or signs.

This might be considered an uninteresting piece of descriptive or classificatory work if no experience appealed to our judgement other than the facts of memory, or the cases of association by unconscious links. The well-known experiment, however, of the 'post-hypnotic suggestion' teaches us to insist upon the importance of the distinction between *conscious* and *unconscious* and seems to increase its value.

In this experiment, as performed by Bernheim, a person is put into a hypnotic state and is subsequently aroused. While he was in the hypnotic state, under the influence of the physician, he was ordered to execute a certain action at a certain fixed moment after his awakening, say half an hour later. He awakes, and seems fully conscious and in his ordinary condition; he has no recollection of his hypnotic state, and yet at the prearranged moment there rushes into his mind the impulse to do such and such a thing, and he does it consciously, though not knowing why. It seems impossible to give any other description of the phenomenon than to say that the order had been present in the mind of the person in a condition of latency, or had been present unconsciously, until the given moment came, and then had become conscious. But not the whole of it emerged into consciousness: only the conception of the act to be executed. All the other ideas associated with this conception—the order, the influence of the physician, the recollection of the hypnotic state, remained unconscious even then.

But we have more to learn from such an experiment. We are led from the purely descriptive to a *dynamic* view of the phenomenon. The idea of the action ordered in hypnosis not only became an object of consciousness at a certain moment, but the more striking aspect of the fact is that this idea grew *active*: it was translated into action as soon as consciousness became aware of its presence. The real stimulus to the action being the order of the physician, it is hard not to concede that the idea of the physician's order became active too. Yet this last idea did not reveal itself to consciousness, as did its outcome, the idea of the action; it remained unconscious, and so it was *active and unconscious* at the same time.

A post-hypnotic suggestion is a laboratory production, an artificial fact. But if we adopt the theory of hysterical phenomena first put forward by P. Janet and elaborated by Breuer and myself, we shall not be at a loss for plenty of natural facts showing the psychological character of the post-hypnotic suggestion even more clearly and distinctly.

The mind of the hysterical patient is full of active yet unconscious ideas; all her symptoms proceed from such ideas. It is in fact the most striking character of the hysterical mind to be ruled by them. If the hysterical woman vomits, she may do so from the idea of being pregnant. She has, however, no knowledge of this idea, although it can easily be detected in her mind, and made conscious to her, by one of the technical procedures of psycho-analysis. If she is executing the jerks and movements constituting her 'fit', she does not even consciously represent to herself the intended actions, and she may perceive those actions with the detached feelings of an onlooker. Nevertheless analysis will show that she was acting her part in the dramatic reproduction of some incident in her life, the memory of which was unconsciously active during the attack. The same preponderance of active unconscious ideas is revealed by analysis as the essential fact in the psychology of all other forms of neurosis.

We learn therefore by the analysis of neurotic phenomena that a latent or unconscious idea is not necessarily a weak one, and that the presence of such an idea in the mind admits of indirect proofs of the most cogent kind, which are equivalent to the direct proof furnished by consciousness. We feel justified in making our classification agree with this addition to our knowledge by introducing a fundamental distinction between different kinds of latent or unconscious ideas. We were accustomed to think that every latent idea was so because it was weak and that it grew conscious as soon as it became strong. We have now gained the conviction that there are some latent ideas which do not penetrate into consciousness, however strong they may have become. Therefore we may call the latent ideas of the first type *foreconscious*,[2] while we reserve the term *unconscious* (proper) for the latter type which we came to study in the neuroses. The term *unconscious*, which was used in the purely descriptive sense before, now comes to imply something more. It designates not only latent ideas in general, but especially ideas with a certain dynamic character, ideas keeping apart from consciousness in spite of their intensity and activity.

Before continuing my exposition I will refer to two objections which are likely to be raised at this point. The first of these may be stated thus: instead of subscribing to the hypothesis of unconscious ideas of which we know nothing, we had better assume that consciousness can be split up, so that certain ideas or other psychical acts may constitute a consciousness apart, which has become detached and estranged from the bulk of conscious psychical activity.

[2][In the 1925 English version, throughout the paper, 'foreconscious' was altered to 'preconscious', which has, of course, become the regular translation of the German 'vorbewusst'.]

Well-known pathological cases like that of Dr. Azam seem to go far to show that the splitting up of consciousness is no fanciful imagination.*

I venture to urge against this theory that it is a gratuitous assumption, based on the abuse of the word 'conscious'. We have no right to extend the meaning of this word so far as to make it include a consciousness of which its owner himself is not aware. If philosophers find difficulty in accepting the existence of unconscious ideas, the existence of an unconscious consciousness seems to me even more objectionable. The cases described as splitting of consciousness, like Dr. Azam's, might better be denoted as shifting of consciousness,—that function—or whatever it be—oscillating between two different psychical complexes which become conscious and unconscious in alternation.

The other objection that may probably be raised would be that we apply to normal psychology conclusions which are drawn chiefly from the study of pathological conditions. We are enabled to answer it by another fact, the knowledge of which we owe to psycho-analysis. Certain deficiencies of function of most frequent occurrence among healthy people, e.g., *lapsus linguae*, errors in memory and speech, forgetting of names, etc., may easily be shown to depend on the action of strong unconscious ideas in the same way as neurotic symptoms. We shall meet with another still more convincing argument at a later stage of this discussion.

By the differentiation of foreconscious and unconscious ideas, we are led on to leave the field of classification and to form an opinion about functional and dynamical relations in psychical action. We have found a *foreconscious activity* passing into consciousness with no difficulty, and an *unconscious activity* which remains so and seems to be cut off from consciousness.

Now we do not know whether these two modes of psychical activity are identical or essentially divergent from their beginning, but we may ask why they should become different in the course of psychical action. To this last question psycho-analysis gives a clear and unhesitating answer. It is by no means impossible for the product of unconscious activity to pierce into consciousness, but a certain amount of exertion is needed for this task. When we try to do it in ourselves, we become aware of a distinct feeling of *repulsion*[3] which must be overcome, and when we produce it in a patient we get the most unquestionable signs of what we call his *resistance* to it. So we learn that the unconscious idea is excluded from consciousness by living forces which

---

*Freud's paper appeared in a symposium organized by the Society for Psychical Research. It followed two papers by Dr. T. W. Mitchell on multiple personality and hysteria. In one of these Mitchell drew attention to a certain type of "double personality," in which a large section of consciousness is at one time split off, and hence dissociated from the rest; but which is then reinstated, so that we are confronted by "an alternation of two selves whose relation to each other might not be readily recognised." Mitchell then says that "the classical example of this form of double personality is Azam's Felida X"; and he refers us to the account of it in Binet's *Les Alterations de la Personnalité* (1891), *Alterations of Personality* (1896), translated by H. G. Baldwin, with notes and preface by J. M. Baldwin. London.—B. A. F.

[3][In the German translation the word 'repulsion', here and lower down, is rendered by ' *Abwehr*', of which the usual English version is 'defence' or 'fending off'.]

oppose themselves to its reception, while they do not object to other ideas, the foreconscious ones. Psycho-analysis leaves no room for doubt that the repulsion from unconscious ideas is only provoked by the tendencies embodied in their contents. The next and most probable theory which can be formulated at this stage of our knowledge is the following. Unconsciousness is a regular and inevitable phase in the processes constituting our psychical activity; every psychical act begins as an unconscious one, and it may either remain so or go on developing into consciousness, according as it meets with resistance or not. The distinction between foreconscious and unconscious activity is not a primary one, but comes to be established after repulsion has sprung up. Only then the difference between foreconscious ideas, which can appear in consciousness and reappear at any moment, and unconscious ideas which cannot do so gains a theoretical as well as a practical value. A rough but not inadequate analogy to this supposed relation of conscious to unconscious activity might be drawn from the field of ordinary photography. The first stage of the photograph is the 'negative'; every photographic picture has to pass through the 'negative process', and some of these negatives which have held good in examination are admitted to the 'positive process' ending in the picture.

But the distinction between foreconscious and unconscious activity, and the recognition of the barrier which keeps them asunder, is not the last or the most important result of the psycho-analytic investigation of psychical life. There is one psychical product to be met with in the most normal persons, which yet presents a very striking analogy to the wildest productions of insanity, and was no more intelligible to philosophers than insanity itself. I refer to dreams. Psycho-analysis is founded upon the analysis of dreams; the interpretation of dreams is the most complete piece of work the young science has done up to the present. One of the most common types of dream-formation may be described as follows: a train of thoughts has been aroused by the working of the mind in the daytime, and retained some of its activity, escaping from the general inhibition of interests which introduces sleep and constitutes the psychical preparation for sleeping. During the night this train of thoughts succeeds in finding connections with one of the unconscious tendencies present ever since his childhood in the mind of the dreamer, but ordinarily *repressed* and excluded from his conscious life. By the borrowed force of this unconscious help, the thoughts, the residue of the day's work,[4] now become active again, and emerge into consciousness in the shape of the dream. Now three things have happened:

1. The thoughts have undergone a change, a disguise and a distortion, which represents the part of the unconscious helpmate.

[4][In the 1925 English version the word 'mental' was inserted before 'work'. In the German translation the whole phrase is rendered '*Tagesreste*', for which the usual English equivalent is 'day's residues'.]

2. The thoughts have occupied consciousness at a time when they ought not.

3. Some part of the unconscious, which could not otherwise have done so, has emerged into consciousness.

We have learnt the art of finding out the 'residual thoughts', the *latent thoughts of the dream*, and, by comparing them with the apparent[5] *dream*, we are able to form a judgement on the changes they underwent and the manner in which these were brought about.

The latent thoughts of the dream differ in no respect from the products of our regular conscious activity; they deserve the name of foreconscious thoughts, and may indeed have been conscious at some moment of waking life. But by entering into connection with the unconscious tendencies during the night they have become assimilated to the latter, degraded as it were to the condition of unconscious thoughts, and subjected to the laws by which unconscious activity is governed. And here is the opportunity to learn what we could not have guessed from speculation, or from another source of empirical information—that the laws of unconscious activity differ widely from those of the conscious. We gather in detail what the peculiarities of the *Unconscious* are, and we may hope to learn still more about them by a profounder investigation of the processes of dream-formation.

This inquiry is not yet half finished, and an exposition of the results obtained hitherto is scarcely possible without entering into the most intricate problems of dream-analysis. But I would not break off this discussion without indicating the change and progress in our comprehension of the Unconscious which are due to our psycho-analytic study of dreams.

Unconsciousness seemed to us at first only an enigmatical characteristic of a definite psychical act. Now it means more for us. It is a sign that this act partakes of the nature of a certain psychical category known to us by other and more important characters[6] and that it belongs to a system of psychical activity which is deserving of our fullest attention. The index-value of the unconscious has far outgrown its importance as a property. The system revealed by the sign that the single acts forming parts of it are unconscious we designate by the name 'The Unconscious', for want of a better and less ambiguous term. In German, I propose to denote this system by the letters *Ubw*, an abbreviation of the German word 'Unbewusst'.[7] And this is the third and most significant sense which the term 'unconscious' has acquired in psycho-analysis.

---

[5][This word was altered to 'manifest' in the 1925 English version.]
[6][This was altered to 'features' in the 1925 English version.]
[7][The equivalent English abbreviation is, of course, '*Ucs.*'.]

2

JEAN-PAUL SARTRE

Bad Faith

THE HUMAN BEING is not only the being by whom *négatités* are disclosed in the world; he is also the one who can take negative attitudes with respect to himself. . . . Attitudes of negation toward the self permit us to raise a new question: What are we to say is the being of man who has the possibility of denying himself? But it is out of the question to discuss the attitude of "self-negation" in its universality. The kinds of behavior which can be ranked under this heading are too diverse; we risk retaining only the abstract form of them. It is best to choose and to examine one determined attitude which is essential to human reality and which is such that consciousness instead of directing its negation outward turns it toward itself. This attitude, it seems to me, is *bad faith (mauvaise foi)*.

Frequently this is identified with falsehood. We say indifferently of a person that he shows signs of bad faith or that he lies to himself. We shall willingly grant that bad faith is a lie to oneself, on condition that we distinguish the lie to oneself from lying in general. Lying is a negative attitude, we will agree to that. But this negation does not bear on consciousness itself; it aims only at the transcendent. The essence of the lie implies in fact that the liar actually is in complete possession of the truth which he is hiding. A man does not lie about what he is ignorant of; he does not lie when he spreads an error of which he himself is the dupe; he does not lie when he is mistaken. The ideal description of the liar would be a cynical consciousness, affirming truth

From Jean-Paul Sartre, *Being and Nothingness*, translated by Hazel E. Barnes (New York and London: Philosophical Library, 1957), chapter 2, pp. 47–52. Reprinted by permission.

within himself, denying it in his words, and denying that negation as such. Now this doubly negative attitude rests on the transcendent; the fact expressed is transcendent since it does not exist, and the original negation rests on a *truth*; that is, on a particular type of transcendence. As for the inner negation which I effect correlatively with the affirmation for myself of the truth, this rests on *words*; that is, on an event in the world. Furthermore the inner disposition of the liar is positive; it could be the object of an affirmative judgment. The liar intends to deceive and he does not seek to hide this intention from himself nor to disguise the translucency of consciousness; on the contrary, he has recourse to it when there is a question of deciding secondary behavior. It explicitly exercises a regulatory control over all attitudes. As for his flaunted intention of telling the truth ("I'd never want to deceive you! This is true! I swear it!")—all this, of course, is the object of an inner negation, but also it is not recognized by the liar as *his* intention. It is played, imitated, it is the intention of the character which he plays in the eyes of his questioner, but this character, precisely because he *does not exist*, is a transcendent. Thus the lie does not put into the play the inner structure of present consciousness; all the negations which constitute it bear on objects which by this fact are removed from consciousness. The lie then does not require special ontological foundation, and the explanations which the existence of negation in general requires are valid without change in the case of deceit. Of course we have described the ideal lie; doubtless it happens often enough that the liar is more or less the victim of his lie, that he half persuades himself of it. But these common, popular forms of the lie are also degenerate aspects of it; they represent intermediaries between falsehood and bad faith. The lie is a behavior of transcendence.

The lie is also a normal phenomenon of what Heidegger calls the "*Mitsein.*"[1] It presupposes my existence, the existence of the *Other*, my existence *for* the Other, and the existence of the Other *for* me. Thus there is no difficulty in holding that the liar must make the project of the lie in entire clarity and that he must possess a complete comprehension of the lie and of the truth which he is altering. It is sufficient that an over-all opacity hide his intentions from the *Other*; it is sufficient that the Other can take the lie for truth. By the lie consciousness affirms that it exists by nature as *hidden from the Other*; it utilizes for its own profit the ontological duality of myself and myself in the eyes of the Other.

The situation can not be the same for bad faith if this, as we have said, is indeed a lie to oneself. To be sure, the one who practices bad faith is hiding a displeasing truth or presenting as truth a pleasing untruth. Bad faith then has in appearance the structure of falsehood. Only what changes everything is the fact that in bad faith it is from myself that I am hiding the truth. Thus the duality of the deceiver and the deceived does not exist here. Bad faith on the

---

[1] A "being-with" others in the world. Tr.

contrary implies in essence the unity of a *single* consciousness. This does not mean that it can not be conditioned by the *Mit-sein* like all other phenomena of human reality, but the *Mit-sein* can call forth bad faith only by presenting itself as a *situation* which bad faith permits surpassing; bad faith does not come from outside to human reality. One does not undergo his bad faith; one is not infected with it; it is not a *state*. But consciousness affects itself with bad faith. There must be an original intention and a project of bad faith; this project implies a comprehension of bad faith as such and a pre-reflective apprehension (of) consciousness as affecting itself with bad faith. It follows first that the one to whom the lie is told and the one who lies are one and the same person, which means that I must know in my capacity as deceiver the truth which is hidden from me in my capacity as the one deceived. Better yet I must know the truth very exactly *in order* to conceal it more carefully—and this not at two different moments, which at a pinch would allow us to reestablish a semblance of duality—but in the unitary structure of a single project. How then can the lie subsist if the duality which conditions it is suppressed?

To this difficulty is added another which is derived from the total translucency of consciousness. That which affects itself with bad faith must be conscious (of) its bad faith since the being of consciousness is consciousness of being. It appears then that I must be in good faith, at least to the extent that I am conscious of my bad faith. But then this whole psychic system is annihilated. We must agree in fact that if I deliberately and cynically attempt to lie to myself, I fail completely in this undertaking; the lie falls back and collapses beneath my look; it is ruined *from behind* by the very consciousness of lying to myself which pitilessly constitutes itself well within my project as its very condition. We have here an *evanescent* phenomenon which exists only in and through its own differentiation. To be sure, these phenomena are frequent and we shall see that there is in fact an "evanescence" of bad faith, which, it is evident, vacillates continually between good faith and cynicism: Even though the existence of bad faith is very precarious, and though it belongs to the kind of psychic structures which we might call "metastable,"[2] it presents nonetheless an autonomous and durable form. It can even be the normal aspect of life for a very great number of people. A person can *live* in bad faith, which does not mean that he does not have abrupt awakenings to cynicism or to good faith, but which implies a constant and particular style of life. Our embarrassment then appears extreme since we can neither reject nor comprehend bad faith.

To escape from these difficulties people gladly have recourse to the unconscious. In the psychoanalytical interpretation, for example, they use the hypothesis of a censor, conceived as a line of demarcation with customs, passport division, currency control, *etc.*, to reestablish the duality of the deceiver and the deceived. Here instinct or, if you prefer, original drives and

---

[2]Sartre's own word, meaning subject to sudden changes or transitions.—Tr.

complexes of drives constituted by our individual history, make up *reality*. It is neither *true* nor *false* since it does not *exist for itself*. It simply *is*, exactly like this table, which is neither true nor false *in itself* but simply *real*. As for the conscious symbols of the instinct, this interpretation takes them not for appearances but for real psychic facts. Fear, forgetting, dreams exist really in the capacity of concrete facts of consciousness in the same way as the words and the attitudes of the liar are concrete, really existing patterns of behavior. The subject has the same relation to these phenomena as the deceived to the behavior of the deceiver. He establishes them in their reality and must interpret them. There is a *truth* in the activities of the deceiver; if the deceived could reattach them to the situation where the deceiver establishes himself and to his project of the lie, they would become integral parts of truth, by virtue of being lying conduct. Similarly there is a truth in the symbolic acts; it is what the psychoanalyst discovers when he reattaches them to the historical situation of the patient, to the unconscious complexes which they express, to the blocking of the censor. Thus the subject deceives himself about the *meaning* of his conduct, he apprehends it in its concrete existence but not in its *truth*, simply because he cannot derive it from an original situation and from a psychic constitution which remain alien to him.

By the distinction between the "id" and the "ego," Freud has cut the psychic whole into two. I *am* the ego but I *am not* the *id*. I hold no privileged position in relation to my unconscious psyche. I *am* my own psychic phenomena in so far as I establish them in their conscious reality. For example I am the impulse to steal this or that book from this bookstall. I am an integral part of the impulse; I bring it to light and I determine myself hand-in-hand with it to commit the theft. But I *am* not those psychic facts, in so far as I receive them passively and am obliged to resort to hypotheses about their origin and their true meaning, just as the scholar makes conjectures about the nature and essence of an external phenomenon. This theft, for example, which I interpret as an immediate impulse determined by the rarity, the interest, or the price of the volume which I am going to steal—it is in truth a process derived from self-punishment, which is attached more or less directly to an Oedipus complex. The impulse toward the theft contains a truth which can be reached only by more or less probable hypotheses. The criterion of this truth will be the number of conscious psychic facts which it explains; from a more pragmatic point of view it will be also the success of the psychiatric cure which it allows. Finally the discovery of this truth will necessitate the cooperation of the psychoanalyst, who appears as the *mediator* between my unconscious drives and my conscious life. The Other appears as being able to effect the synthesis between the unconscious thesis and the conscious antithesis. I can know myself only through the mediation of the other, which means that I stand in relation to *my* "id," in the position of the *Other*. If I have a little knowledge of psychoanalysis, I can, under circumstances particularly favorable, try to psychoanalyze myself. But this attempt can succeed only if I distrust every kind of intuition, only if I apply to my case *from the outside*, abstract schemes and

rules already learned. As for the results, whether they are obtained by my efforts alone or with the cooperation of a technician, they will never have the
certainty which intuition confers; they will possess simply the always increasing probability of scientific hypotheses. The hypothesis of the Oedipus complex, like the atomic theory, is nothing but an "experimental idea;" as Pierce
said, it is not to be distinguished from the totality of experiences which it allows to be realized and the results which it enables us to foresee. Thus psychoanalysis substitutes for the notion of bad faith, the idea of a lie without a
liar; it allows me to understand how it is possible for me to be lied to without
lying to myself since it places me in the same relation to myself that the Other
is in respect to me; it replaces the duality of the deceiver and the deceived,
the essential condition of the lie, by that of the "id" and the "ego." It introduces into my subjectivity the deepest intersubjective structure of the *Mit-
sein*. Can this explanation satisfy us?

Considered more closely the psychoanalytic theory is not as simple as it
first appears. It is not accurate to hold that the "id" is presented as a thing in
relation to the hypothesis of the psychoanalyst, for a thing is indifferent to the
conjectures which we make concerning it, while the "id" on the contrary is
sensitive to them when we approach the truth. Freud in fact reports resistance when at the end of the first period the doctor is approaching the truth.
This resistance is objective behavior apprehended from without: the patient
shows defiance, refuses to speak, gives fantastic accounts of his dreams, sometimes even removes himself completely from the psychoanalytic treatment. It
is a fair question to ask what part of himself can thus resist. It can not be the
"Ego," envisaged as a psychic totality of the facts of consciousness; this could
not suspect that the psychiatrist is approaching the end since the ego's relation to the *meaning* of its own reactions is exactly like that of the psychiatrist
himself. At the very most it is possible for the ego to appreciate objectively the
degree of probability in the hypotheses set forth, as a witness of the psycho-
analysis might be able to do, according to the number of subjective facts
which they explain. Furthermore, this probability would appear to the ego to
border on certainty, which he could not take offence at since most of the time
it is he who by a *conscious* decision is in pursuit of the psychoanalytic therapy.
Are we to say that the patient is disturbed by the daily revelations which the
psychoanalyst makes to him and that he seeks to remove himself, at the same
time pretending in his own eyes to wish to continue the treatment? In this
case it is no longer possible to resort to the unconscious to explain bad faith; it
is there in full consciousness, with all its contradictions. But this is not the
way that the psychoanalyst means to explain this resistance; for him it is secret
and deep, it comes from afar; it has its roots in the very thing which the psychoanalyst is trying to make clear.

Furthermore it is equally impossible to explain the resistance as emanating
from the complex which the psychoanalyst wishes to bring to light. The complex as such is rather the collaborator of the psychoanalyst since it aims at expressing itself in clear consciousness, since it plays tricks on the censor and

seeks to elude it. The only level on which we can locate the refusal of the subject is that of the censor. It alone can comprehend the questions or the revelations of the psychoanalyst as approaching more or less near to the real drives which it strives to repress—it alone because it alone *knows* what it is repressing.

If we reject the language and the materialistic mythology of psychoanalysis, we perceive that the censor in order to apply its activity with discernment must know what it is repressing. In fact if we abandon all the metaphors representing the repression as the impact of blind forces, we are compelled to admit that the censor must choose and in order to choose must be aware of so doing. How could it happen otherwise that the censor allows lawful sexual impulses to pass through, that it permits needs (hunger, thirst, sleep) to be expressed in clear consciousness? And how are we to explain that it can relax its surveillance, that it can even be deceived by the disguises of the instinct? But it is not sufficient that it discern the condemned drives; it must also apprehend them *as to be repressed*, which implies in it at the very least an awareness of its activity. In a word, how could the censor discern the impulses needing to be repressed without being conscious of discerning them? How can we conceive of a knowledge which is ignorant of itself? To know is to know that one knows, said Alain. Let us say rather: All knowing is consciousness of knowing. Thus the resistance of the patient implies on the level of the censor an awareness of the thing repressed as such, a comprehension of the end toward which the questions of the psychoanalyst are leading, and an act of synthetic connection by which it compares the *truth* of the repressed complex to the psychoanalytic hypothesis which aims at it. These various operations in their turn imply that the censor is conscious (of) itself. But what type of self-consciousness can the censor have? It must be the consciousness (of) being conscious of the drive to be repressed, but precisely *in order not to be conscious of it*. What does this mean if not that the censor is in bad faith?

Psychoanalysis has not gained anything for us since in order to overcome bad faith, it has established between the unconscious and consciousness an autonomous consciousness in bad faith. The effort to establish a veritable duality and even a trinity (*Es, Ich, Ueberich* expressing themselves through the censor) has resulted in a mere verbal terminology. The very essence of the reflexive idea of hiding something from oneself implies the unity of one and the same psychic mechanism and consequently a double activity in the heart of unity, tending on the one hand to maintain and locate the thing to be concealed and on the other hand to repress and disguise it. Each of the two aspects of this activity is complementary to the other; that is, it implies the other in its being. By separating consciousness from the unconscious by means of the censor, psychoanalysis has not succeeded in dissociating the two phases of the act, since the libido is a blind conatus toward conscious expression and since the conscious phenomenon is a passive, faked result. Psychoanalysis has merely localized this double activity of repulsion and attraction on the level of the censor.

Furthermore the problem still remains of accounting for the unity of the total phenomenon (repression of the drive which disguises itself and "passes" in symbolic form), to establish comprehensible connections among its different phases. How can the repressed drive "disguise itself" if it does not include (1) the consciousness of being repressed, (2) the consciousness of having been pushed back because it is what it is, (3) a project of disguise? No mechanistic theory of condensation or of transference can explain these modifications by which the drive itself is affected, for the description of the process of disguise implies a veiled appeal to finality. And similarly how are we to account for the pleasure or the anguish which accompanies the symbolic and conscious satisfaction of the drive if consciousness does not include—beyond the censor—an obscure comprehension of the end to be attained as simultaneously desired and forbidden. By rejecting the conscious unity of the psyche, Freud is obliged to imply everywhere a magic unity linking distant phenomena across obstacles, just as sympathetic magic unites the spellbound person and the wax image fashioned in his likeness. The unconscious drive (*Trieb*) through magic is endowed with the character "repressed" or "condemned," which completely pervades it, colors it, and magically provokes its symbolism. Similarly the conscious phenomenon is entirely colored by its symbolic meaning although it can not apprehend this meaning by itself in clear consciousness.

Aside from its inferiority in principle, the explanation by magic does not avoid the coexistence—on the level of the unconscious, on that of the censor, and on that of consciousness—of two contradictory, complementary structures which reciprocally imply and destroy each other. Proponents of the theory have hypostasized and "reified" bad faith; they have not escaped it. This is what has inspired a Viennese psychiatrist, Steckel, to depart from the psychoanalytical tradition and to write in *La femme frigide*:"Every time that I have been able to carry my investigations far enough, I have established that the crux of the psychosis was conscious." In addition the cases which he reports in his work bear witness to a pathological bad faith which the Freudian doctrine can not account for. There is the question, for example, of women whom marital infidelity has made frigid; that is, they succeed in hiding from themselves not complexes deeply sunk in half physiological darkness, but acts of conduct which are objectively discoverable, which they can not fail to record at the moment when they perform them. Frequently in fact the husband reveals to Steckel that his wife has given objective signs of pleasure, but the women when questioned will fiercely deny them. Here we find a pattern of *distraction*. Admissions which Steckel was able to draw out inform us that these pathologically frigid women apply themselves to becoming distracted in advance from the pleasure which they dread; many for example at the time of the sexual act, turn their thoughts away toward their daily occupations, make up their household accounts. Will anyone speak of an unconscious here? Yet if the frigid woman thus distracts her consciousness from the pleasure which she experiences, it is by no means cynically and in full agreement with herself; *it is in order to prove to herself* that she is frigid. We have in fact to deal with a phenomenon of bad faith since the efforts taken in order not to be present to the experienced pleasure imply the recognition that the pleasure is experienced; they imply it *in order to deny it.* But we are no longer on the ground of psychoanalysis. Thus on the one hand the explanation by means of the unconscious, due to the fact that it breaks the psychic unity, can not account for the facts which at first sight it appeared to explain. And on the other hand, there exists an infinity of types of behavior in bad faith which explicitly reject this kind of explanation because their essence implies that they can appear only in the translucency of consciousness. We find that the problem which we had attempted to resolve is still untouched.

3

T. R. MILES

The Unconscious

I SHALL ARGUE that the use of the substantive term "the unconscious" is unnecessary. To put the matter crudely, no such entity as "the unconscious" exists.

This point, however, requires elucidation, since the "denial of existence" idiom is liable to be misleading. Thus if someone denies the existence of extra-sensory perception he is implicitly claiming that attempts to investigate it will never lead to positive results. It might seem, therefore, that if a person denies the existence of the unconscious he is saying that those who try to study the unconscious (viz. psycho-analysts) are similarly chasing a will o' the wisp. This, however, is a misunderstanding. I am not attacking what analysts do, but proposing that we should categorise their findings in a different way. On my view psycho-analysis is not the study of an entity called "the unconscious"; it is the study of what people say and do in response to somewhat unusual environmental stimuli. If a group of sociologists were investigating public opinion in Ruritania and believed that their findings constituted a major breakthrough, these findings would not cease to be interesting simply because someone pointed out that there was no such thing as public opinion but only the holding of individual opinions by individual people. My lenial of the existence of the unconscious is no more a disparagement of psycho-analysis than the denial of the existence of public opinion would be a disparagement o such a group of sociologists.

From T. R. Miles, *Eliminating the Unconscious* (Oxford: Pergamon Press, 1966), Chapter 6. Reprinted by permission.

In the discussion which follows I shall consider two main lines of approach, viz. (i) the view which suggests, explicitly or implicitly, that the words "the unconscious" stand for a real thing, and (ii) the view which commends the use of the words "the unconscious" but without commitment as to its "reality". I shall argue that both views are mistaken, and that in place of the noun *"the* unconscious" the adjective "unconscious" or the adverb "unconsciously" can be substituted throughout.

"THE UNCONSCIOUS" AS A REAL THING

At the time when the *Introductory Lectures* were first written, Freud clearly believed that the words "the unconscious" stood for something real. Here are some characteristic passages.*

> The unconscious is a special realm (6, p. 178).
> You will . . . understand that we cannot dispense with the unconscious part of the mind in psycho-analysis, and that we are accustomed to deal with it as with something actual and tangible (6, p. 235).
> Since then, however, Janet has taken up an attitude of undue reserve, as if he meant to imply that the unconscious had been nothing more to him than a manner of speaking, a makeshift,† *une façon de parler,* and that he had nothing "real" in mind (6, p. 218).
> When anyone objects that in a scientific sense the unconscious has no reality, that it is a mere makeshift, *une façon de parler,* we must resign ourselves with a shrug to rejecting his statement as incomprehensible. Something unreal, which can nevertheless produce something so real and palpable as an obsessive action! (6, pp. 234–5).

I shall argue that, whatever the findings of the analytic session, the words "the unconscious" cannot have the function which Freud here ascribes to them.

The first point which requires elucidation is the distinction drawn by Freud between a "real thing" and a *"façon de parler".* Let us therefore begin by considering possible uses of the word "real".

In many contexts the word "real" is used to indicate genuineness in some form. Objects can be genuine, however, in different ways. Thus "a real dog" means "not a stuffed one" or, in some contexts, "not a foppish lap-dog"; "a real oasis" means "not a mirage", and "real coffee" means "not ersatz coffee" (compare Austin[1]). An important criterion of reality is in many contexts the power of *doing* things. Thus a real dog has the power of chasing rabbits, a real oasis will quench one's thirst, and real coffee will satisfy one in a way that ersatz

---

*It should be remembered, of course, that the original passages were written in German, and that the feelings of discomfort which English readers sometimes undergo may be due in part to difficulties over translation. In what follows I shall consider only the English versions of what Freud said; this seems to me not unreasonable in view of the large numbers of people who now read his work in English. Whether Freud's conceptual scheme would have been radically different had he written in English and not German is an interesting point of speculation but cannot be answered with any confidence.

†The original German word is *Notbehelf.* Perhaps "verbal device" would bring out the intended meaning more clearly.

[1]Austin, J. L., Other Minds, *Aristotelian Society,* Suppl. vol. xx, 1946.

coffee will not. A comprehensive account, however, of all possible uses of the word "real" would at best be very difficult to give, and indeed it may well be that no single formula could ever be adequate.

What concerns us here is a special type of sentence containing the word "real", viz. sentences of the form "Is X a real entity?", e.g. "Is the memory a real entity?" or "Is public opinion a real entity?" An important characteristic of such questions is that they can be more adequately understood if one brings in inverted commas. Thus "Is the memory a real entity?" means, in effect, "Does the word 'memory' (in inverted commas) stand for a real entity?", and "Is public opinion a real entity?" means in effect "Do the words 'public opinion' (in inverted commas) stand for a real entity?" These can helpfully be characterised as *second-order* (or philosophical) questions, in contrast with first-order questions such as "Has he a good memory?" or "What is the state of public opinion?" Second-order sentences involve *talking about* concepts (hence the inverted commas) while in first-order sentences concepts are used rather than discussed.

What, then, are the criteria which lead us to say that a concept stands for a real entity? There is no "official" list of such criteria; but if one examines the rules which are implicit in this kind of discussion one can arrive at certain tentative suggestions. This I have already done elsewhere (Miles[2], Chapter IV). In my opinion some of the relevant criteria are: (a) whether the alleged entity can act and be acted upon, (b) whether the alleged entity lasts through a period of time, (c) whether the alleged entity has spatial boundaries, (d) whether the alleged entity is visible and tangible, and (e) whether for any reason it is valuable or important to treat the alleged entity as a unity. Ordinary usage gives little guidance as to how many of these criteria need to be satisfied, but it is clear that where several of them fail to be satisfied one is very hesitant about speaking of "real entities". Thus by these criteria one ought to be reluctant (as indeed one is) to say that the memory is a real entity or that there exists a real entity called "public opinion".

An alternative procedure for determining if a concept stands for a "real entity" is to ask if the alleged real entity can be "translated out of existence". The notion of being "translated out of existence" can be illustrated by once again using the examples of "memory" and "public opinion". If we say of someone that he has a good memory, this is commonly agreed to mean that if he is asked questions about past events in his life he tends to report on them accurately; to put the matter this way is to reorganise our concepts so that we do not need to believe in a thing or entity called "the memory" at all. Similarly, as has been pointed out already, "Public opinion has veered round in support of the Prime Minister" is commonly agreed to mean "There are more people who now believe in the Prime Minister's policy than there were previously"; here the words "public opinion" have been translated out of existence in the sense that we do not need a substantial entity called "public opinion" in addition to the indisputably substantial entities, viz. people, who are now behaving differ-

---

[2]Miles, T. R., *Religion and the Scientific Outlook*. Allen & Unwin, 1959.

ently. If these equivalences are agreed, then the words "the memory" and "public opinion" are *façons de parler* in a way in which words for familiar objects such as "gatepost" are not. To put the matter another way, if we had no word "gatepost" or its equivalent, we should be seriously handicapped in talking of gateposts, whereas if we had no word "memory" or no word "public opinion" we could get round the difficulty by saying that people are able to remember or that they are behaving on political issues in certain specified ways.

Now to ask if "the unconscious" stands for something real is to ask the same sort of question as we have been asking about "the memory", "public opinion", and "gatepost". Is the term "the unconscious" like the term "gatepost" or is it like the terms "memory" and "public opinion"? Is it that we simply have a use for the words "the unconscious" just as we have a use for the words "memory" and "public opinion", or is there a real entity called "the unconscious" which exists in its own right just as a gatepost is thought (at any rate by common-sense standards) to exist in its own right? This, I think, is the sort of question which Freud is implicitly asking.

His answer, of course, is that the unconscious is something actual, a real thing; in other words he is implicitly claiming that the term (in quotes) "the unconscious" is more like "gatepost" than it is like "memory" and "public opinion".

Now it is plain that the term "the unconscious" cannot in any literal sense stand for something visible and tangible: no analyst, or anyone else for that matter, supposes that during analytic sessions or even outside them a visible and tangible entity called "the unconscious" is scrutinised. Freud's carefully chosen remark that we "are accustomed to think" of the unconscious as actual and tangible is a tacit admission of this. He still wants to say, however, that the unconscious must be postulated as a hidden cause to explain the things which we do in fact observe—viz. the obsessive acts or whatever it may be. What is important on this view is that the unconscious has dynamic properties; it can cause things to happen. Hence the justification for using adjectives like "real" and "actual" and indeed for introducing the word "it" to stand for the noun to which they apply.

Now the objection to all this is not that intangible causal agencies are necessarily an absurdity. Such an objection suggests a traditional tough-minded materialism, which cannot easily be justified by argument and which simply provokes the reply, "Why shouldn't I postulate intangible causes?"* What is objectionable is the vacuousness of any such explanation, since the only evidence which can be adduced for the existence of "the unconscious" is the behavioural manifestations which require to be explained!

*It is also a point of considerable interest that we have almost daily experience of the operation of an intangible cause when we observe the effects of the wind. Another familiar experience is that which occurs when we ourselves cause things to happen. It is not surprising that both these experiences should give rise to the claim that someting "spiritual" (or windlike) is operating as a cause and that there can therefore be "non-material" agencies. As descriptions of experience there seems to me nothing objectionable in such talk. All that I am objecting to as a behaviourist is the suggestion that because I and others can cause things to happen it follows that the universe comprises two kinds of reality, "mental" and "physical".

Let us look at this question of vacuous explanations in more detail. Whatever our views about intangible causes there can clearly be no objection to inferring tangible ones, even though these causes happen temporarily to be unobservable. Thus it is perfectly legitimate to argue from footprints in the flower beds to an inferred burglar or from the movements of puppets to a person behind who is controlling them; and, to quote the classic case, astronomers legitimately inferred the presence of Neptune from the occurrence of irregularities in nearby planets. In all these cases, however, the inferred entity—the burglar, the puppet-operator, or Neptune—is observable in principle; its presence is an explanation precisely because the events to be explained are linked with something independently discoverable. The words "the unconscious", however, are agreed *not* to stand for anything independently discoverable, and cannot therefore explain any occurrence in the way in which the presence of a burglar, a puppet-operator, or the planet Neptune explain occurrences. The arguments against using the concept of "the unconscious" as the name of a hidden cause are in effect precisely the same as those used by Berkeley in rejecting the notion of "material substance" as a hidden cause. As Berkeley[3] (section 20) in effect pointed out, we can do our Newtonian physics perfectly well without the concept of "material substance" and if there were no such thing we should have precisely the same reasons for believing in its existence as we have now.* Similarly to introduce "the unconscious" as the name of a hidden cause contributes nothing to psycho-analysis.

I conclude, therefore, that if the term "the unconscious" is thought of as standing for something real in the sense of a causal agency there is no justification for postulating its existence. As with all such entities it requires to be eliminated under the principle of Occam's razor.

Not only, however, is the concept of "the unconscious" (if interpreted as standing for a "real thing") unnecessary; it is positively misleading. In particular it leads to an erroneous account of where Freud's achievement lay, since it invites us to picture him as a Columbus who discovered a new continent rather than as someone who invites us to look at our existing data in a new way.† It is widely assumed that the discovery of the unconscious mind was

---

[3]Berkeley, G., *Principles of Human Knowledge*. 1710.

*Berkeley, of course, uses the "denial of existence" idiom; but this has sometimes generated misunderstandings (e.g., Dr. Johnson's celebrated attempt to refute him by kicking a stone) similar to those which I have mentioned. For further discussion of the parallels between Berkeley's work and the approach of modern psychology see Miles[4].

[4]Miles, T. R., Berkeley and Ryle: Some comparisons, *Philosophy* xxxviii, 104, 1953.

†It would be interesting to examine in detail the different types of accusative that follow the word "discover". For example such accusatives can be proper names (e.g., America, Neptune), gerunds (e.g., the circulation of the blood), substances which from the very fact of their discovery require names (e.g., oxygen, radium), as well as familiar objects which one finds by changing one's position in space (e.g., rats in the coal shed) or by remaining static but looking at things in a new way (e.g., the hidden face in the puzzle-picture). I am not, of course, claiming that the phrase "looking at our existing data in a new way" is in any sense adequate to characterise Freud's achievement, only that it is more adequate than the "Columbus" type of analogy or even than the analogy with the person who notices hitherto undiscovered rats in the coal shed. No one wants to claim that slips of the tongue, incestuous dreams, totem feasts, etc., were unknown before the time of Freud; it is rather that, as a result of Freud, we now look at such things differently.

Freud's great contribution to knowledge; and indeed this claim is continually reiterated by analysts. For example Glover[5] (p. 16) speaks of "Freud's discovery of the unconscious mind"; Rivière[6] (p. 2) says that "Freud discovered the unconscious mind of man", and in giving a popular account Ernest Jones[7] (p. 589) says: "What did Freud really do? That can be most shortly answered by saying that he discovered a *previously inaccessible region of the mind* we now call the unconscious" (my italics). Now if traditional dualism is taken for granted then it is scarcely surprising that Freud's achievement should be described in dualistic terms. It is clear, however, on reflection—as Glover and others would no doubt agree—that Freud did not discover the *hidden causes* of infantile sexuality, slips of the tongue, obsessional behavior, etc., in the sense in which one might discover that a hidden rat had gnawed a hole in the coal shed; what he observed was the behaviour-patterns themselves, and his achievement was in effect to make people look at their significance in a new way. Yet this point is lost if we continue to think of Freud as a Columbus who discovered new regions in a non-physical entity.

THE UNCONSCIOUS AS A *FAÇON DE PARLER*

Even, however, if the term "the unconscious" does not stand for something real in the sense described, there might still be a case for retaining it as a *façon de parler*. Its position would in that case be comparable to that of the word "memory", which is retained in our discourse not as an explanation of the fact that people remember but simply as a restatement of this fact.

Another possible comparison is the example, originally derived from Molière, of *vertus dormitiva*. Asked why opium makes people go to sleep, a certain medical student replied "Because there is in it a *vertus dormitiva* whose nature is to assuage the senses." As an explanation this, of course, is vacuous; to make it informative one would need to specify how *vertus dormitiva* could be independently recognised (as would be done if one specified the defining properties of morphia). Yet "opium contains *vertus dormitiva*" can be a perfectly proper thing to say, provided one is not trying to explain its sleep-giving properties but only to call attention to them; and it would be an argument at cross-purposes if someone protested against this usage and was then criticised for overlooking the important new discovery that opium sends people to sleep.

The suggestion would then be that, somehow or other, perhaps in an indirect way, the term "the unconscious" refers to the obsessional and other behaviour which Freud and others have studied, and should therefore be retained in our discourse even though, unlike the word "gatepost", it is not

---

[5]Glover, E., *Freud or Jung*. Allen & Unwin, 1950.
    [6]Rivière, Joan, General Introduction to *Developments in Psycho-analysis* by Melanie Klein and others. Hogarth Press, 1952.
    [7]Jones, Ernest, *The Listener*, 10 May, 1956.

the name of a real thing. Two different accounts of its function seem to me possible here: the first is that it functions as a "link"-concept, i.e., as a concept which serves to link together behavioural events which would otherwise be disconnected; the second is that it offers a pictorial model.

If "the unconscious" is a "link"-concept, then we should not think in terms of hidden causes of obsessional behaviour; the important point is the connexion between such behaviour and other events in the patient's life. In the case, for example, of the woman whose obsession took the form of running into the next room and ringing for her maid (see Freud[8], pp. 221–2), the important discovery (if we assume Freud is right) is the link between this behaviour and the events on her wedding night. Similarly, one might find links of a more general kind between, for example, dreams or slips of the tongue and uncooperative or hostile behaviour in ostensibly quite different circumstances. The concept of "the unconscious" serves, on this view, to link all these many different events together, and to say that we all have an unconscious is to say that such behaviour is liable to occur in all of us. In that case one is not explaining behaviour in terms of independently discoverable events, in the way in which one might, for example, explain the breaking of a window in terms of the movement of a stone; one is explaining it by reference to general laws, somewhat, for example, as one might explain the breaking of a window by reference to the fact that the glass was brittle. Explanations by reference to general laws are different from explanations in terms of independently discoverable events, but are none the worse for that.

To adopt the terminology of some American learning theorists one could say, on this view, that, while the "data-language" is agreed to be that which describes what the patient says and does, there is still scope for introducing the concept of "the unconscious" as an "intervening variable"—i.e., as a concept which makes inferences and predictions possible but does not stand for anything whose reality could meaningfully be either asserted or denied.* "The unconscious" would in that case be a concept which intervenes between one set of data and another but does not itself stand for any kind of datum.

The fatal objection to regarding "the unconscious" as an intervening variable or "link"-concept is that for this purpose a substantive is entirely unnecessary. What makes much better sense is not the postulation of a hidden cause but a doctrine of unconscious purposes. It is interesting to note in this connexion that Freud himself does not always speak of hidden causes but sometimes refers to purposes and motives.† Thus he speaks of "the *purpose* she had in performing the action" and then adds that "it took her a long time to grasp, and admit to me, that such a *motive* as this alone could have been the driving

[8]Freud, S., *Introductory Lectures on Psycho-analysis*, tr. Joan Rivière. Allen & Unwin, 1922.
*For further discussion of the concepts "data-language" and "intervening variable" see William K. Estes and others, *Modern Learning Theory*, New York, 1954 (especially pp. 17 *seq.*).
†For an excellent discussion of this point see A. G. N. Flew, "Psycho-analytic Explanation," *Analysis* 10, 1, 1949 (pp. 8–15).

force behind the obsessive act" (Freud[9], p. 234, my italics). Later he says "By means of analysis we can always find the *purpose* behind the neurotic symptom" (Freud[10], p. 251, my italics). In general it seems clear from all passages of this kind that no explanatory result is achieved by the doctrine of "*the* unconscious" which cannot also be achieved by a doctrine of unconscious purposes or motives. Indeed, as Malan has suggested,* the noun "the unconscious" can be replaced without loss by the adjective "unconscious" or by the adverb "unconsciously".

A final line of defence is to say that talk of "the unconscious" is justified since such language gives us a useful pictorial model. Now clearly there can be no objection to models as such, provided that they genuinely help our understanding. Thus one might suppose that there is a large ante-room representing the unconscious part of the mind, and that ideas are prevented from entering the smaller reception room (in which consciousness resides) by the activity of a door-keeper ("resistance"). Freud[11] (pp. 249–50) agrees that "these conceptions are as crude as they are fantastic", but goes on to say that "they are useful aids to understanding, like Ampère's manikin swimming in the electric current, and, in so far as they do assist comprehension, are not to be despised". He continues, "I should like to assure you that these crude hypotheses, the two chambers, the doorkeeper on the threshold between the two, and consciousness as a spectator at the end of the second room, must indicate an extensive approximation to the actual reality."

Another well-known analogy is that of the iceberg; only a small top part is open to inspection, the rest—and indeed by far the greatest part—lying below the surface.

Now I am not suggesting for one moment that such pictures are entirely uninformative. One could, of course, be captious and ask *how much* of whatever it is lies below the surface, or one could ask if the doorkeeper *himself* has disreputable wishes, which would presumably be kept from his consciousness by another, miniature doorkeeper, and so on *ad infinitum*; but no one expects models to be without their inadequacies, and many models, if examined closely, would no doubt be found to yield similar absurdities. The real difficulty arises if one asks, Of what is this supposed to be a model? The customary answer is to say that it is "the mind" which is like an iceberg or a suite of rooms; the model tells us what "the mind" is like. Thus the ante-room and the below-surface part of the iceberg are models representing a special area of "the mind", viz. "the unconscious mind". On this showing, however, "the unconscious" itself is not part of the model at all, but an independently existing "thing" whose nature we try to understand by reference to the model, and in that case the difficulties as to how such an entity could be known have not been removed.

[9]Freud, *Introductory Lectures.*
[10]Freud, *Introductory Lectures.*
*Personal communication.
[11]Freud, *Introductory Lectures.*

In the same way when Freud[12] (*passim*) speaks of "the psychical apparatus", he certainly gives no suggestion that these words are to be understood in any way except a literal one. Admittedly it is often conceded that "spatial metaphors" are inadequate; thus Lee[13] (p. 32) tells us that to speak of "areas of the mind" is misleading, and Glover[14] (p. 21) says explicitly that "the psychologist is not concerned with the locality of mind". Yet despite half-hearted concessions of this kind it appears to be taken for granted among most psycho-analytic writers that "the mind" itself exists in an entirely literal sense, however much we may resort to metaphor when we try to describe "it". Sometimes the issue becomes further complicated by the substitution of temporal characteristics for spatial ones, as when Friedlander[15] (p. 14) speaks of the unconscious as "that buried part of the mind which reaches down into the early years of existence". Even if *per impossibile* the idea of "regions" of the mind, stretching spatially to great "depths", were taken as legitimate, the idea of a stretch backwards in time seems particularly puzzling.

The truth is that, from many passages, one receives the impression that Freud is offering a sort of "para-physics" or "para-physiology" involving counterpart entities (of a "psychological" kind) to those of ordinary physics and ordinary physiology. Discussing the "psychic apparatus" he writes: "We thus ascribe to the apparatus a sensible and a motor end . . . this is only in compliance with the demand long familiar to us that the psychic apparatus must be constructed like a reflex apparatus" (Freud[16], p. 426). On the other hand he clearly does not regard his theory as in any sense a contribution to physiology. Psycho-analysis, he says, "must dissociate itself from every foreign preconception, whether anatomical, chemical, or physiological, and must work throughout with conceptions of a purely psychological order" (Freud[17], p. 16). Moreover the laws governing the "psychological" world are as deterministic as those of traditional physics, and belief in free-will is "quite unscientific, and . . . must give ground before a determinism which governs even mental life" (Freud[18], p. 187). From these and similar passages it is plain that Freud regularly thought in dualistic terms, and that the "psychological world" was to him some kind of counterpart to the "physical" world. Thus just as structures of clockwork explain the regular, and highly predictable behaviour of clocks, so structures of non-physical not-clockwork must be postulated to explain the similarly determined, though less easily predictable, behaviour of human beings. The position has been admirably described by MacIntyre[19] (p. 23) in his excellent book on Freud's concept of "the unconscious".

[12]Freud, S., *The Interpretation of Dreams*, tr. A. A. Brill. Allen & Unwin, 1927.
[13]Lee, R. S., *Freud and Christianity*. James Clarke & Co., London, 1948.
[14]Glover, *Freud or Jung*.
[15]Friedlander, K., *Psycho-analytic Approach to Juvenile Deliquency*. Kegan Paul, Trench, Trubner & Co., 1947.
[16]Freud, *Interpretation of Dreams*.
[17]Freud, *Introductory Lectures*.
[18]Freud, *Introductory Lectures*.
[19]MacIntyre, A. C., *The Unconscious*. Routledge & Kegan Paul, 1958.

Freud's picture of the world [According to MacIntyre:] as a series of places where various entities move about is, to borrow and distort an expression of Hobbes, "the ghost of the central nervous system sitting crowned upon the grave thereof". What Freud in fact does is to bring a scheme of explanation derived from neurology to the phenomena which his psychological studies had forced on his attention.

There is nothing objectionable about pictorial models as such. But the words "the unconscious", whether regarded as a pictorial model or not, are still tied inescapably to traditional dualism, since even as a model they would seem to be a model for better understanding of "the mind". I do not dispute that concepts such as "system", "structure", and "core" could be used for model-building, but it needs to be made clear that such models are models for understanding human behaviour, not models for understanding a recondite entity called "the mind".*

CONCLUSIONS

I have argued in this chapter that the concept of "the unconscious" requires to be abandoned. To regard this concept as referring to something "real" is both unnecessary and misleading; as a link-concept (or intervening variable) linking apparently disparate events it is valueless, since it achieves nothing which cannot also be achieved by the concept of "unconscious purposes" or "unconscious motives"; and as part of a pictorial model it continues to generate confusion since it is inextricably tied to traditional dualism and suggests a picture of what "the mind" is like. Psycho-analysis can manage perfectly well without it.

---

*I am grateful to Dr. J. D. Sutherland for letting me see an interesting formulation of such a model. In this formulation the key-note is that of integration of those "sub-systems" which were "split off" from the main system. Compare also the title of Dr. R. D. Laing's book, *The Divided Self* (Tavistock Publications, 1960).

4

M. H. ERDELYI

Modelling the Unconscious

MEANING AND EVOLUTION OF THE REPRESSION/DEFENSE CONCEPT

Freud's use of the concept of defense (if not the term itself) antedates psychoanalysis. . . . In his report, "A Case of Successful Treatment by Hypnotism" (1892–1893), Freud advanced a dynamic conception of hysteria, in which one side of a conflict is intentionally barred—"suppressed," "excluded," "dissociated"—from consciousness: "The distressing antithetic idea, which seems to be inhibited, is removed from association with the intention and continues to exist as a disconnected idea, often unconsciously, to the patient himself" (Freud, 1892–1893, p. 122).

This basic notion was developed over the next several years through a bewildering profusion of more-or-less interchangeable rubrics, including "repression," "suppression," "inhibition," "exclusion," "removal," "censorship," "defense," "resistance," "forcible repudiation," "intentional forgetting," and "disavowal" (denial). Not surprisingly, such terminological sprawl produced confusions in both terminology and concept (cf. Brenner, 1957; Erdelyi and Goldberg, 1979; Eriksen and Pierce, 1968; Holmes, 1974; MacKinnon and Dukes, 1964; Madison, 1956; 1961; Sjöbäck, 1973; Wolitzky, Klein, and Dworkin, 1976).

After an initial burst of terminological experimentation, which never altogether subsided and which for a brief period saw *defense* emerge as a key term synonymous with repression, Freud settled upon repression (*Verdräng-ung*) as the generic construct, though never with complete consistency or generality. In his late writings (e.g., Freud, 1926), he sought to reverse himself and supplant repression with defense; but he never managed to maintain consistency in this regard, and so the terms *repression* and *defense* are to be regarded as synonymous (except in one sense, to be explained below). Although psychoanalysts today tend to favor the general term, *defense*, most of Freud's important theoretical writings on the topic are formulated in terms of *repression*. Thus, when he states that "repression is the foundation stone on which the whole structure of psychoanalysis rests, the most essential part of it" (Freud, 1914b, p. 16), we are to understand that he is speaking of defense processes in general.

The terminological problem is almost surely not one merely of carelessness but involves a subtle evolution of the concept itself, one that bears some parallels to the evolution of the force concept in physics. In Freud's earliest writings, *repression* referred to the (apparently) simple notion that some distressing wish, idea, or memory was forced out or kept out of consciousness. Thus: "*A hysterical subject seeks intentionally to forget an experience or forcibly repudiates, inhibits and suppresses an intention or idea*" (Freud, 1892/ 1940, p. 153); "it was a question of things which the patient wished to forget, and therefore intentionally repressed from his conscious thought and inhibited and suppressed" (Breuer and Freud, 1893, p. 10). In hysterics, his earliest patients, the effect of this repression was rather straightforward: It resulted in amnesia for the rejected material. However, it very soon became obvious that the process was often more subtle. As early as 1894, for example, Freud observed in connection with obsessive-compulsive patients, who as a rule do not exhibit amnesia for distressing events, that repression can take another form: What these patients repress are not the actual facts or details of a painful event but their emotional component. Thus, "[the] defense against the incompatible idea was effected by separating it from its affect; the idea itself remained in consciousness" (Freud, 1894, p. 58). This affective form of repression, which already resists expression in simple force-vector terms (requiring some kind of previous splitting or dissociation between cognition and affect) has come to be known in psychoanalysis as the defense mechanism of *isolation*. In Freud's terminology (at least until 1926) isolation was to be understood, simply, as a form of repression.

With the accumulation of additional clinical experience, it became clear that there were actually many ways in which distressing or "unbearable" mental contents could be excluded (or partially excluded) from consciousness. In just two published case histories, the "Rat Man" (1909) and the "Psychotic Dr. Schreber" (1911) Freud deals with more than a dozen of such specific devices (not always by actual name), including omission and ellipsis, symbolization, isolation, displacement, doubt, regression, reaction formation, undoing, rationalization, denial, and projection. These constructs are no longer synonyms of one another but are used to describe distinct mechanisms by which repression (defense) can be implemented.

With the progressive broadening of the repression concept, the problem eventually had to be faced: How was repression in this general sense (subsuming a multiplicity of specific techniques) to be distinguished from the original, simplistic notion of repression as the forcing out or keeping out of some specific mental content from consciousness? It is this problem that Freud sought to resolve in his monograph, *Inhibitions, Symptoms and Anxiety* (1926), where he proposed that the term *defense* (*Abwehr*) replace the by then overgrown construct of *repression*, and that the original term be reserved for the early, simple meaning, namely, motivated amnesia or forgetting. Although the suggestion is implemented by some later psychoanalysts (e.g., Fenichel, 1945; A. Freud, 1936), Freud himself did not pursue it with any consistency. *Repression* in Freud's later writings continues to be, on the whole, synonymous with *defense*, although from time to time Freud distinguishes the two senses of the term by speaking of "repression in the broadest sense" (defense) and "repression in the narrow sense" (motivated forgetting). We shall here follow Freud's general practice of equating repression with defense, qualifying the term on those occasions when it is intended narrowly.

Having touched on some of the terminological issues, let us now turn to the more substantive question of meaning. Nomenclature aside, what does the concept of repression (defense) signify? Since there are unresolved problems in this connection also, we decompose what might be regarded as the "standard" definition in contemporary psychoanalysis (e.g., Brenner, 1973) into its constituent elements, only the first two of which, in the author's judgment, are actually crucial.

Defense mechanisms constitute:

1. techniques for distorting or outrightly rejecting from consciousness some feature of reality (physical or psychological)

2. for the purpose of avoiding the unbearable psychological pain ("anxiety") which it would provoke in consciousness.

3. Defense mechanisms are often conceived of as ego devices which

4. are prototypically unconscious.

The first component of the definition is essentially a paraphrase of Freud's own statement in his article on the topic, "Repression" (Freud, 1915a): "*the essence of repression lies simply in the function of rejecting and keeping something out of consciousness*" (p. 105).

The second element of the definition incorporates Freud's statement in the same article and many of his other writings that the rejection from consciousness has a defensive purpose (hence *defense* mechanisms), that of "avoiding 'pain'" (p. 105). In *Inhibitions, Symptoms and Anxiety* (1926) the psychological pain motivating defense is reconceptualized as "anxiety," which Freud uses in the broadest possible sense to mean realistic fears ("reality anxiety"), irrational fears ("neurotic anxiety"), and guilt ("moral anxiety").

The third component of the definition makes sense in the framework of the structural model, but it is hardly crucial for the concept (note that the structural model was introduced in 1923, more than a quarter of a century after the concept of repression/defense). It would be possible to jettison the structural model without in the slightest degree undermining the viability of the theory of defense. Thus, the notion that defense mechanisms are *ego* mechanisms (Freud, 1923; 1933; A. Freud, 1936) is a subsidiary idea grafted onto the basic repression/defense concept.

As regards the last component of the definition, there is wide consensus among contemporary psychoanalysts that the defenses are unconscious. However, this feature is by no means basic to Freud's own stance. In his later writings (perhaps under the influence of Anna Freud), Freud does stipulate that defense processes are themselves unconscious. However, up to 1915 if not later (cf. Erdelyi and Goldberg, 1979), defense or repression was often treated as conscious, so much so, that at one juncture Freud felt compelled to remind the reader that defenses are not *necessarily* conscious (Freud, 1915a, p. 106). It is often suggested in textbooks that repression is the unconscious mechanism of which *suppression* is the conscious counterpart. This is not so. As Erdelyi and Goldberg (1979) have demonstrated, there is no real basis for such a distinction in the writings of Freud, who, from his earliest writings (e.g., Breuer and Freud, 1893) to his last (Freud, 1940), treated repression and suppression interchangeably.

Although clinical experience shows that defenses are often used unconsciously, there exists no theoretical necessity to foist a sharp distinction upon their conscious and unconscious deployment. Such a distinction would not only be artificial but theoretically pernicious as well. It would confuse the question of defense with the question of the unconscious, producing an error that is the obverse counterpart of the pre-Freudian philosophical fiat that unconscious processes are (by definition) not psychological. With such an imposed dissociation upon the continuity of mental life, no meaningful science of psychology is possible, as Freud emphasized. . . . To turn around now and exclude conscious activity from the continuity of mental life—to impose another gratuitous theoretical discontinuity—would be equally inappropriate and unpromising. If the question of unconsciousness should be at issue in a particular clinical or experimental context one need only qualify the defenses under consideration as conscious or unconscious—conscious versus unconscious repression, conscious versus unconscious displacement, and so forth.

REPRESSION (IN THE NARROW SENSE): SUPPRESSION, CENSORSHIP, DENIAL, AND ISOLATION

In this section we deal with defense processes that are similar in postulated mechanisms, or which are in effect synonyms of one another. It has been already suggested that *repression* (in the narrow sense) and *suppression* are used interchangeably in Freud's writings (if not in the psychoanalytic literature). *Censorship*, discussed in some detail in Chapter 4, is included here because, except for the fact that it is the term of choice in Freud's discussions of dream life, it corresponds substantially to the repression-suppression notion.

Isolation is obviously a cognate notion. In a sense, it is a special form of censorship: It excludes affect from consciousness while allowing the "cold facts" to register.

Denial is a highly problematic term (see Sjöbäck, 1973, Chap. 8), sometimes distinguished from, sometimes equated with repression. One distinction, proposed as well as contradicted by Freud (see also A. Freud, 1936; Janis, Mahl, Kagan, and Holt, 1969) is that denial is a special type of repression, one involving external rather than internal events; in some sense, then, it is a failure of sight. The distinction, as usually applied, turns out to be artificial and ultimately misleading (see Sjöbäck). Denial will be treated here as a failure of sight, but only in a special sense—in the sense of "I see your point" versus "I see a point of light." It is a form of repression which excludes from consciousness not the manifest event(s), . . . but some latent content. . . . Thus, it is not so much a failure of sight as a failure of insight. We shall return to this point later. . . . The neobehavioristic approach to repression is starkly simple. In this lies its attractiveness—as well as its weakness. It takes the extensively investigated behavior of laboratory animals, such as rats, dogs, cats, and pigeons, and treats them as analogs of human cognitive processes.

Perhaps the most brilliant, certainly the most influential version of this perspective, is that of Dollard and Miller (1950). Consciousness is treated as behaving like a frightened laboratory rat, which tries by every means possible to escape from the source of its fright. This conception dovetails nicely with Freud's frequently voiced formula (e.g., Freud, 1926, p. 153), that "repression . . . is, fundamentally, an attempt at flight."

To understand this perspective in concrete terms, we turn to the prototypic experimental situation to which Dollard and Miller's treatment is anchored. A rat is placed in a "Miller Box," which is a rectangular enclosure divided into two compartments by a partition in the middle. One compartment is all white, the other is all black. The floor of the white compartment consists of a metal grill through which electric shock may be administered to the rat. An interesting feature of the partition is that it contains a closed door which opens if the rat performs some specific action, such as turning a wheel or pressing a lever, allowing the rat to scurry from one compartment to the other.

At the beginning of the experiment the tame rat is not frightened of either compartment. It is then placed in the shock compartment (the white side) and exposed to shock. The rat shows every sign of intense fright (it jumps around, urinates, defecates, and so forth). In this agitated state it eventually emits the crucial response of, say, pressing the lever (either by accident or through previous behavior "shaping"), whereupon the compartment door opens, and the rat scampers through it to safety. The procedure is repeated several times until the rat shows clear evidence of having learned the critical instrumental response (pressing the lever).

This part of the experiment demonstrates the phenomenon of instrumental (or Skinnerian) conditioning: The animal learns to respond to a stimulus, S_i (the lever), with a particular response, R_i (pressing), as a result of previous reinforcement, S_j (in this case negative reinforcement, namely, the cessation of shock). Schematically, the instrumental conditioning may be rendered as:

$$S_i \rightarrow R_i \rightarrow S_j$$

Now a second phase of the experiment begins. The rat is placed in the shock compartment but without any further shock being administered. Despite the absence of shock the rat dashes to the lever, presses it, and runs through to the safe compartment. Why does the rat escape in the absence of shock? Dollard and Miller (1950) explain it in terms of classical conditioning: The previously neutral white compartment (CS), through its association with electric shock (UCS), which produces intense fright (UCR), now also elicits fright (CR). Schematically, several trials of:

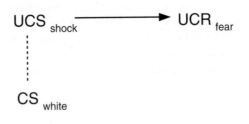

results in:

Thus, the rat's behavior in the second, no-shock phase of the experiment, is explained by a dual-factor theory of conditioning: (1) through *classical conditioning* the rat learns to associate fear with the white compartment; (2) through *instrumental conditioning* it learns to avoid the white compartment.

In humans, consciousness is assumed to behave like the conditioned laboratory rat: Memories previously associated with trauma are avoided (by consciousness). This is another way of saying that memories associated with trauma in the past are rejected or kept out of consciousness, even though, as in the case of the rat, the events in question—perhaps from childhood—are no longer realistically dangerous.

The following question often arises in connection with this rat analogy: The rat avoids the physical compartment that was associated with shock, but why should the human subject avoid thoughts or memories when these (as opposed to the physical events that gave rise to them) were never directly punished? For example, a child may have been severely punished for some misbehavior, and it is understandable that he might avoid emitting the punished *behavior*. But why should he avoid thoughts and feelings associated with the behavior, which are impossible for parents to punish (unless they read minds)?

The answer follows from another well-established conditioning phenomenon, that of generalization. In both instrumental and classical conditioning, it has been amply demonstrated (e.g., Dollard and Miller, 1950) that conditioned responses (R_i CR) are emitted not just to the actual conditioned stimulus (S_i, CS) but also to stimuli that are *similar* to them. Dollard and Miller (1950) argue that in humans the conditioned response of anxiety which motivates avoidance—"cognitive avoidance" (Eriksen and Pierce, 1968; Mischel, 1980)—generalizes to thoughts and impulses related to the punished behavior. Neal Miller has substantiated this hypothesis experimentally:

Human subjects were asked to read aloud a sequence of the letter T and the number 4 (to say "T," "four," "T," "four," and so forth). The saying of *one* of these (for example "T" but not "four") was followed by shock. In short order, the subjects learned (through classical conditioning) to be anxious whenever they pronounced the critical item. The conditioned anxiety was objectively indexed through the monitoring of the galvanic skin response (GSR), which showed selective deflections to T but not to 4. In the second phase of the study, the subjects were informed that no more shock would be administered for the remainder of the experiment. Further, they were told that a series of dots were going to be presented to them. On the appearance of the first dot, they were to *think* (not say) "4"; on the presentation of the second dot they were to think "T"; on the third presentation of the dot, to think "4"; and so forth. They were in every case to *think* of the appropriate stimulus but never to pronounce it aloud. The question of interest was whether the conditioned anxiety (CR) would generalize from the punished *behavior* (the *saying* of "T") to the *thinking* of the item (T). The results [as the Figure on page 34 shows] were unequivocally positive. Subjects became anxious when *thinking* of the stimulus, even though they had been punished only for *saying* it aloud. Dollard and Miller concluded that thoughts (feelings, impulses, and so on) associated with punishment are themselves subject to conditioned avoidance, that is, exclusion from consciousness.

Dollard and Miller additionally suggest that in conjunction with conditioning, there may be a supplementary phylogenetic disposition to adopt a "freeze" or "possum" reaction in response to intense fright involving cessation of motor activity, vocalization, and (one may assume) thinking.

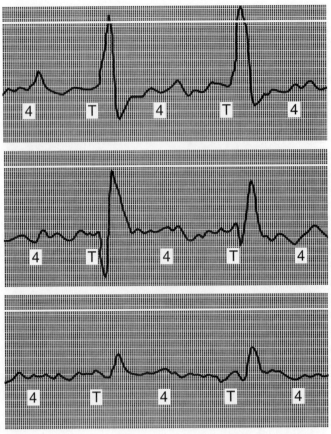

Figure 4.1 "The generalization of conditioned galvanic skin responses from words pronounced aloud to thoughts. The subject was presented with T followed by an electric shock and 4 not followed by shock in an unpredictable order. He named each symbol when he saw it. After a discrimination had been established, the subject was presented with a series of dots and instructed to think 4 when he saw the first dot, T when he saw the second, etc. These are his galvanic responses to presentations 1–5, 11–15, 21–25" (from Dollard & Miller, 1950, p. 206).

Dollard and Miller's theory is termed *neobehavioristic* because of its inclusion of a protocognitive description of the covert processes involved. The model is framed in stimulus-response terminology but incorporates, nevertheless, hypothesized events in the "black box" intervening between the observable stimulus, S, and the response, R. This model, which resembles in important respects Freud's linear compound-instrument model,* . . . pro-

---

*S. Freud, *The Interpretation of Dreams* (1900), *The Standard Edition* 4 and 5 (London: Hogarth Press, 1953), pp. 537–538.—B. A. F.

vides some insights into the way in which conscious repression may become unconscious and how unconscious mentation may result in a shift away from secondary- to primary-process types of thinking.

The model is straightforward. It is assumed that the overt response, R, to the observed stimulus, S, is mediated by a sequence of internal stimulus-response events, which Dollard and Miller term, *cue-producing responses* (this terminology is meant to convey the notion that a mediating event in a sequential chain functions both as a response—to the previous event—and as a stimulus or cue—to the subsequent event.) Schematically:

$$S \longrightarrow [r\text{-}s\text{-}r\text{-}s\text{-}r\text{-}s\text{-}r\text{-}s \ldots r\text{-}s\text{-}r\text{-}s\text{-}r\text{-}s\text{-}r\text{-}s] \longrightarrow R$$

It is assumed by Dollard and Miller (like Freud) that regions close to the terminal response, R, are associated with consciousness. Specifically, to Dollard and Miller (following an isolated suggestion by Freud), this terminal region, prior to R, is associated with verbal-symbolic processes that are conscious. In terms of the scheme:

Region of
verbal/conscious
mediation

$$S \longrightarrow [r\text{-}s\text{-}r\text{-}s\text{-}r\text{-}s \ldots r\text{-}s\text{-}r\text{-}\overset{\frown}{s\text{-}r\text{-}s}\text{-}r\text{-}s] \longrightarrow R$$

The notion that *behavioral* avoidance generalizes to *thought* may be alternately conceptualized as a form of backward temporal generalization—responses generalize not only to stimuli that are physically similar but also to stimuli that are temporally close. Such backward temporal generalization results in anticipatory response inhibition, that is, the inhibition of not just the behavior but of the thoughts that precede the behavior. If the human subject thinks as the rat behaves in the Miller Box, then it may be assumed that response inhibition (or avoidance) generalizes backward in the mediating chain. Hence, the subject may both avoid speaking of certain things—as well as thinking of certain things:

$$S \longrightarrow \left[r\text{-}s\text{-}r\text{-}s\text{-}r\text{-}s \ldots r\text{-}s\text{-}r\text{-}s\text{-}r\text{-}s\text{-}r\text{-}s \right] \longrightarrow R$$

behavior inhibition
conscious repression

Up to this point, the conscious, symbolic system is intact enough for the maintenance of consciousness of the fact that inhibition (repression/suppression) is taking place. Under more extreme circumstances, when potential anxiety is very intense, the anticipatory inhibition/avoidance extends further back (there being ample experimental evidence that under high motivation or drive, generalization increases), to the mediation regions prior to consciousness. In this case, the subject loses consciousness of both the material avoided and of the avoidance itself:

> We would expect the response of stopping thinking to tend to become anticipatory like any other strongly reinforced response. Therefore, the patient should stop thinking, or veer off onto a different line of thought before he reaches the memory of the traumatic incident. [Moreover] he should learn to avoid not only thoughts about the fear-provoking incident but also the associations leading to these thoughts. (Dollard and Miller, 1950, p. 202)

Schematically:

$$S \longrightarrow \left[\text{r-s-r-s-r-s} \ldots \text{r-s-r-s-r-s-r-s-r-s-r-s} \right] \longrightarrow R$$

behavior inhibition
conscious repression
unconscious repression

Although the process of anticipatory avoidance/inhibition is viewed as a "more-or-less" rather than "all-or-none" phenomenon (the greater the anxiety, the greater the backward temporal generalization), the consequence of engaging in conscious rather than unconscious inhibition is seen as critical. As long as basic verbal-symbolic functions are not inhibited, the subject may engage in higher-order discriminations and generalizations, that is, discriminations and generalizations based on symbolic versus physical differences and similarities; when inhibition extends further back, to a point prior to symbolic mediation, discriminations and generalizations are reduced to physical similarities or differences (for example, knife $\cong$ penis, mother $\cong$ wife, and so forth).

An excessive reliance on unconscious repression results in "neurotic stupidity." Not only are major areas of thought excluded from consciousness (in what might be thought of as functional ablations) but the generalizations and discriminations critical to intelligent thinking become dependent on primitive, concretistic (versus abstract) similarities and differences.

A major problem with this approach is the same as that encountered in Freud's linear model. . . . There is no feedback built into the model, which tends to be crudely mechanical as a result. There is, for example, no place in it for subtle, symbolic analyses of the input prior to the decision whether it is to be avoided or permitted access to consciousness.

INFORMATION-PROCESSING APPROACH. We take up here not a specific model but a general approach, one that emphasizes the processing (or misprocessing) of information. The neobehavioristic model, though it is couched in stimulus-response terminology, nevertheless has as its focus the unfolding or inhibition of informational ("cue-producing") mediational sequences. Similarly, Freud's compound-instrument model, and the implicit neurological notions that influenced it (Pribram and Gill, 1976; Sulloway, 1979), are likewise, as has been already emphasized, information-processing in nature.

In the most general sense—the sense that a model deals in some way with the processing or misprocessing of information—probably most models of psychological functioning are information-processing in character. What gives modern information-processing approaches their unique flavor is their espousal (unlike that of previous approaches) of the computer analog. Although this is in no sense an "ultimate" analog, it is nevertheless fundamental in its consequence, for it provides psychology a viable metaphor system for the higher mental processes that allows for "tailor-made" as opposed to "ready-made" models much as mathematics does for physics. Thus, the crucial feature of computer-based information-processing conceptualizations is that they are theoretically malleable; the metaphor system allows, within broad limits, a flexible specification of precisely the type of description one desires to achieve and, also, the possibility of substantive adjustments at a later point. Quite different models can be created within the same metaphor system. Actually, Dollard and Miller's scheme, is capable of expression in precise information-processing terms and of computer simulation.

This last point brings us to another fundamental advantage of the computer metaphor system, its ability, like mathematics, to articulate theory with minute and unambiguous precision. The flowcharts that are the usual summaries of information-processing theories are shorthand for processes that in principle can be simulated through a full fledged computer program. Flaws or hidden paradoxes . . . emerge unmistakably in such simulations and cannot be camouflaged with clever writing or rhetoric. Further, such simulations can prove, with mathematical precision, that notions that might be considered logically or "common-sensically" untenable may not in fact be so. It had been suggested, for example (cf. Erdelyi, 1974), that the phenomenon of "perceptual defense" (perceptual repression) was impossible, because in order to know that one had to defend against seeing something, one had first to see it. (Sartre [1943] raised similar objections to the notion of self-deception or repression.) Moreover, it was argued that such a process as perceptual defense was scientifically untenable because it implied the existence of a homunculus—a little man—in the head, responsible for making decisions about defense. The computer information-processing approach has shown such misgivings to be unfounded (Erdelyi, 1974), for computers easily simulate the processes that had been considered impossible. . . .

In contemporary information-processing flowcharts the "censors" or "screens" (or "filters") in the model* would be usually rendered as "decision nodes." In Figure 5.9 [*Figure 4.2*] this simple model of repression/censorship is paraphrased in modern flowchart form with decision- and command-nodes supplanting the earlier censors. The first censor corresponds to the decision node (in first triangle), "Is anxiety level $x \geq \mu$?" (where "μ" is the current criterion of "unbearability"). Thus, if the level of anxiety that the information would provoke in consciousness matches or exceeds the unbearability criterion, the information-processing is aborted ("Stop processing/accessing information"), without it being transferred to *Pcs.* (a preconscious information buffer). Note that the value of μ may actually vary, so that when the individual feels in a particularly vulnerable state the criterion value, μ, may be set very low, whereas under more auspicious circumstances, it might be set much higher (allowing for the possibility of consciousness for the painful material that is excluded from consciousness in other circumstances). Also, any agent (such as hypnosis or sodium pentothal) that would lower the level of anxiety, x, associated with the information, would necessarily result in greater potential consciousness for the material.

If $x < \mu$ (that is, x is not $\geq \mu$), then the information is processed/transferred into the buffer *Pcs.* Here the material is subjected to another censorship, in the guise of a new decision test, "Is $x \geq \nu$?" where ν is an anxiety criterion that is laxer than the former, μ. If the material is still too anxiety-provoking by this criterion ($x \geq \nu$) then, again, it fails to be processed, and is not made accessible to consciousness. (Freud's discussion of the preconscious would suggest that a subject might consciously alter, "through a decision of will," the criterion value of ν so as to access, if necessary, material that may be fairly, but not unbearably, distressing; thus, material in the preconscious buffer may be rendered accessible with effort.)

In the flowchart, an additional decision node has been added, namely, "Is $x \geq \omega$?" which determines whether material in consciousness (which may be quite anxiety-provoking, even if $x < \nu$) is to be acted out or communicated (through free association, for example). In the experimental literature the subject's failure to *report* anxiety-provoking (perhaps embarrassing) conscious *thoughts* is termed response suppression. It is with this decision node, which concerns overt-response decisions, that mathematical decision theory has concerned itself (cf. Erdelyi, 1974; Green and Swets, 1966; Swets, 1964). As Erdelyi and Goldberg (1979) have argued, there is no theoretical reason why this extremely fruitful mathematical framework should not be conceptually generalized to earlier decision nodes, resulting in a grand unification within a highly formal theoretical system of dynamic phenomena. It is for this reason in part that the author argued earlier against the exclusion of conscious defenses from the domain of defense processes in general.

---

*Offered by Freud in *The Interpretation of Dreams*, chapter 7, vol. 4.—B. A. F.

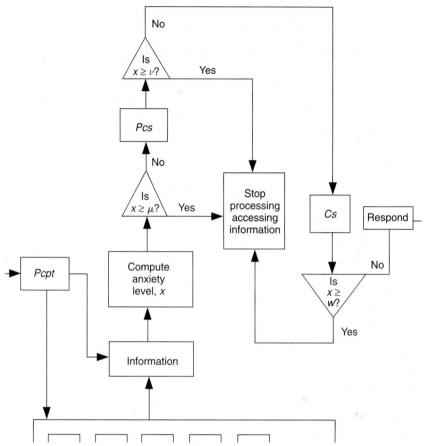

Figure 4.2 Freud's repression/censorship notion in modern information-processing terms.

Although Freud did not specifically include this third "screen" in his Chapter VII model, it is implicit in his overall theory—and therapeutic experience. The withholding of embarrassing conscious ideas in psychoanalytic psychotherapy—the breaking of the "basic rule"—is standard fare. By including two censors in his Chapter VII model, Freud's intent was not to suggest that there were merely two such sites, but rather that there were more than one: "We shall do well . . . to assume that to every transition from one system to that immediately above it (that is, every advance to a higher stage of psychical organization) there corresponds a new censorship" (Freud, 1915b, p. 192).

The author (Erdelyi, 1974; Erdelyi and Goldberg, 1979) has shown how biased decisions are in fact ubiquitous at all levels, starting at the perceptual periphery (for example, "Shall I look?") extending to the response periphery ("Shall I report what I have seen/thought?"). Thus, "there is no single locus or set of loci at which tendentious processing (censoring, filtering, etc.) occurs; rather, *bias begins at the beginning and ends only at the very end of information processing"* (Erdelyi and Goldberg, 1979, p. 391).

Obviously, then, the flowchart in Figure 5.9 [*Figure 4.2*] is a *very* schematic summary of the model. It oversimplifies in conceptual as well as in trivial ways. For example, as rendered here, without certain necessary subroutines there is no provision for clearing information from the various buffers once the information has been entered into them. At a more conceptual level, it is clear that variants of repression, such as isolation, would require another set of decision and command nodes. In the case of isolation, the nodes would have to bring about the dissociation between affect and factual information in order to allow the facts (minus the affect) to be experienced in consciousness (assuming that the affectless facts do not breach the decision criteria, μ and ν). Because of the immense complexity of defense processes, probably any general model would be oversimple. Nevertheless, actual simulations of complex defensive maneuvers have been written and tested by Colby and his associates (e.g., Colby, 1981; Faught, Colby, and Parkinson, 1977). In their work, they report on a sophisticated self-deceiver, the paranoid PARRY (a program), which manages to pass Turing-like tests of indistinguishability vis-à-vis human paranoids (Colby, Hilf, Weber, and Kraemer, 1972). When PARRY is sufficiently threatened, its reality-testing routine (the INFERENCE process) is overridden by the reality-distorting PARANOID MODE, which defends it against unbearable mental distress, "shame." Thus: "if shame crosses a threshold for paranoia (SHAME equal to 10), the paranoid mode is activated. The first consequence of the paranoid mode is the rejection of the belief that led to the increase in shame by resetting the truth value of the belief. . . . Instead an alternate belief is inferred" (Faught, Colby, and Parkinson, 1977, pp. 175–176). It should be noted, moreover, that in the simulation, the paranoid intention is "activated outside the normal intention process on condition of extreme shame affect. Such a process is a clear example of unconscious processing, an intentional process that is not available to conscious inspection either during or after its performance" (p. 179).

REFERENCES

Brenner, C. 1957. The Nature and development of the concept of repression in Freud's writings. *Psychoanalytic Study of the Child* 12:19–46.
———. 1973. *An Elementary Textbook of Psychoanalysis* (2nd Ed.) Garden City, N.Y.: Doubleday.
Breuer, J., and S. Freud (1893). On the psychical mechanism of hysterical phenomena: Preliminary Communication. Trans. by A. Strachey and J. Strachey. In *The Standard Edition*, ed. by J. Strachey. Vol. 2. London: Hogarth Press, 1955.
Colby, K. M. 1981. Modelling a paranoid mind. *The Behavioral and Brain Sciences* 4: 515–560.
Colby, K. M., F. D. Hilf, S. Weber, and H. C. Kraemer 1972. Turing-like indistinguishability tests for the validation of a computer simulation of paranoid processes. *Artificial Intelligence* 3:199–221.

Dollar, J., and N. E. Miller 1950. *Personality and Psychotherapy*. New York: McGraw-Hill.

Erdelyi, M. H. 1974. A new look at the New Look: Perceptual defence and vigilance. *Psychological Review* 81:1–25.

Erdelyi, M. H., and B. Goldberg 1979. Let's not sweep repression under the rug: Toward a cognitive psychology of repression. In *Functional Disorders of Memory*, ed. by J. F. Kihlstrom and F. J. Evans. Hillsdale, N.J.: Erlbaum.

Eriksen, C. W., and J. Pierce 1968. Defense mechanisms. In *Handbook of Personality Theory and Research*, ed. by E. Borgatta and W. Lambert. Chicago: Rand McNally.

Faught, W. S., K. M. Colby, and R. C. Parkinson 1977. Inferences, affects and intentions in a model of paranoia. *Cognitive Psychology* 9:153–187.

Fenichel, O. 1945. *The Psychoanalytic Theory of Neurosis*. New York: Norton.

Freud, A. (1936) *The Ego and the Mechanisms of Defense*. Trans. by C. Baines. New York: International Universities Press, 1946.

Freud, S. (1892b). Sketches for the "preliminary communication" of 1893: (C) On the theory of hysterical attacks. In *The Standard Edition*, ed. and trans. by J. Strachey. Vol. 1. London: Hogarth Press, 1966. (Written possibly with J. Breuer, in Nov. 1892; originally published, 1940).

————. (1892–1893). A case of successful treatment by hypnotism: With some remarks on the origin of hysterical symptoms through "counter-will." *The Standard Edition*, ed. and trans. by J. Strachey. Vol. 1. London: Hogarth Press, 1966.

————. (1900). *The Interpretation of Dreams*. In *The Standard Edition*, ed. and trans. by J. Strachey. Vols. 4 and 5. London: Hogarth Press, 1953.

————. (1909). Notes upon a case of obsessional neurosis. Trans. by A. Strachey and J. Strachey. *The Standard Edition*, ed. by J. Strachey. Vol. 10. London: Hogarth Press, 1955.

————. (1911). Psychoanalytic notes upon an autobiographical account of a case of paranoia (dementia paranoides). Trans. by A. Strachey and J. Strachey. *The Standard Edition*, ed. by J. Strachey. Vol 12. London: Hogarth Press, 1958.

————. (1914b). The History of the Psychoanalytic Movement. Trans. by J. Rivière and J. Strachey. *The Standard Edition*, ed. by J. Strachey. Vol 14. London: Hogarth Press, 1957.

————. (1915a). Repression. Trans. by C. M. Baines and J. Strachey. *The Standard Edition*, ed. by J. Strachey. Vol. 14. London: Hogarth Press, 1957.

————. (1915b). The Unconscious. Trans. by C. M. Baines and J. Strachey. *The Standard Edition*, ed. by J. Strachey. Vol 14. London: Hogarth Press, 1957.

————. (1926). Inhibitions, Symptoms and Anxiety. Trans. by A. Strachey and J. Strachey. *The Standard Edition*, ed. by J. Strachey. Vol 20. London: Hogarth Press.

————. (1940). An Outline of Psycho-Analysis. *The Standard Edition*, ed. and trans. by J. Strachey. Vol. 23. London: Hogarth Press, 1964.

Green, D. M., and J. A. Swets 1966. *Signal Detection Theory and Psychophysics*. New York: Wiley.

Holmes, D. S. 1974. Investigations of repression: Differential recall of material experimentally or naturally associated with ego threat. *Psychological Bulletin* 81:632–653.

Janis, I., G. Mahl, J. Kagan, and R. Holt 1969. *Personality; Dynamics, Development and Assessment*. New York: Harcourt Brace and World.

MacKinnon, D., and W. Dukes 1964. Repression. In *Psychology in the Making*, ed. by L. Postman. New York: Knopf.

Madison, P. 1956. Freud's repression concept. *Inter. J. of Psychoanalysis* 37:75–81.

————. 1961. *Freud's Concept of Repression and Defense, Its Theoretical and Observational Language*. Minneapolis: University of Minnesota Press.

Mischel, W. 1976. *Introduction to Personality*. 2nd ed. New York: Holt, Rinehart and Winston.

Pribram, K. H., and M. M. Gill 1976. *Freud's Project Reassessed*. New York: Basic Books.

Sjöbäck, H. 1973. *The Psychoanalytic Theory of Defensive Processes*. New York: Wiley.

Sulloway, F. J. 1979. *Freud: Biologist of the Mind*. New York: Basic Books.

Swets, J. A. (Ed.) 1964. *Signal Detection and Recognition by Human Observers*. New York: Wiley.

Wolitzky, D. L., G. S. Klein, and S. F. Dworkin 1976. An Experimental approach to the study of repression: Effects of a hypnotically induced fantasy. In *Psychoanalysis and Contemporary Science*, ed. by D. P. Spence. Vol 4. New York: International Universities Press.

5

JÜRGEN HABERMAS

The Interpretation of a Case

FREUD'S GENERAL INTERPRETATIONS* contain assumptions about interaction patterns of the child and his primary reference persons, about corresponding conflicts and forms of conflict mastery, and about the personality structures that result at the end of the process of early childhood socialization, with their potential for subsequent life history. These personality structures even make possible conditional predictions. Since learning processes take place in the course of communicative action, theory can take the form of a narrative that depicts the psychodynamic development of the child as a course of action: with typical role assignments, successively appearing basic conflicts, recurrent patterns of interaction, dangers, crises, solutions, triumphs, and defeats. On the other hand, conflicts are comprehended metapsychologically from the viewpoint of defense, as are personality structures in terms of the relations between ego, id, and super-ego. Consequently this history is represented schematically as a self-formative process that goes through various stages of self-objectivation and that has its telos in the self-consciousness of a reflectively appropriated life history.

Only the metapsychology that is presupposed allows the *systematic generalization* of what otherwise would remain pure *history*. It provides a set of categories and basic assumptions that apply to the connections between language deformation and behavioral pathology in general. The general inter-

From Jürgen Habermas, *Knowledge and Human Interests*, translated by J. J. Shapiro (London: Heinemann, 1972), chapter 11, pp. 258–267. Reprinted by permission of Basil Blackwell, Oxford.
*I.e., of the "empirical" material which the "analytic dialogue" gives to the analyst.—B. A. F.

pretations developed in this framework are the result of numerous and repeated clinical experiences. They have been derived according to the elastic procedure of hermeneutic anticipations (*Vorgriffe*), with their circular corroboration. But these experiences were already subject to the *general anticipation of the schema of disturbed self-formative processes.* In addition, an interpretation, once it claims the status of "generality," is removed from the hermeneutic procedure of continually correcting one's preunderstanding on the basis of the text. In contrast to the hermeneutic anticipation of the philologist, general interpretation is "fixed" and, like a general theory, must prove itself through predictions deduced from it. If psychoanalysis offers a narrative background against which interrupted self-formative processes can be filled out and become a complete history, the predictions that have been obtained with its help serve the reconstruction of the past. But they, too, are hypotheses that can prove wrong.

A general interpretation defines self-formative processes as lawlike successions of states of a system: Each succession varies in accordance with its initial conditions. Therefore the relevant variables of developmental history can be analyzed in their dependence on the system as a whole. However, the objective-intentional structure of life history, which is accessible only through self-reflection, is not functionalistic in the normal sense of this term. The elementary events are processes in a drama, they do not appear within the instrumentalist viewpoint of the purposive-rational organization of means or of adaptive behavior. The functional structure is interpreted in accordance with a dramatic model. That is, the elementary processes appear as parts of a structure of interactions through which a "meaning" is realized. We cannot equate this meaning with ends that are realized through means, on the model of the craftsman. What is at issue is not a category of meaning that is taken from the behavioral system of instrumental action, such as the maintenance of the state of a system under changing external conditions. It is a question, rather, of a meaning that, even if it is not intended as such, takes form in the course of communicative action and articulates itself reflectively as the experience of life history. This is the way in which "meaning" discloses itself in the course of a drama. But in our own self-formative process, we are at once both actor and critic. In the final instance, the meaning of the process itself must be capable of becoming part of our consciousness in a critical manner, entangled as we are in the drama of life history. The subject must be able to relate his own history and have comprehended the inhibitions that blocked the path of self-reflection. For the final state of a self-formative process is attained only if the subject remembers its identifications and alienations, the objectivations forced upon it and the reflections it arrived at, as the path upon which it constituted itself.

Only the *metapsychologically founded and systematically generalized history* of infantile development with its typical developmental variants puts the physician in the position of so combining the fragmentary information obtained in analytic dialogue that he can reconstruct the gaps of memory and hypothetically anticipate the experience of reflection of which the patient is at first incapable. He makes interpretive suggestions for a story that the patient cannot tell. Yet they can be verified in fact only if the patient adopts them and tells his own story with their aid. The interpretation of the case is corroborated only by the successful continuation of an interrupted self-formative process.

General interpretations occupy a singular position between the inquiring subject and the object domain being investigated. Whereas in other areas theories contain statements about an object domain to which they remain external as statements, the validity of general interpretations depends directly on statements about the object domain being applied by the "objects," that is the persons concerned, to *themselves.* Information in the empirical sciences usually has meaning only for participants in the process of inquiry and, subsequently, for those who use this information. In both cases, the validity of information is measured only by the standards of cogency and empirical accuracy. This information represents cognitions that have been tested on objects through application to reality; but it is valid only for subjects. To the contrary, analytic insights possess validity for the analyst only after they have been accepted as knowledge by the analysand himself. For the empirical accuracy of general interpretations depends not on controlled observation and subsequent communication among investigators but rather on the accomplishment of self-reflection and subsequent communication between the investigator and his "object."

It may be objected that, just as with general theories, the empirical validity of general interpretations is determined by repeated applications to real initial conditions and that, once demonstrated, it is binding for all subjects who have any access to knowledge. Although correct in its way, this formulation conceals the specific difference between general theories and general interpretations. In the case of testing theories through observation (that is in the behavioral system of instrumental action), the application of assumptions to reality is a matter for the inquiring subject. In the case of testing general interpretations through self-reflection (that is in the framework of communication between physician and patient), this application becomes *self-application* by the object of inquiry, who participates in the process of inquiry. The process of inquiry can lead to valid information only via a transformation in the patient's self-inquiry. When valid, theories hold for all who can adopt the position of the inquiring subject. When valid, general interpretations hold for the inquiring subject and all who can adopt its position only to the degree that those who are made the object of individual interpretations *know and recognize themselves* in these interpretations. The subject cannot obtain knowledge of the object unless it becomes knowledge for the object—and unless the latter thereby emancipates itself by becoming a subject.

This is not as odd as it may sound. Every accurate interpretation, including those in the cultural sciences, is possible only in a language *common* to the interpreter and his object, owing to the fact that interpretation restores an intersubjectivity of mutual understanding that had been disturbed. Therefore it must hold likewise for both subject and object. But this function of thought has consequences for general interpretations of self-formative processes that do not occur in the case of interpretations in the cultural sciences. For general interpretations share with general theories the additional claim of allowing causal explanations and conditional predictions. In distinction from the strict empirical sciences, however, psychoanalysis cannot make good this claim on the basis of a methodologically clear separation of the object domain from the level of theoretical statements. This has implications (1) for the construction of the language of interpretation, (2) for the conditions of empirical verification, and (3) for the logic of explanation itself.

Like all interpretations, (1) general interpretations also remain rooted in the dimension of ordinary language. Although they are systematically generalized narratives, they remain historical. Historical representation makes use of narrative statements. They are narrative because they represent events as elements of histories. We explain an event narratively if we show how a subject is involved in a history. In every history, individual names appear, because a history is always concerned with changes in the state of a subject or of a group of subjects who consider themselves as belonging together. The unity of the history is provided by the identity of the horizon of expectations that can be ascribed to them. The narrative tells of the influence of subjectively experienced events that change the state of the subject or group of subjects by interviewing in a life-world and attaining significance for acting subjects. In such histories, the subjects must be able to understand both themselves and their world. The historical significance of events always refers implicitly to the meaning structure of a life history unified by ego identity or of a collective history defined by group identity. That is why narrative representation is tied to ordinary language. For only the peculiar reflexivity of ordinary language makes possible communicating what is individual in inevitably general expressions.

By representing an individuated temporal structure, every history is a particular history. Every historical representation implies the claim of *uniqueness*. A *general* interpretation, on the contrary, must break this spell of the historical without departing from the level of narrative representation. It has the form of a narrative, because it is to aid subjects in reconstructing their own life history in narrative form. But it can serve as the background of *many* such narrations only because it does not hold merely for an individual case. It is a *systematically generalized history*, because it provides a scheme for many histories with foreseeable alternative courses. Yet, at the same time, each of these histories must then be able to appear with the claim of being the autobiographical narrative of something individuated. How is such a generalization possible? In every history, no matter how contingent, there is something general, for someone else can find something exemplary in it. Histories are understood as examples in direct proportion to the typicality of their content. Here the concept of type designates a quality of translatability: a history or story is typical in a given situation and for a specific public, if the "action" can be easily taken out of its context and transferred to other life situations that are just as individuated. We can apply the "typical" case to our own. It is we ourselves who undertake the application, abstract the comparable from the differences, and concretize the derived model under the specific life circumstances of our own case.

So the physician, too, proceeds when reconstructing the life history of a patient on the basis of given material. So the patient proceeds himself when, on the basis of the scheme offered him, he recounts his life history even in its previously forgotten phases. Both physician and patient orient themselves not toward an example but, indeed, toward a *scheme.* In a general interpretation, the individual features of an example are missing; the step of abstraction has already been taken. Physician and patient have only to take the further step of application. What characterizes systematic generalization, therefore, is that in hermeneutic experiences, which are relatively a priori to application, the abstraction from many typical histories with regard to many individual cases has already taken place. A general interpretation contains no names of individuals but only anonymous roles. It contains no contingent circumstances, but recurring configurations and patterns of action. It contains no idiomatic use of language, but only a standardized vocabulary. It does not represent a typical process, but describes in type-concepts the scheme of an action with conditional variants. This is how Freud presents the Oedipal conflict and its solutions: by means of structural concepts such as ego, id, and super-ego (derived from the experience of analytic dialogue); by means of roles, persons, and patterns of interaction (arising from the structure of the family); and by means of mechanisms of action and communication (such as object-choice, identification, and internalization). The terminological use of ordinary language is not just an attribute of an accidental stage in the development of psychoanalysis. Rather, all attempts to provide metapsychology with a more rigorous form have failed, because the conditions of the application of general interpretations exclude the formalization of ordinary language. For the terms used in it serve the structuring of narratives. It is their presence in the patient's ordinary language which the analyst and the patient make use of in completing an analytic narrative scheme by making it into a history. By putting individual names in the place of anonymous roles and filling out interaction patterns as experienced scenes, they develop ad hoc a new language, in which the language of general interpretation is brought into accord with the patient's own language.

This step reveals application to be a translation. This remains concealed as long as, owing to the common social background of bourgeois origins and college education, the terminological ordinary language of the theory meets the patient's language halfway. The problem of translation becomes explicit as such when the linguistic distance increases on account of social distance. Freud is aware of this. This is shown in his discussion of the possibility that in the future psychoanalysis might be propagated on a mass basis:

We shall then be faced by the task of adapting our technique to the new conditions. I have no doubt that the validity of our psychological assumptions
will make its impression on the uneducated too, but we shall need to look for
the simplest and most easily intelligible ways of expressing our theoretical
doctrines.[1]

The problems of application that arise with theories in the empirical sciences
only seem to be analogous. In the application of lawlike hypotheses to initial
conditions, it is true that the singular events expressed in existential statements ("this stone") have to be brought into relation to the universal expressions of theoretical statements. But this subsumption is unproblematic, since
the singular events only come into consideration insofar as they satisfy the criteria of general predicates ("this stone" is considered, for example, as "mass").
Thus it suffices to establish whether the singular event corresponds to the operational definition through which the theoretical expression is determined.
This operational application necessarily proceeds within the framework of instrumental action. Consequently it does not suffice for the application of the
theoretical expressions of general interpretations. The material to which the
latter are applied consists not of singular events but of symbolic expressions of
a fragmentary life history, that is of components of a structure that is individuated in a specific way. In this case it depends on the hermeneutic understanding of the person providing the material whether an element of his life
history is adequately interpreted by a suggested theoretical expression. This
hermeneutic application necessarily proceeds in the framework of communication in ordinary language. It does not do the same job as operational application. In the latter case, the deciding factor is whether given empirical
conditions may count as a case for the application of the theory, leaving untouched the theoretical deductions as such. In contrast, hermeneutic application is concerned with *completing* the narrative background of a general
interpretation by creating a narrative, that is the narrative presentation of an
individual history. The conditions of application define a *realization* of the interpretation, which was precluded on the level of general interpretation itself.
Although theoretical deductions are mediated by communication with the
physician, they must be made by the patient himself.

This is the context of (2) the methodological peculiarity that general interpretations do not obey the same criteria of refutation as general theories. If a
conditional prediction deduced from a lawlike hypothesis and initial conditions is falsified, then the hypothesis may be considered refuted. A general interpretation can be tested analogously if we derive a construction from one of
its implications and the communications of a patient. We can give this construction the form of a conditional prediction. If it is correct, the patient will
be moved to produce certain memories, reflect on a specific portion of forgotten life history, and overcome disturbances of both communication and

---

[1]"Lines of Advance in Psycho-Analytic Therapy" (1919), *The Standard Edition* 17 (London:
Hogarth Press, 1955).

behavior. But here the method of falsification is not the same as for general theories. For if the patient rejects a construction, the interpretation from which it has been derived cannot yet be considered refuted at all. For psychoanalytic assumptions refer to conditions in which the very experience in which they must corroborate themselves is suspended: the experience of reflection is the only criterion for the corroboration or failure of hypotheses. If it does not come about, there is still an alternative: either the interpretation is false (that is, the theory or its application to a given case) or, to the contrary, the resistances, which have been correctly diagnosed, are too strong. The criterion in virtue of which false constructions fail does not coincide with either controlled observation or communicative experience. The interpretation of a case is corroborated only by the successful *continuation of a self-formative process,* that is by the completion of self-reflection, and not in any unmistakable way by what the patient says or how he *behaves.* Here success and failure cannot be intersubjectively established, as is possible in the framework of instrumental action or that of communicative action, each in its way. Even the disappearance of symptoms does not allow a compelling conclusion. For they may have been replaced by other symptoms that at first are inaccessible to observation or the experience of interaction. For the symptom, too, is bound in principle to the meaning that it has *for* the subject engaged in defense. It is incorporated in the structure of self-objectivation and self-reflection and has no falsifying or verifying power independent of it.

6

ADOLF GRÜNBAUM

The Cognitive Enthronement of the Patient

THE LOGIC OF validating the general hypotheses of Freud's clinical theory is one of the major themes of Habermas's hermeneutic epistemology. The pivotal claim of his account is that the patient is the ultimate epistemic arbiter of these general psychoanalytic postulates, which he calls "general interpretations" (1971: 261). Within the confines of analytic therapy, these universal hypotheses are used to generate *particular* interpretations pertaining to the individual lives of specific patients. For example, the analyst employs psychoanalytic generalizations retrodictively to construct an etiologic scenario for the pathogenesis of a patient's disorder.

In the context of the clinical setting, Habermas downgrades the doctor cognitively vis-à-vis his patient by endowing the analysand with an epistemic *monopoly* in the testing of the *particular* interpretations pertaining to his own life history. As he puts it, "analytic insights possess validity for the analyst only after they have been accepted as knowledge by the analysand himself" (1971: 261). Having claimed that the patient is thus cognitively preeminent, Habermas infers that "the success and failure [of a psychoanalytic construction] cannot be intersubjectively established" (p. 266). Thereupon, he assumes that induction from just such particular interpretations is the *sole* means for *validating* Freud's universal hypotheses, and not merely for elaborating these generalizations heuristically (p. 259). Hence, he concludes that patients enjoy privileged epistemic access as follows: "the validity of general interpretations

From Adolf Grünbaum, *The Foundations of Psychoanalysis* (Berkeley: University of California Press, 1984). Reprinted by permission.

depends directly on statements about the object domain being applied by the 'objects,' that is the persons concerned, to themselves" (p. 261). Habermas relies on this contention, in turn, to arrive at the methodological dichotomy that general interpretations are not governed by the same criteria of validation as the universal hypotheses of the empirical sciences (pp. 261–266).

It appears that the tenability of this dichotomy depends on the merits of Habermas's cognitive tribute to the patient. Note that if the analysand were actually the ultimate epistemic arbiter, as depicted by Habermas, then the patients treated by psychoanalysts would have truly formidable cognitive powers. Each patient would be not only the best judge but ultimately the *sole* judge of what was in fact the cause of his neurotic disorder, what engendered his sundry dreams, and what induced his lapses of memory, various slips of the tongue, and other bungled actions. Moreover, in Habermas's account, the cognitive monopoly of patients, taken collectively, likewise extends to *universal* psychoanalytic hypotheses. Hence, the validation of Freud's etiology of paranoia, for example, would then ultimately rest entirely on the collective verdicts of those treated for this delusional affliction. I contend that this epistemic thesis is no less untenable than Habermas's two alleged causal dichotomies.

The pillar of Habermas's account of clinical validation is that the patient is the ultimate epistemic arbiter of the general interpretations used retrodictively by the doctor to construct an etiologic scenario for the explanation of the patient's neurosis. He states this thesis of privileged epistemic access on the part of the analysand as follows:

> General interpretations occupy a singular position between the inquiring subject and the object domain being investigated. Whereas in other areas theories contain statements about an object domain to which they remain external as statements, the validity of general interpretations depends directly on statements about the object domain being applied by the "objects," that is the persons concerned, to themselves. . . . analytic insights possess validity for the analyst only after they have been accepted as knowledge by the analysand himself. For the empirical accuracy of general interpretations depends not on controlled observation and subsequent communication among investigators but rather on the accomplishment of self-reflection and subsequent communication between the investigator and his "object." [P. 261]

Thus, his more specific claim is that the application of general interpretations by patients *to themselves* makes them—to the exclusion of their analysts—the decisive epistemic arbiters of the *validity* of these general hypotheses.

But just what *argument* does he offer to show that such self-application by the patients—which occurs in the context of the application made by their analysts—confers the stated *cognitive monopoly* on the former? Why, for example, should the self-application of principles of somatic medicine made by physicians to themselves—alongside the application made by specialists who treat them—not likewise make for a corresponding cognitive monopoly on the part of the former? Habermas's case for endowing the *psychoanalytic* patient with such epistemic primacy rests entirely on his allegation that there is a "specific difference between general theories [of the received empirical sciences] and general interpretations." And he proceeds to state that purported difference as follows:

> In the case of testing theories through observation (that is in the behavioral system of instrumental action), the application of assumptions to reality is a matter for the inquiring subject. In the case of testing general interpretations through self-reflection (that is in the framework of communication between physician and patient), this application becomes self-application by the object of inquiry, who participates in the process of inquiry. The process of inquiry can lead to valid information only via a transformation in the patient's self-inquiry. [P. 261]

I submit that Habermas simply begs the question. Note that in the second sentence he turns to "the case of testing general interpretations" in order to substantiate his claim as to the patient's cognitive preeminence vis-à-vis the analyst in their validation. But this opening phrase of the sentence in question is immediately followed by the *proviso* "through self-reflection." Habermas then tacitly trades on the ambiguity of this term to beg the question at issue. Obviously, the production of free associations and of various responses by the patient in the presence of the analyst—including the *reacting* to interpretations offered by the therapist—is an *intrinsic* part of the clinical testing of analytic interpretations pertaining to the patient. But this commonplace is hardly enough to yield Habermas's desired conclusion. For, if the phrase "testing through self-reflection" were to encapsulate no more than the stated platitude, it would be unavailing to the deduction of Habermas's claim. What he concludes is that the patient enjoys a *cognitive monopoly of appraisal* of interpretations as to their validity *vis-à-vis the analyst*. In order to manage the deduction of the latter thesis of privileged epistemic access—a thesis he states by speaking of "self-application by the object of inquiry"—Habermas relies on the ambiguity of the phrase "testing through *self*-reflection" to build into it the following sort of restriction: The *definitive appraisal* of a particular explanatory interpretation pertaining to a patient *A* as to truth or falsity is to be reserved *de jure* to none other than *A*, to the exclusion of the therapist. Though cognizant that the analyst rather than the patient may well have generated the interpretation, Habermas presupposes from the outset that probatively the therapist must *always* rely on his patient's appraisal of it. For he explicitly tells us that the testing of general interpretations *within the treatment setting* "becomes self-application by the object of inquiry" (1971: 261).

It emerges that Habermas has begged the question at issue by construing the otherwise innocuous phrase "testing through self-reflection" so as to *stipulate* that only the patient's own appraisal can carry out the application of general interpretations to his particular life situation. Of course, it then follows trivially from Habermas's proviso that the patient will be the sole or privileged epistemic arbiter of *any* such clinical hypothesis.

Indeed, note that when Habermas characterized the testing of the ordinary theories of empirical science as being effected "by observation," he studiously refrained from considering the large class of such hypotheses in which the inquiring person who tests the hypothesis is able to apply it to himself/herself in the sense of appraising it himself/herself by means of *self*-observation. Clearly, such self-application is feasible not only in, say, somatic medicine but extends also to all those hypotheses in physics, for example, whose purview includes the human body of a physicist or of some other person capable of testing the hypothesis on his or her own body. This class of self-applications can now serve to construct a reductio ad absurdum of Habermas's argument, which boomerangs. For he was concerned to contrast the testing of general theories of empirical science with the clinical appraisal of general explanatory hypotheses in psychoanalysis, and the burden of this alleged difference is that *only* in the latter validation is there an epistemic preeminence of the *object* of knowledge.

It is ironic, therefore, that by parity with his question-begging reasoning the same cognitive preeminence of the *object* of knowledge will now turn out to be deducible *in physics* for the validation of any hypothesis that is applied to the body of a person A. All that is needed is to proceed à la Habermas, mutatis mutandis, and to require that the very same person A not only be the one to whose body the hypothesis *pertains*, but also be the one who *appraises* the hypothesis as to its truth or falsity. It will be seen to be immaterial to this deduction that the *self*-observation carried out by A while fulfilling this cognitive assignment serves to appraise a physical hypothesis concerning his body, whereas the corresponding "self-reflective" appraisal by the patient in analysis is addressed to a hypothesis about his mental processes.

Thus, consider the physical hypothesis that in an elevator or space rocket falling *freely* in the earth's gravitational field, a weight scale on the floor will register zero for a body placed upon it. Obviously, this hypothesis of weightlessness applies equally well to the bodies of humans trapped in an elevator whose cable has been cut or to the more fortunate astronauts in their space rocket. Now, while emulating Habermas, let us require that some of these persons not only step onto the weight scale during free-fall but also be the ones who ascertain its reading after having examined the scale for defects of operation with the aid of the pertinent auxiliary hypotheses. By analogy with Habermas's initial exclusion of the analyst or other third person from the appraisal of the interpretation in favor of the patient, we have likewise excluded from ascertaining the weight scale readings any one not actually on the scale.

Clearly, under the *stipulated* initial restriction that none other than the person A appraise a hypothesis pertaining to himself, the conclusion reached by Habermas will follow trivially in physics no less than in psychoanalysis. The simple reason is that once his restrictive proviso has been imposed, *only* the *object of inquiry* himself/herself can carry out the *particular* sort of appraisal that has been mandated by the question-begging restriction. Thus, it then follows in physics no less than in psychoanalysis that "the application of assumptions to reality . . . becomes self-application by the object of inquiry." No wonder that, having traded on the ambiguity of his proviso, Habermas is then able to conclude misleadingly: "analytic insights possess validity for the analyst only after they have been accepted as knowledge by the analysand himself" (1971: 261).

In fact, several weighty considerations tell against Habermas's thesis that only the patient's memory-assisted "self-reflection"—to the *exclusion* of the *intersubjective* methods of an outside analytic observer—can attest the validity of analytic interpretations (1971: 266). In outline, these objections are as follows.

1. Substantial evidence recently marshaled by cognitive psychologists has shown that even in the case of *consciously* motivated behavior, a subject does not enjoy privileged cognitive access to the discernment of the motivational causes of his various actions (see Grünbaum 1980: 354–367, for an account of the relevant studies). Though the subject often does have direct access to the individual contents of his mental states, he/she has only *inferential* access—just like outside observers—to such causal linkages as actually connect some of his own mental states. No less than in the case of causal hypotheses pertaining to physical states, the subject's avowal of causal connections between his own mental states is based either on the fallible inferences drawn by himself, or on those carried out by members of his subculture to whom he gives credence. Hence, these avowed causal linkages may be fancied or actual. In short, when a subject attributes a causal relation to some of his own mental states, he does so—just like outside observers—by invoking theory-based causal schemata endorsed by the prevailing belief-system. More often than not, a patient who seeks treatment from a Freudian doctor already brings some psychoanalytic beliefs into the therapy, or is at least receptive to etiologic interpretations of his conduct based on the analyst's theoretical stance. No wonder that analytic patients then find the rationale offered to them credible. But this credulity is hardly tantamount to privileged cognitive access.

By the same token, when a patient deems his own analysis to have issued in the alleviation of his suffering, he is no better able to certify whether this gain was actually wrought through the mediation of Freudian etiologic insights than are outside students of therapeutic *process*. Indeed, two such students, who are analysts, have issued the following disclaimer (Luborsky and Spence 1978: 360): "Psychoanalysts, like other psychotherapists, literally *do not know* how they achieve their results." If Habermas's *ipse dixit* paean to the patient's "self-reflection" is to be believed, all that these investigators need to do to dispel their avowed ignorance is ask the patient to give them the benefit of his truly formidable epistemic powers. A concrete example will now illustrate the fanciful nature of this cognitive enthronement of the patient.

For simplicity, I shall take a well-known instance of forgetting, which Freud sought to explain by pointing to a short-term repression as the cause. I discuss this case in depth in chapter 4. Hence, suffice it to say here that when a young man omitted the Latin word "aliquis" (someone) in his recitation of a line from Virgil's *Aeneid* and Freud supplied the missing word, the young man's associations issuing from this word—interspersed by some of Freud's interjections—yielded, in due course, that he had harbored a presumably repressed fear. He suspected that an Italian girlfriend had become pregnant by him. Freud then informed him that this repressed anxiety had "undeniably" produced his "*aliquis*" lapse, whereas the subject was skeptical that his worry—though genuine—had any causal bearing on his forgetting.

In chapter 4 I argue that Freud has not given any good reason at all for his attribution of this instance of forgetting to the pregnancy fear elicited by the subject's associations. But here, I must ask Habermas: how could the subject possibly know *better than Freud* or any of the rest of us whether his unconscious fear had actually caused his memory slip? A *fortiori*, how can Habermas expect us to believe in the analysand's privileged cognitive access to the validity of the far more ambitious causal claims that are central to the etiologic reconstruction of his neurotic affliction?

2. There is a second set of considerations that undermine Habermas's cognitive enthronement of the patient. Notoriously, neurotics are quite suggestible (Möller 1976: 71). By the same token, their beliefs are quite malleable. Thus, often enough, patients do claim to confirm the etiologic interpretations and sundry causal attributions made by their analysts. But, as subsequent chapters will document, such purported confirmations can be warrantedly explained by the well-attested doctrinal compliance of patients with the subtly communicated theoretical expectations of the healing authority figure to whom they have turned for help. As Freud himself appreciated all too keenly (S.E. 1917, 16: Lectures 27 and 28), even if the analyst does his best to forego overt or covert suggestion, there are myriad ways in which he can unconsciously but persuasively mold the analysand's convictions and engender a compliant pseudocorroboration. Hence, it plainly will not do to adduce the analyst's professional integrity and avowed intent not to abuse his suggestive influence as an adequate safeguard against the elicitation of *spurious confirmations* from the patient.

In an earlier book, Habermas (1971: 268–269) touched on the reproach of spurious corroboration by the patient's doctrinal deference to his therapist. There he deals with this complaint in the course of citing Freud's 1937 article on "Constructions in Analysis," a paper that he had adduced quite misleadingly (1971: 230). . . . It turns out that, in this connection as well, Habermas cites tendentiously from that same paper.

There Freud explains that the patient's verbal agreement with a psychoanalytic construction is not to be taken at face value in and of itself, any more than his denial. Instead, Freud maintains (S.E. 1937, 23: 263), "there are indirect forms of confirmation which are in every respect trustworthy." On the strength of these other indicators, a construction is to be considered validated by the convergence or "consilience" of a whole array of clinical inductions, based on diverse data from the patient's various productions. I shall argue in chapter 10 that reliance on such congruence of clinical inductions from data other than patient assent or denial likewise affords no protection against suggestive adulteration of the patient's responses and the ensuing spurious corroboration. But, for argument's sake, let me nonetheless assume here, as Habermas (1971: 267–269) does, that the confluence of seemingly independent clinical inductions does have probative value, as claimed by Freud.

Then, to the grave detriment of Habermas's allegations, let me call attention to two points.

(i) On the heels of paying his tribute to the probative value of the stated convergence of clinical inductions, Freud (S.E. 1937, 23: 265–266) asserts—now that he is armed with just such inductions—that *the analyst's inference* can *reliably* fill up the serious gaps in the patient's memory. As we recall, such reliance on the analyst's inference is necessary because, as Freud emphasized, the patient's poor mnemonic performance can readily fail to supply the information vital to the reconstruction of his pathogenically crucial past. Thus, if the confluence marshaled by Freud does have probative cogency, while the patient's "yes" or "no" may be discounted, then there is good reason for according cognitive primacy to the analyst's inference over the patient's "self-reflection." And just such an epistemic elevation of the analyst's inference as the ultimate epistemic arbiter of a psychoanalytic construction is both the logical import and explicit tenor of Freud's entire paper. Hence, its conclusion obviously gainsays Habermas's bald, peremptory, though repeated, assertion that "the patient himself is the final authority." Yet Habermas studiously refrains from giving the reader any intimation of this upshot of the pertinent 1937 paper by Freud, any more than he had earlier reported Freud's remark therein about the disappointingly poor showing of the patient's recall.

(ii) As is clear from the context of Habermas's digression (1971: 266–269) into Freud's aforementioned 1937 views on the consilience of inductions, this excursion was occasioned by Habermas's concern to deny that clinical testability can be *intersubjective*. But his approving rehearsal of Freud's ideas on the consilience of clinical inductions is also patently unavailing to his contention that "the success and failure [of a construction] cannot be intersubjectively established" (1971: 266).

This brings me to the appraisal of Habermas's separate statement on the *falsification* of psychoanalytic interpretations (1970: 302; 1971: 266). His aim is to exhibit "the methodological peculiarity that general interpretations do not obey the same criteria of refutation as general theories" (1971: 266). True to form, he begins with a misdepiction of falsifications in the received empirical sciences. Habermas wrote some half century after the publication of the French original of Pierre Duhem's *The Aim and Structure of Physical Theory*. By that time, Duhem's elucidation of falsification in physics had become a staple of elementary courses in the philosophy of science. As Duhem had explained, when a hypothesis H is at issue in a given inquiry, then observational predictions p made by means of H are typically deduced not from H and some initial condition *I* alone, but only from their *conjunction* with some of the auxiliary hypotheses *A* of the larger theoretical system of which *H* is a part. What, then, can the physicist infer deductively from the failure of the predictions *p* under experimental test? Duhem replies:

> when the experiment is in disagreement with his predictions, what he learns is that at least one of the hypotheses constituting this group [*H*, *I*, and *A*] is unacceptable and ought to be modified; but the experiment does not designate which one should be changed. [1954: 187]

In the face of this, Habermas is either unaware of—or chooses to ignore—the typical, if not ineluctable, copresence of the collateral hypotheses *A* with *H* in the very deduction of *p*. And this untutored disregard would seem to be the basis of his case. Thus, speaking of the refutation of the general theories of the received empirical sciences, such as physics, he says (1971: 266): "If a conditional prediction [*p*] deduced from a lawlike hypothesis [*H*] and initial conditions [*I*] is falsified, then the hypothesis may be considered refuted." Oblivious to Duhem's point as to why, on the contrary, the falsity of *p* does *not* entail the falsity of *H* in physics, Habermas then deems it noteworthy that falsification is uncertain in psychoanalysis. Says he:

> if the patient rejects a construction, the interpretation from which it has been derived cannot yet be considered refuted at all. . . . there is still an alternative: either the interpretation is false (that is, the theory or its application to a given case) or, to the contrary, the resistances, which have been correctly diagnosed, are too strong. [1971: 266]

Habermas fails to note that, to the detriment of his thesis of "methodological peculiarity," precisely the same logical situation prevails in physics: The experimental failure of *p* allows that *H* be true, while the falsity of *A* (or of *I*) may be to blame for the falsity of *p*. In short, the logical situation in psychoanalysis is commonplace in any and all sophisticated theories that purport to have observable import. But by simply denying this fact, well known since Duhem, Habermas has manufactured yet another pseudoasymmetry between the methodology of the natural sciences and that of psychoanalysis. Presumably, it was his quest for yet another asymmetry that prompted him to give a separate statement on falsifiability. Be that as it may, his conclusion that, for general interpretations in psychoanalysis, "the method of falsification is not the same as for general theories" (1971: 266) is itself unsound.

REFERENCES

Duhem, P. *The Aim and Structure of Physical Theory*, trans. by P. P. Wiener. Princeton: Princeton University Press, 1954.
Eissler, K. R. Irreverent remarks about the present and the future of psychoanalysis. *Intern. J. of Psycho-analysis* 50 (1969): 461–471.
Grünbaum, A. Epistemological liabilities of the clinical appraisal of psychoanalytic theory. *Nous* 14 (1980):307–385.
Habermas, J. *Zur Logik der Sozialwissenschaften*. Frankfurt: Suhrkamp Verlag, 1970.

———. *Knowledge and Human Interests*, trans. by J. J. Shapiro. Boston: Beacon Press, 1971; London: Heinemann, 1972.

Luborsky, L., and D. P. Spence. Quantitative research on psychoanalytic therapy. In *Handbook of Psychotherapy and Behavior Change*, ed. by S. L. Garfield and A. E. Bergin, 2nd. ed. New York: Wiley, 1978.

Möller, H. J. *Methodische Grundprobleme der Psychiatrie*. Stuttgart: W. Kohlhammer Verlag, 1976.

7

LUDWIG WITTGENSTEIN

Remarks on Freud

15. GIVING A REASON sometimes means 'I actually went this way,' sometimes 'I could have gone this way,' i.e, sometimes what we say acts as a justification, not as a report of what was done, e.g., I *remember* the answer to a question; when asked why I give this answer, I gave a process leading to it, though I didn't go through this process.[1]

16. "Why did you do it?" Answer: "I said to myself such and such . . ." In many cases the motive is just what we give on being asked.[2]

17. When you ask: "Why did you do it?", in an enormous number of cases people give an answer—apodictic—and are unshakable about it, and in an enormous number of cases we accept the answer given. There are other cases where people say they have forgotten their motive. Other cases where you are puzzled immediately after you have done something and ask: "Why did I do

From Ludwig Wittgenstein, *Lectures and Conversations on Aesthetics, Psychology and Religious Belief*, edited by Cyril Barrett (Oxford: Basil Blackwell, 1966) pp. 22–27 and pp. 42–52. Reprinted by permission.

These lectures and conversations were compiled from notes taken by students of Wittgenstein. Those reprinted here were taken by Rush Rhees and James Taylor. The differences between the notes are shown in the footnotes. The editorial notes are by Cyril Barrett.—B. A. F.

[1]We may give the process which led to it before. Or it may be what we now see would justify it.—Rush Rhees [R.]

(It is not a natural usage of 'motive'.) You might say: 'He knows what he was doing, nobody else does.'—James Taylor [T.]

[2]Thus 'reason' does not always mean the same thing. And similarly with 'motive.' 'Why did you do it?' One sometimes answers: 'Well, I said to myself: "I must see him because he is ill."'—actually remembering having said things to oneself. Or again, in many cases the motive is the justification we give on being asked—just that.—R.

this?"[3] Suppose Taylor was in this state and I said: "Look here, Taylor. The molecules in the sofa attract the molecules in your brain, etc . . . and so . . ."

18. Suppose Taylor and I are walking along the river and Taylor stretches out his hand and pushes me in the river. When I ask why he did this he says: "I was pointing out something to you," whereas the psycho-analyst says that Taylor subconsciously hated me.[4] Suppose, e.g., it often happened that when two people were walking along a river:

1. they were talking amicably;

2. one was obviously pointing out something and pushed the other in the river;

3. the person pushed in had a similarity with the father of the other person.

Here we have two explanations:

1. He subconsciously hated the other man.

2. He was pointing at something.

19. Both explanations may be correct. When would we say that Taylor's explanation was correct? When he had never shown any unfriendly feelings, when a church-steeple and I were in his field of vision, and Taylor was known to be truthful. But, under the same circumstances, the psycho-analyst's explanation may also be correct.[5] Here there are two motives—conscious and unconscious. The games played with the two motives are utterly different.[6] The explanations could in a sense be contradictory and yet both be correct. (Love and Hate.)[7]

20. This connects up with something that Freud does. Freud does something which seems to me immensely wrong. He gives what he calls an interpretation of dreams. In his book *The Interpretation of Dreams* he describes one dream which he calls a 'beautiful dream' ['Ein schöner Traum'—R].[8] A patient, after saying that she had had a beautiful dream, described a dream in

---

[3]But is it clear why one should be puzzled?—R.

[4]A lot of things confirm this. At the same time a psycho-analyst has another explanation.—T. We might have evidence that the psycho-analyst's explanation is correct.—R.

[5]He hated me because I reminded him of something. And the psychoanalyst's statement is then corroborated. *How* corroborated?—R.

[6]Utterly different things are done with the statement of conscious motive and with the statement of unconscious motive.—R.

[7]One could be love and one could be hatred.—R.

[8]Freud's 'Ein schöner Traum' (*Die Traumdeutung* Frankfurt: Fischer Bücherei, 1961, p. 240) does not contain the features of the 'beautiful dream' described here. But the dream which does contain them (the 'flowery dream'—'Blumentraum'—p. 289) is in fact described as 'beautiful' or 'pretty' ('schöne'): 'Der schöne Traum wollte der Träumerin nach der Deutung gar nicht mehr gefallen.'—Ed.

which she descended from a height, saw flowers and shrubs, broke off the branch of a tree, etc. Freud shows what he calls the 'meaning' of the dream. The coarsest sexual stuff, bawdy of the worst kind—if you wish to call it that—bawdy from A to Z. We know what we mean by bawdy. A remark sounds to the uninitiated harmless, but the initiated, say, chuckle when they hear it. Freud says the dream is bawdy. *Is* it bawdy? He shows relations between the dream images and certain objects of a sexual nature. The relation he establishes is roughly this. By a chain of associations which comes naturally under certain circumstances, this leads to that, etc.[9] Does this prove that the dream is what is called bawdy? Obviously not. If a person talks bawdy he doesn't say something which seems to him harmless, and is then psycho-analysed.[10] Freud called this dream 'beautiful,' putting 'beautiful' in inverted commas. But *wasn't* the dream beautiful? I would say to the patient: "Do these associations make the dream not beautiful? It was beautiful.[11] Why shouldn't it be?" I would say Freud had cheated the patient. Cf. scents made of things having intolerable smells. Could we therefore say: "The 'best' scent is really all sulphuric acid"?[12] Why did Freud give this explanation at all? Two things people might say:

1. He wishes to explain everything nice in a nasty way, meaning almost that he is fond of bawdy. This is obviously not the case.

2. The connections he makes interest people immensely. They have a charm. It is charming[13] to destroy prejudice.

21. Cf. "If we boil Redpath at 200°C. all that is left when the water vapour is gone is some ashes, etc.[14] This is all Redpath really is." Saying this might have a certain charm, but would be misleading to say the least.

22. The attraction of certain kinds of explanation is overwhelming. At a given time the attraction of a certain kind of explanation is greater than you can conceive.[15] In particular, explanation of the kind 'This is really only this.'

23. There is a strong tendency to say: "We can't get round the fact that this dream is really such and such."[16] It may be the fact that the explanation is extremely repellent that drives you to adopt it.

24. If someone says: "Why do you say it is really this? Obviously it is not this at all," it is in fact even difficult to see it as something else.

---

[9]From a flower to this, a tree to that, etc.—R.

[10]You don't say a person talks bawdy when his intention is innocent.—T.

[11]This is what is called beautiful.—T.

[12]If there is a connection between butyric acid which stinks and the best perfumes, could we on that account put 'the best perfume' in quotes.—T.

[13]To some people.—R.

[14]If we heat this man to 200 degrees Centigrade, the water evaporates . . .'—R.

[15]If you haven't just the right examples in mind.—T.

[16]If we add the connection of something like this beautiful dream to something ugly . . . —R.

25. Here is an extremely interesting psychological phenomenon, that this ugly explanation makes you say you really had these thoughts, whereas in any ordinary sense you really didn't.

1. There is the process ['freier Einfall'—R] which connects certain parts of the dream with certain objects.

2. There is the process 'So this is what I meant.' There is a maze for people to go astray in here.[17]

26. Suppose you were analysed when you had a stammer. (1) You may say that that explanation [analysis—R] is correct which cures the stammer. (2) If the stammer is not cured the criterion may be the person analysed saying: "This explanation is correct,"[18] or agreeing that the explanation given him is correct. (3) Another criterion is that according to certain rules of experience[19] the explanation given is the correct one, whether the person to whom it is given adopts it or not.[20] Many of these explanations are adopted because they have a peculiar charm. The picture of people having subconscious thoughts has a charm. The idea of an underworld, a secret cellar. Something hidden, uncanny. Cf. Keller's two children putting a live fly in the head of a doll, burying the doll and then running away.[21] (Why do we do this sort of thing? This is the sort of thing we do do.) A lot of things one is ready to believe because they are uncanny.

27. One of the most important things about an explanation [in Physics R, T] is that it should work, that it should enable us to predict something [successfully—T]. Physics is connected with Engineering. The bridge must not fall down.

28. Freud says: "There are several instances (cf. Law) in the mind."[22] Many of these explanations (i.e. of psycho-analysis) are not borne out by experience, as an explanation in Physics is.[23] The *attitude* they express is important. They give us a picture which has a peculiar attraction for us.[24]

29. Freud has very intelligent reasons for saying what he says, great imagination and colossal prejudice, and prejudice which is very likely to mislead people.[25]

---

[17]These two need not go together. Either might work and the other not.—R.

[18]'Oh yes, that's what I meant.'—R. Or you may say that the analogy is correct which the person analysed agrees to.—T.

[19]Of explaining such phenomena.—R.

[20]Or you may say that the correct analogy is the accepted one. The one ordinarily given.—T.

[21]Gottfried Keller (1819–1890). A Swiss poet, novelist and short-story writer. The incident to which Wittgenstein refers occurs in *Romeo und Julia auf dem Dorfe*, *Werke* V–VI, Berlin, 1889, p. 84.—Ed.

[22]If you look at what Freud says in explanation—not in his clinical procedure, but, for instance, what we say about the different 'Instanzen' ('instances,' in the sense in which we speak of a court of higher instance) of the mind.—R.

[23]An explanation in a different sense often. Its attractiveness is important, more important than in the case of an explanation in physics.—T.

[24]This does not help us to *predict* anything, but it has a peculiar attraction.—R.

[25]People can be convinced of many things according to what you tell them.—R.

30. Suppose someone like Freud stresses enormously the importance of sexual motives:

1. Sexual motives are immensely important.

2. Often people have good reason to hide a sexual motive as a motive.[26]

31. Isn't this also a good reason for *admitting* sex as a motive for everything, for saying: "This is really at the bottom of everything"? Isn't it clear that a particular way of explaining can bring you to admit another thing. Suppose I show Redpath fifty cases where he admits a certain motive, twenty cases where this motive is an important link. I could make him admit it as a motive in all cases.[27]

32. Cf. The Darwin upheaval. One circle of admirers who said: "Of course," and another circle [of enemies—R] who said: "Of course not."[28] Why in the Hell should a man say 'of course'? (The idea was that of monocellular organisms becoming more and more complicated until they became mammals, men, etc.) Did anyone see this process happening? No. Has anyone seen it happening now? No. The evidence of breeding is just a drop in the bucket. But there were thousands of books in which this was said to be *the* obvious solution. People were *certain* on grounds which were extremely thin. Couldn't there have been an attitude which said: "I don't know. It is an interesting hypothesis which may eventually be well confirmed"?[29] This shows how you can be persuaded of a certain thing. In the end you forget entirely every question of verification, you are just sure it must have been like that.

33. If you are led by psycho-analysis to say that really you thought so and so or that really your motive was so and so, this is not a matter of discovery, but of persuasion.[30] In a different way you could have been persuaded of something different. Of course, if psycho-analysis cures your stammer, it cures it, and that is an achievement. One thinks of certain results of psycho-analysis as a discovery Freud made, as apart from something persuaded to you by a psycho-analyst, and I wish to say this is not the case.

34. Those sentences have the form of persuasion in particular which say 'This is *really* this.' [This means—R] there are certain differences which you have been persuaded to neglect.[31] It reminds me of that marvellous motto:

---

[26]It is disagreeable to have to admit it so often.—R.

[27]If you get him to admit that *this* is at the bottom of everything, is it therefore at the bottom of everything? All you can say is that you can bring certain people to think that it is.—T.

[28]What does their saying this mean?—T. We could say the same thing against both of them. —R.

[29]But people were immensely attracted by the unity of the theory, by the single principle— which was taken to be the obvious solution. The certainty ('of course') was created by the enormous charm of this unity. People could have said: '. . . Perhaps sometime we shall find grounds.' But hardly anyone said this; they were either sure that it was so, or sure that it was not so.—R.

[30]We are likely to think of a person's admitting in analysis that he thought so and so as a kind of discovery which is independent of having been persuaded by a psychoanalyst.—R.

[31]This means you are neglecting certain things and have been persuaded to neglect them.—R.

'Everything is what it is and not another thing.' The dream is not bawdy, it is
something else.

NOTES BY R. R. AFTER A CONVERSATION, SUMMER 1942.

When we are studying psychology we may feel there is something unsatisfactory, some difficulty about the whole subject or study—because we are taking
physics as our ideal science. We think of formulating laws as in physics. And
then we find we cannot use the same sort of 'metric,' the same ideas of mea-
surement as in physics. This is especially clear when we try to describe appearances: the least noticeable differences of colours; the least noticeable
differences of length, and so on. Here it seems that we cannot say: "If A=B,
and B=C, then A=C," for instance. And this sort of trouble goes all through
the subject.

Or suppose you want to speak of causality in the operation of feelings. "Determinism applies to the mind as truly as to physical things." This is obscure
because when we think of causal laws in physical things we think of *experiments*. We have nothing like this in connexion with feelings and motivation.
And yet psychologists want to say: "There *must* be some law"—although no
law has been found. (Freud: "Do you want to say, gentlemen, that changes in
mental phenomena are guided by *chance*?") Whereas to me the fact that there
aren't actually any such laws seems important.

Freud's theory of dreams. He wants to say that whatever happens in a
dream will be found to be connected with some wish which analysis can bring
to light. But this procedure of free association and so on is queer, because
Freud never shows how we know where to stop—where is the right solution.
Sometimes he says that the right solution, or the right analysis, is the one
which satisfies the patient. Sometimes he says that the doctor knows what the
right solution or analysis of the dream is whereas the patient doesn't: the doctor can say that the patient is wrong.

The reason why he calls one sort of analysis the right one, does not seem to
be a matter of evidence. Neither is the proposition that hallucinations, and so
dreams, are wish fulfilments. Suppose a starving man has an hallucination of
food. Freud wants to say the hallucination of anything requires tremendous
energy: it is not something that could normally happen, but the energy is provided in the exceptional circumstances where a man's wish for food is overpowering. This is a *speculation*. It is the sort of explanation we are inclined to
accept. It is not put forward as a result of detailed examination of varieties of
hallucinations.

Freud in his analysis provides explanations which many people are inclined
to accept. He emphasizes that people are *dis*-inclined to accept them. But if
the explanation is one which people are disinclined to accept, it is highly
probable that it is also one which they are *inclined* to accept. And this is what
Freud had actually brought out. Take Freud's view that anxiety is always a
repetition in some way of the anxiety we felt at birth. He does not establish

this by reference to evidence—for he could not do so. But it is an idea which has a marked attraction. It has the attraction which mythological explanations have, explanations which say that this is all a repetition of something that has happened before. And when people do accept or adopt this, then certain things seem much clearer and easier for them. So it is with the notion of the unconscious also. Freud does claim to find evidence in memories brought to light in analysis. But at a certain stage it is not clear how far such memories are due to the analyst. In any case, do they show that the anxiety was necessarily a repetition of the original anxiety?

Symbolizing in dreams. The idea of a dream language. Think of recognizing a painting as a dream. I (L.W.) was once looking at an exhibition of paintings by a young woman artist in Vienna. There was one painting of a bare room, like a cellar. Two men in top hats were sitting on chairs. Nothing else. And the title: "Besuch" ("Visit"). When I saw this I said at once "This is a dream." (My sister described the picture to Freud, and he said 'Oh yes, that is quite a common dream'—connected with virginity.) Note that the title is what clinches it as a dream—by which I do not mean that anything like this was dreamt by the painter while asleep. You would not say of *every* painting 'This is a dream.' And this does show that there is something like a dream language.

Freud mentions various symbols: top hats are regularly phallic symbols, wooden things like tables are women, etc. His historical explanation of these symbols is absurd. We might say it is not needed anyway: it is the most natural thing in the world that a table should be that sort of symbol.

But dreaming—using this sort of language—although it *may* be used to refer to a woman or to a phallus, may *also* be used not to refer to that at all. If some activity is shown to be carried out often for a certain purpose—striking someone to inflict pain—then a hundred to one it is also carried out under other circumstances *not* for that purpose. He may just want to strike him without thinking of inflicting pain at all. The fact that we are inclined to recognize the hat as a phallic symbol does not mean that the artist was necessarily referring to a phallus in any way when she painted it.

Consider the difficulty that if a symbol in a dream is not understood, it does not seem to be a symbol at all. So why call it one? But suppose I have a dream and accept a certain interpretation of it. *Then*—when I superimpose the interpretation on the dream—I can say "Oh yes, the table obviously corresponds to the woman, this to that etc."

I might be making scratches on the wall. It seems in a way like writing, but it is not a writing which either I or anyone else would recognize or understand. So we say I'm doodling. Then an analyst begins to ask me questions, trace associations and so on; and we come to an explanation of why I'm doing this. We may then correlate various scratches which I make with various elements in the interpretation. And we may then refer to the doodling as a kind of writing, as using a kind of language, although it was not understood by anyone.

Freud is constantly claiming to be scientific. But what he gives is *specula-tion*—something prior even to the formation of an hypothesis.

He speaks of overcoming resistance. One "instance" is deluded by another "instance." (In the sense in which we speak of "a court of higher instance" with authority to overrule the judgment of the lower court. R.R.) The analyst is supposed to be stronger, able to combat and overcome the delusion of the instance. But there is no way of showing that the whole result of analysis may not be "delusion." It is something which people are inclined to accept and which makes it easier for them to go certain ways: it makes certain ways of be-having and thinking natural for them. They have given up one way of thinking and adopted another.

Can we say we have laid bare the essential nature of mind? "Concept for-mation." Couldn't the whole thing have been differently treated?

NOTES BY R. R. FOLLOWING CONVERSATIONS IN 1943.

DREAMS. The interpretation of dreams. Symbolism.

When Freud speaks of certain images—say the image of a hat—as symbols, or when he says the image "means" so and so, he is speaking of interpretation; and of what the dreamer can be brought to accept as an interpretation.

It is characteristic of dreams that often they seem to the dreamer to call for an interpretation. One is hardly ever inclined to write down a day dream, or recount it to someone else, or to ask "What does it mean?" But dreams do seem to have something puzzling and in a special way interesting about them—so that we want an interpretation of them. (They were often regarded as messages.)

There seems to be something in dream images that has a certain resem-blance to the signs of a language. As a series of marks on paper or on sand might have. There might be no mark which we recognized as a conventional sign in any alphabet we knew, and yet we might have a strong feeling that they must be a language of some sort: that they mean something. There is a cathedral in Moscow with five spires. On each of these there is a different sort of curving configuration. One gets the strong impression that these different shapes and arrangements must mean something.

When a dream is interpreted we might say that it is fitted into a context in which it ceases to be puzzling. In a sense the dreamer re-dreams his dream in surroundings such that its aspect changes. It is as though we were presented with a bit of canvas on which were painted a hand and a part of a face and cer-tain other shapes, arranged in a puzzling and incongruous manner. Suppose this bit is surrounded by considerable stretches of blank canvas, and that we now paint in forms—say an arm, a trunk, etc.—leading up to and fitting on to the shapes on the original bit; and that the result is that we say: "Ah, now I see why it is like that, how it all comes to be arranged in that way, and what these various bits are . . . " and so on.

Mixed up with the shapes on the original bit of canvas there might be cer-tain forms of which we should say that they do not join on to further figures in the wider canvas; they are not parts of bodies or trees, etc., but bits of writing. We might say this of a snake, perhaps, or a hat or some such. (These would be like the configurations of the Moscow cathedral.)

What is done in interpreting dreams is not all of one sort. There is a work of interpretation which, so to speak, still belongs to the dream itself. In considering what a dream is, it is important to consider what happens to it, the way its aspect changes when it is brought into relation with other things remembered, for instance. On first awaking a dream may impress one in various ways. One may be terrified and anxious; or when one has written the dream down one may have a certain sort of thrill, feel a very lively interest in it, feel intrigued by it. If one now remembers certain events in the previous day and connects what was dreamed with these, this already makes a difference, changes the aspect of the dream. If reflecting on the dream then leads one to remember certain things in early childhood, this will give it a different aspect still. And so on. (All this is connected with what was said about dreaming the dream over again. It still belongs to the dream, in a way.)

On the other hand, one might form an hypothesis. On reading the report of the dream, one might predict that the dreamer can be brought to recall such and such memories. And this hypothesis might or might not be verified. This might be called a scientific treatment of the dream.

Freier Einfall and wish fulfilments. There are various criteria for the right interpretation: e.g., (1) what the analyst says or predicts, on the basis of his previous experience; (2) what the dreamer is led to by *freier Einfall*. It would be interesting and important if these two generally coincided. But it would be queer to claim (as Freud seems to) that they *must always* coincide.

What goes on in *freier Einfall* is probably conditioned by a whole host of circumstances. There seems to be no reason for saying that it must be conditioned only by the sort of wish in which the analyst is interested and of which he has reason to say that it must have been playing a part. If you want to complete what seems to be a fragment of a picture, you might be advised to give up trying to think hard about what is the most likely way the picture went, and instead simply to stare at the picture and make whatever dash first comes into your mind, without thinking. This might in many cases be very fruitful advice to give. But it would be astonishing if it *always* produced the best results. What dashes you make, is likely to be conditioned by everything that is going on about you and within you. And if I knew one of the factors present, this could not tell me with certainty what dash you were going to make.

To say that dreams are wish fulfilments is very important chiefly because it points to the sort of interpretation that is wanted—the sort of thing that would be an interpretation of a dream. As contrasted with an interpretation which said that dreams were simply memories of what had happened, for instance. (We don't feel that memories call for an interpretation in the same way as we feel this about dreams.) And some dreams obviously are wish fulfilments; such as the sexual dreams of adults, for instance. But it seems muddled to say that *all* dreams are hallucinated wish fulfilments. (Freud very commonly gives what we might call a sexual interpretation. But it is interesting that among all the reports of dreams which he gives, there is not a single example of a straightforward sexual dream. Yet these are common as rain.) Partly because this doesn't seem to fit with dreams that spring from fear rather than from longing. Partly because the majority of dreams Freud considers have to be regarded as *camouflaged* wish fulfilments; and in this case they simply don't fulfil the wish. Ex hypothesi the wish is not allowed to be fulfilled, and something else is hallucinated instead. If the wish is cheated in this way, then the dream can hardly be called a fulfilment of it. Also it becomes impossible to say whether it is the wish or the censor that is cheated. Apparently both are, and the result is that neither is satisfied. So that the dream is not an hallucinated satisfaction of anything.

It is probable that there are many different sorts of dreams, and that there is no single line of explanation for all of them. Just as there are many different sorts of jokes. Or just as there are many different sorts of language.

Freud was influenced by the 19th century idea of dynamics—an idea which has influenced the whole treatment of psychology. He wanted to find some one explanation which would show what dreaming is. He wanted to find the *essence* of dreaming. And he would have rejected any suggestion that he might be partly right but not altogether so. If he was partly wrong, that would have meant for him that he was wrong altogether—that he had not really found the essence of dreaming.

NOTES BY R. R. FOLLOWING CONVERSATIONS, 1943.

Whether a dream is a thought. Whether dreaming is thinking about something.

Suppose you look on a dream as a kind of language. A way of saying something, or a way of symbolizing something. There might be a regular symbolism, not necessarily alphabetical—it might be like Chinese, say. We might then find a way of translating this symbolism into the language of ordinary speech, ordinary thoughts. But then the translation ought to be possible both ways. It ought to be possible by employing the same technique to translate ordinary thoughts into dream language. As Freud recognizes, this never is done and cannot be done. So we might question whether dreaming is a way of thinking something, whether it is a language at all.

Obviously there are certain similarities with language.

Suppose there were a picture in a comic paper, dated shortly after the last war. It might contain one figure of which you would say it was obviously a caricature of Churchill, another figure marked somehow with a hammer and sickle so that you would say it was obviously supposed to be Russia. Suppose the title of the picture was lacking. Still you might be sure that, in view of two figures mentioned, the whole picture was obviously trying to make some point about the political situation at that time.

The question is whether you would always be justified in assuming that there is some one joke or some one point which is *the* point which the cartoon is making. Perhaps even the picture as a whole has no "right interpretation" at all. You might say: "There are indications—such as the two figures mentioned—which suggest that it has." And I might answer that perhaps these indications are all that there is. Once you have got an interpretation of these two figures, there may be no ground for saying that there *must* be an interpretation of the whole thing or of every detail of it on similar lines.

The situation may be similar in dreams.

Freud would ask: "What made you hallucinate that situation at all?" One might answer that there need not have been anything that *made* me hallucinate it.

Freud seems to have certain prejudices about when an interpretation could be regarded as complete—and so about when it still requires completion, when further interpretation is needed. Suppose someone were ignorant of the tradition among sculptors of making busts. If he then came upon the finished bust of some man, he might say that obviously this is a fragment and that there must have been other parts belonging to it, making it a whole body.

Suppose you recognized certain things in the dream which can be interpreted in the Freudian manner. Is there any ground at all for assuming that there must be an interpretation for everything else in the dream as well? that it makes any sense to ask what is the right interpretation of the other things there?

Freud asks "Are you asking me to believe that there is anything which happens without a cause?" But this means nothing. If under 'cause' you include things like physiological causes, then we know nothing about these, and in any case they are not relevant to the question of interpretation. Certainly you can't argue from Freud's question to the proposition that everything in the dream must have a cause in the sense of some past event with which it is connected by association in that way.

Suppose we were to regard a dream as a kind of game which the dreamer played. (And by the way, there is no one cause or one reason why children always play. This is where theories of play generally go wrong.) There might be a game in which paper figures were put together to form a story, or at any rate were somehow assembled. The materials might be collected and stored in a scrap-book, full of pictures and anecdotes. The child might then take various bits from the scrap-book to put into the construction; and he might take a considerable picture because it had something in it which he wanted and he might just include the rest because it was there.

Compare the question of why we dream and why we write stories. Not everything in the story is allegorical. What would be meant by trying to explain why he has written just that story in just that way?

There is no one reason why people talk. A small child babbles often just for the pleasure of making noises. This is also one reason why adults talk. And there are countless others.

Freud seems constantly to be influenced by the thought that a hallucination is something requiring a tremendous mental force—*seelische Kraft*. 'Ein

Traum findet sich niemals mit Halbheiten ab.' And he thinks that the only force strong enough to produce the hallucinations of dreams is to be found in the deep wishes of early childhood. One might question this. Supposing it is true that hallucinations in waking state require an extraordinary mental force—why should not dream hallucinations be the perfectly normal thing in sleep, not requiring any extraordinary force at all?

(Compare the question: "Why do we punish criminals? Is it from a desire for revenge? Is it in order to prevent a repetition of the crime?" And so on. The truth is that there is no one reason. There is the institution of punishing criminals. Different people support this for different reasons, and for different reasons in different cases and at different times. Some people support it out of a desire for revenge, some perhaps out of a desire for justice, some out of a wish to prevent a repetition of the crime, and so on. And so punishments are carried out.)

Notes by R. R. following conversation, 1946.

I have been going through Freud's "Interpretation of Dreams" with H. And it has made me feel how much this whole way of thinking wants combatting.

If I take any one of the dream reports (reports of his own dreams) which Freud gives, I can by the use of free association arrive at the same results as those he reaches in his analysis—although it was not my dream. And the association will proceed through my own experiences and so on.

The fact is that whenever you are preoccupied with something, with some trouble or with some problem which is a big thing in your life—as sex is, for instance—then no matter what you start from, the association will lead finally and inevitably back to that same theme. Freud remarks on how, after the analysis of it, the dream appears so very logical. And of course it does.

You could start with any of the objects on this table—which certainly are not put there through your dream activity—and you could find that they all could be connected in a pattern like that; and the pattern would be logical in the same way.

One may be able to discover certain things about oneself by this sort of free association, but it does not explain why the dream occurred.

Freud refers to various ancient myths in these connexions, and claims that his researches have now explained how it came about that anybody should think or propound a myth of that sort.

Whereas in fact Freud has done something different. He has not given a scientific explanation of the ancient myth. What he has done is to propound a new myth. The attractiveness of the suggestion, for instance, that all anxiety is a repetition of the anxiety of the birth trauma, is just the attractiveness of a mythology. "It is all the outcome of something that happened long ago." Almost like referring to a totem.

Much the same could be said of the notion of an 'Urszene.' This often has the attractiveness of giving a sort of tragic pattern to one's life. It is all the repetition of the same pattern which was settled long ago. Like a tragic figure carrying out the decrees under which the fates had placed him at birth. Many people have, at some period, serious trouble in their lives—so serious as to lead to thoughts of suicide. This is likely to appear to one as something nasty, as a situation which is too foul to be a subject of a tragedy. And it may then be an immense relief if it can be shown that one's life has the pattern rather of a tragedy—the tragic working out and repetition of a pattern which was determined by the primal scene.

There is of course the difficulty of determining what scene is the primal scene—whether it is the scene which the patient recognizes as such, or whether it is the one whose recollection effects the cure. In practice these criteria are mingled together.

Analysis is likely to do harm. Because although one may discover in the course of it various things about oneself, one must have a very strong and keen and persistent criticism in order to recognize and see through the mythology that is offered or imposed on one. There is an inducement to say, 'Yes, of course, it must be like that.' A powerful mythology.

8

DAVID MALAN

Some Stories About People in Difficulties

NINE STORIES

The aim is to illustrate the ways in which human beings try to avoid mental pain; how they try to control unacceptable behaviour or feelings; how sometimes what is unacceptable creeps in by the back door; and finally the kinds of consequence that may ensue from all these processes. The stories will be told in the first place with no elucidation, and it might be a good exercise for the reader to analyse them for himself, using no more than self-knowledge and intuition. It is worth saying, however, that most of them are a good deal more complex than they probably at first appear.

THE SPOILT SON

A young solicitor, an only child, who in recent years had begun to make his unhappiness clear for everyone to see, told how his mother was always saying that his father had spoilt him. The truth seemed to be rather that she herself had always been suffocatingly possessive and over-protective; and the father, who was effective enough at work but under his wife's thumb at home, had gone along with her in his ineffective and passive way.

From David Malan, *Individual Psychotherapy and the Science of Psychodynamics* (London: Butterworths, 1979), chapter 2, pp. 5–15. Reprinted by permission.

THE ANTHROPOLOGIST AND THE CAT

A young woman with a degree in anthropology was going through yet another crisis with her man-friend, Dick, whose pattern of letting her down seemed chronic and compulsive. She was visiting the house of a woman friend, where Dick had promised to phone her, but of course he didn't. She was sitting with her friend's cat in her lap, and her friend said to her. 'Of course you know Dick was never any good for you'. She hurled the cat across the room (who, in the way of cats, fell on his feet uninjured), and walked out of the house. When she later returned, her friend was naturally furious, and could not leave the incident alone for a long time.

UPSETTING THE SUGAR

One evening a mother came into her little girl's bedroom, to find the walls smeared with faeces. Though revolted, she did not scold her daughter and simply cleaned it all up. The next day the girl accidentally upset the sugar, and the mother completely lost control and hit her.

THE FRANCISCANS IN THE MIDDLE AGES

This religious Order was founded by St. Francis of Assisi in the early part of the 13th century. One of the basic principles laid down by the founder was the vow of poverty, according to which the Order renounced possessions of any kind. This even applied to the *ownership* of churches and friaries, but it did not apply to their *occupation*.

In the latter part of the century the Order found itself in competition with the parish clergy not only for churches, but also for such religious duties as burials and the hearing of confessions. The members of the Order also set up their own teaching at universities and found themselves in competition with the ordinary dons, both for pupils and for teaching appointments. There was also competition for *holiness*, since their vow of poverty gave them a certain 'holier than thou' attitude towards the other clergy. Moreover their hearing of deathbed confessions often resulted in substantial legacies which they would use for building finer churches and friaries, and also for such items as books necessary for their status as a learned order. Thus they gave the appearance of a considerable degree of prosperity, and all these factors together brought down upon them a great deal of envy and hostility. A way out of the weaknesses in their position was then found when they induced the Papacy to take upon itself the ownership of all their possessions. The crisis occurred, however, when Pope John XXII withdrew his ownership. . . .

SOUR GRAPES

'A hungry fox tried to reach some clusters of grapes which he saw hanging from a vine trained on a tree, but they were too high. So he went off, . . . saying "They weren't ripe anyhow"'.

Roberta in Hospital

A physicist was in hospital for an operation. In the next ward was a little girl of four, Roberta, who was in for a tonsillectomy, and with whom he made friends. The day after her operation her mother visited her, but Roberta refused to respond. The physicist witnessed the incident and afterwards saw Roberta lying frozen, almost as if she was paralysed, staring at the ceiling, with the mother in another part of the ward ignoring her and talking to some other parents. He went up to Roberta's bed and said very gently, twice, stroking her hair, 'Yes it's awful being in hospital without your mother'. She let out a heart-rending sob, and the mother came over angrily, saying, 'Now look what you've done, she'll have a sore throat for days'. He said to her, through his teeth, 'I had thirty years of stammering because of an episode like this', and walked away. And what was the result? First, Roberta sobbing in her mother's arms; then walking with her up and down the corridor for twenty minutes; and then holding her mother's hand in the ward, the two of them looking happy. Needless to say the physicist received no thanks for what he had done.

The Social Worker and her Father

The father of a social worker, who had left the home when she was eleven but had kept in touch with her, phoned her one evening to say that he was in London. At the time she was needing comfort very badly and she asked him if he would come and see her there and then, but he said he couldn't and asked if instead she could come and see him the next day. In reply she was very rude, saying 'What do you think I do with my time?', but in the end she agreed. When they met he tried to put his arms round her, but she utterly rejected him and moved to the other side of the room. When she later told this story she said she had realized she didn't love him at all, she disliked him.

The Anatomy Viva

A medical student arrived in the dissecting room to find that his two companions were suggesting that the three of them should be examined on the upper part of the leg that afternoon. He did not feel that he knew enough to be ready to be examined, and protested, but the others insisted. 'All right', he said, 'Let's have the viva this morning'.

The Snake and the Wasp

'A wasp settled on a snake's head and tormented it by continually stinging. The snake, maddened with the pain and not knowing how else to be revenged on its tormentor, put its head under the wheel of a waggon, so they both perished together'.

DISCUSSION

Throughout its history dynamic psychotherapy has aroused a great deal of scepticism and hostility. These particular stories have been chosen because the mechanisms involved in them are easily accessible to introspection, and I would say largely undeniable, and yet they contain many of the essential principles of the theoretical basis of dynamic psychotherapy, a subject which we may call psychodynamics. If even this chapter arouses scepticism in the reader, then I would suggest he should read no further—whatever else his accomplishments, he is not likely to be able to number psychotherapy among them, nor, for that matter, much of human interaction.

As mentioned above, and as always when human reactions are being considered, careful examination reveals that most of these stories are more complex than they seem. Moreover, they lead rapidly by association into profound and often painful truths about human beings.

EXPRESSIVE AND DEFENSIVE MECHANISMS

The best starting point is the story of the Spoilt Son. Here the mechanism is relatively straightforward: the son, by implication, had begun to blame his parents for his unhappiness; and the mother then started to accuse the father of spoiling him, when the truth seemed to be that it was she who was largely responsible for the spoiling. The mechanism that she was using was described by the son in words that cannot be bettered: 'I think she's afraid of being found out, and is trying to put the blame on my father'. According to this, she was both *expressing* something, namely blaming the father, and also *defending* herself against her son's implied accusations, by deflecting them onto the father. In other words she was using the mechanism of *displacement*. Yet even this is not entirely simple, as she was surely defending herself both against her *son's blame* and against *self-blame*, because somewhere within her she must have known about her own guilt in the situation. But this was hardly likely to be something that she would readily acknowledge.

Perhaps most similar to this, though far more complicated, is the story of the Anthropologist and the Cat. Here also displacement is at work—after all, the cat had done her no harm, and the anger was with her friend. In this case, therefore, the main mechanism is largely *expressive* and involves the displacement of an *impulse* from her friend onto the cat. Yet this is only the beginning. First, the displacement was also *defensive* in the sense that, by directing her anger at the cat, she was clearly trying to avoid an angry assault on her friend; but this was only partially successful, since to hurt the cat was to hurt the friend, as was shown by her friend's reaction to the incident. Thus her action was a fusion of *defence* and *impulse*.

Next we need to ask the question, why was her anger of such intensity? Well, her friend had said something disparaging about the man with whom she was involved, which naturally would anger her. But surely this is the lesser of two determinants. The real trouble was that her friend's remark was not merely disparaging but—painfully and unforgivably—true, which she had been trying for a long time not to acknowledge to herself. Therefore there was probably yet another *defensive* function of her reaction, namely to divert her attention from acknowledging this truth. It is the attempt to escape from painful truth that makes the main link with the story of the Spoilt Son.

A third kind of displacement is at work in the story entitled Upsetting the Sugar. Here the original situation was the little girl smearing faeces over her bedroom, which the mother dealt with in the most enlightened fashion by controlling her impulse of anger and simply cleaning it all up. To all outward appearances, the incident was then forgotten. But undischarged impulses seek expression, and what then happened was almost certainly that when the mother was faced with another situation in which her daughter made a mess, her defences were completely taken by surprise, and the original anger immediately overcame her. The displacement here is thus from one *situation* onto another, the *person* towards whom the feelings were directed remaining the same in both cases. It is also an example of what Freud called the *return of the repressed*, since the original impulse suddenly erupted in a disguised form. Further, it is an example of *symbolization*, or something very like it, in the sense that in the second incident the sugar very clearly 'stood for' faeces—and this in turn reveals that symbolization is simply one particular form of displacement.

THE RETURN OF THE REPRESSED

Another example of the *return of the repressed*—which is highly entertaining as long as we temper our feelings with some degree of compassion and fellow-feeling—is provided by the story of the Franciscans. Here the attempt was to control man's basic impulses of acquisitiveness and competitiveness by the vow of poverty, which meant the renunciation of property or possessions of any kind. This sounds very like an example of the mechanism of *over-compensation*, or 'trying to be better than you really are'—which puts a burden on human beings that may be more than they can bear. . . . Anyhow, such was the result in this particular case: first, the acquisitiveness and competitiveness returned in all sorts of disguised forms—the acquisition of, and hence competition for, churches, for religious duties, for pupils, for teaching appointments, and finally for holiness itself. And then, since the proper discharge of their religious function depended in part on material articles such as books, they needed to acquire these; and the distinction from actual material possessions became a very fine one indeed. They then found it necessary to escape from the position into which they had got themselves by what can only be described as a piece of sophistry (dishonesty?): that all these possessions were really the property of the Pope. And so it went on. If anyone had offered them the comment that they really were highly acquisitive and competitive people, I doubt if he would have received a ready acknowledgment of the truth of what he was saying. Let us enjoy our amusement at this piece of human frailty, at the same time remembering that, whatever political party we may support, we have almost certainly become involved at one time or another in similar mechanisms ourselves.

GUILT AND CONCERN

In passing we may perhaps make some remarks about the forces operating in human beings to hold in check their basic, primitive, and selfish impulses. Without question these controlling forces can be of immense power, as the story of the Franciscans shows. If we are religious we may refer to concepts like the Christian ideal, and say that this has been provided for us by our Maker: if we are biologists we may speak of the altruistic forces of *guilt* and *concern*, and say that they have survival value for the species and have been developed by evolution; and of course the two mechanisms are not mutually exclusive. But in my view we should thank our Maker or evolution (or both) for *concern*, but I do not feel inclined to offer any thanks for *guilt*, which is a force too powerful, too lasting, too destructive and in the end often ineffective, as we discover time and again in psychotherapy.

PRELIMINARY SUMMARY

But this is threatening to take us too far afield. What needs to be pointed out is that in these four stories we have illustrated a number of observations, and concepts derived from them, which are necessary to the understanding of almost all neurotic reactions, and hence which play a part every day in the processes of psychotherapy. These are as follows: (1) the concept of *defence mechanisms*, whose function is the attempt to avoid pain or conflict; (2) the observation that, as a result of the defence mechanisms, the painful or conflicting feelings are at least to some degree *kept out of conscious awareness*; (3) the *return of the repressed*, i.e., the observation that the end-product of the defence mechanism often involves in addition the disguised *expression* of the feelings that the person has been trying to avoid; and therefore (4) that the end-product as observed usually does not have a simple explanation, but contains more than one determinant, a phenomenon which is known as *condensation* or *over-determination*.

THE APPLICATION OF THESE CONCEPTS TO SYMPTOMS

In all these examples the end-product of the mental mechanisms consisted of a *piece of behaviour*. Now when patients present themselves for psychotherapy it may often be unwanted behaviour for which they are asking help, but more often it is *symptoms*—e.g., anxiety, obsessions, or depression. In this case the connection between the end-product and inner mechanisms is usually not immediately obvious and not accessible to introspection. Nevertheless, exactly the same concepts may have very great explanatory power.

The Economics Student mentioned earlier in this book[1] can be considered from this point of view. She suffered from an attack of *depression*. It is clear that she was trying to *defend herself* against the *painful* and *guilt-laden* feeling of jealousy. Both the jealousy and the guilt were at first *kept out of conscious awareness*. The *return of the repressed* then occurred in two ways: the guilt appeared in the form of *self-hatred*; and the *jealousy* was effectively expressed by the fit of crying, which forced the other two people to pay attention to her rather than to each other. She was then able to become aware of the hidden feelings and to express them openly, and the depression disappeared.

DEPRECIATION OR REJECTION OF WHAT IS DESIRED

Let us now turn to the best known of all these stories, the Fox and the Sour Grapes. No apology will be offered for using this entirely mythical example, since the type of human situation that it is meant to illustrate is obvious and presumably has existed almost as long as Man himself.

The basic situation is that of being faced with something *desirable* that is also *unattainable*. The natural reaction to this is the pain of frustration and disappointment. However the pain is then eased by a piece of self-deception (or dishonesty): whatever it was that was desirable is made out to have been undesirable—the grapes weren't ripe—so that there is now no longer any cause for disappointment. In other words the function of this mechanism, once more, is to *avoid pain*.

Of course this formulation is correct as far as it goes, and indeed this is clearly what Aesop (if he existed) was intending, since the last sentence as actually written contains the words '*he comforted himself* by saying "They weren't ripe anyhow"'. But in most real-life situations, the reaction is likely to be not only the pain of disappointment, but also the *anger of frustration*; and this will be doubly true if it is *a person* who has made himself (or herself) unattainable, since then the anger is the result of *being rejected*. Careful thought then indicates that the mechanism involves not only the avoidance of pain but the expression of anger, as is made clearer when one sees that the grapes in the story are being *disparaged* or *depreciated*. Of course it doesn't hurt the grapes to be called sour, so that in this situation the expression of anger is purely internal; but if the depreciation can be expressed *to* the person who has done the rejecting, then it is likely to be painful to *him*, and the anger is

---

[1]An economics student in her early twenties travelled to Spain with a young man, who talked intimately to her on the train journey about his life and troubles. On arrival at the villa they were joined by a girl-friend of hers. Some days later the student began to have a depressive attack accompanied by a feeling of self-hatred, which she described as 'like descending into a pit'. After some hours there began to emerge in her mind her intense jealousy of her girl-friend, to whom the young man had been paying more attention than to her, and she went to her room and broke down into an uncontrollable fit of weeping. The other two heard her and came in, and she was able to pour out her feelings to them. The depressive attack disappeared, and from then on not only in the short term did the holiday go well, but in the long term she found herself able to relate to groups of people in a new way—no longer as an outsider, but as a participant.

expressed externally and directly and is effective because it hurts. Taken to the limit, the other person becomes rejected in his turn, 'now you can know what it feels like', and the punishment fits the crime.

The two stories that illustrate this kind of mechanism are those of Roberta in Hospital, and the Social Worker and her Father. Of these the former is probably the simpler. We owe particularly to John Bowlby[2] and James Robertson[3] the realization of the devastating consequences of separating young children from their mothers for any length of time, without an adequate substitute, and an understanding of the mechanisms involved. As Bowlby has described, the first stage is that of *protest*. Driven by extremely painful and intense feelings, the child (without fully knowing what he is doing) does all in his power to create a situation in which his mother will feel forced by her own maternal instincts either not to leave him or else to return; and when this fails, he sinks into a state of *despair*. Both these stages are relatively direct and straightforward, and do not in themselves contain any pathogenic potential.

The two first stages of adult grief are essentially the same; and when all goes well they are followed by what may be called a stage of 'working through', in which the agonies of loss are faced one by one and over and over again, to a point at which they are sufficiently weakened to lose their effect. An alternative outcome, however, when the individual is not strong enough to face the feelings involved—which seems to be the usual situation when the person concerned is a small child—is that they are not weakened, but that they are buried and kept away from consciousness. The end product is Bowlby's third stage, in which the child uses the defence mechanism of *denial* or *detachment*, which is utterly deceptive because to outward appearances he seems to have returned to normal.

If now the lost mother returns, the naive expectation is that the child will be, quite simply and straightforwardly, overjoyed to see her again. Indeed, this is what happens when a master returns to his dog; but with human beings, as the story of Roberta illustrates, the result is often very different. What in fact may happen is that the mother is rejected. The message to the mother is very like that conveyed in the sour grapes reaction—'I don't want you any more'—and the mechanism almost certainly serves the same twin functions, which as always are not as simple as they may at first sight appear. (1) The first function is the *avoidance of pain*—as long as the child keeps up the pretence of not wanting her mother, (a) she saves herself the agonizing recovery of the buried feelings of grief (demonstrated so clearly in Roberta after the physicist

---

[2]John Bowlby, "Some pathological processes set in motion by early mother-child separation," *J. Ment. Sci.* 99 (1953):265. John Bowlby, *Attachment and Loss*, vol. II: Separation: anxiety and anger (London: Hogarth Press, 1973).

[3]J. Robertson, "Some responses of young children to the loss of maternal care," *Nurs. Times* 49 (1953):382. [See also: J. Robertson, A two-year-old goes to hospital (film) (London: Tavistock Child Development Research Unit; New York: New York University Film Library, 1952).—B. A. F.]

had spoken to her): and (b) she forearms herself against having to go through the same stages of useless protest and hopeless agony if the mother should leave again. (2) The second function is almost certainly the *expression of anger*—there is a great deal of direct evidence for anger in young children as a response to loss (see Bowlby, 1973, pp. 146ff.) though it may not be obviously detectable in the initial rejection of the mother, and may be utterly obscured by the overwhelming grief that is later uncovered. It also would be far too sophisticated to suggest that under these circumstances young children are trying to make the mother suffer what they have been suffering themselves. This is only likely to enter at a much later stage.

The story of Roberta, therefore, illustrates much more clearly the defensive or protective function of rejecting the mother who returns. The story of the Social Worker and her Father illustrates the anger quite clearly, and the sour grapes reaction is absolutely clear in her statement that she didn't love him, she disliked him. In this story, too, the element of hurting the other person, and making him suffer what she had suffered herself, is very clear. It is also worth noting the language used, as the word 'disliked' carries with it the defensive manoeuvre of the sour grapes reaction, implying that she never wanted him anyhow, whereas the word 'hated' would have implied an involvement that she obviously did not want to acknowledge at the time.

Unconscious Mechanisms and Feelings

This story leads to one of the crucial points of the present chapter. So far I have described situations in which feelings were *kept out of conscious awareness* but I have deliberately avoided using the word 'unconscious'. The stories can probably be arranged in a series according to the degree to which the true feelings were or were not accessible. Thus, at one end, the Anthropologist, and the mother of the little girl who upset the sugar, both of whom were insightful and sophisticated people, would have readily acknowledged the inner mechanisms at work; in the middle, the mother of the Spoilt Son, and the Franciscans, would probably have had the greatest difficulty in acknowledging their hidden feelings, though they must really have been aware of them; and at the other end, the Economics Student was quite unaware of her jealousy until it finally forced itself on her attention.

We may now ask, at what point are we justified in introducing the word 'unconscious'? This seems to be largely a matter of choice, and surely it must be true that there is really a continuum from being *unwilling to acknowledge* at one end to being *totally unaware* at the other.

Yet, because in the case of the Economics Student the feelings were in the end relatively easily accessible, there may be reluctance to use the word 'unconscious' even here.

This is the importance of the story of the Social Worker. During many years of psychotherapy she had always regarded her father as the perfection of what a man should be. Side by side with this had gone an intense—even compulsive—awareness of the faults of *other men in her life*, to the point at which she used to say that she could never get married because she would destroy any man whom she got close to. Where on earth could such intense hatred of men have originated? She had suffered nothing at the hands of men to justify such a feeling.

Yet of course she had—she had been abandoned by her father at the age of eleven. The whole picture now becomes comprehensible if we postulate that she is using three related defence mechanisms to protect herself against the intolerable pain of hating someone whom she also loved so much: first *idealization*, which is obvious; then *splitting*, which means avoiding conflict by keeping the two kinds of incompatible feelings entirely separate; and finally, when faced with the *return of the repressed*, she is using *displacement*—displacing her anger against her father onto other men. Of course all this is only a hypothesis—and indeed, however many times she was confronted with it in her psychotherapy, she simply denied it and remained totally unaware that it had any validity whatsoever. The importance of incidents like that described in the above story was that at last the hidden anger with her father emerged, and the hypothesis was confirmed by direct evidence. Now the long process of rescuing her from her hatred of men could finally begin. It remains absolutely incontrovertible that until this point in her life the hidden feelings and mechanisms had been, in the full sense of the word, unconscious.

SELF-DEFEATING AND SELF-DESTRUCTIVE MECHANISMS

Further consideration of these two stories may be approached through a diversion introducing the last two stories, the Anatomy Viva and the Snake and the Wasp.

A quick glance at the first of these may raise a naive question: if the medical student was so unprepared that he felt unable to undergo his viva that *afternoon*, why on earth did he suddenly turn round and advocate having the viva that *morning?* A likely consequence would be that all three of them would fail together. The answer is of course very simple, namely that in doing so he hoped to turn the tables on his two fellow-students, making them in their turn face the viva with insufficient preparation. The fact that this made the prospect of the viva even worse for him was ignored *because it was worth it.* This is a mild example of the situation illustrated by the fable of the Snake and the Wasp—'not knowing how else to be revenged on its tormentor, it put its head under the wheel of a wagon, so that they both perished together'.

The point illustrated here is that the forces driving some of these mental mechanisms are often so powerful that the devastatingly self-destructive consequences that may ensue offer no deterrence whatsoever. This is one of the gloomy truths about human beings that face all of us when we undertake psychotherapy; and it results in one of our primary tasks, namely to rescue our patients from the self-destructive consequences of what they are doing, by tracing these mechanisms to their origin and uncovering the feelings that are being expressed indirectly or are being avoided.

This leads us back at once to what the physicist did for Roberta. Her rejection of her mother, if hardened into a pattern, could have set up ripples that extended, for her, to the ends of time. A single sentence, repeated once, aborted them—on this occasion anyhow. This sentence is of course an example of an *interpretation*, i.e., a communication to the suffering person designed to bring out the hidden mechanisms involved and thus to have therapeutic effects.

THE TRIANGLE OF CONFLICT

Here we may introduce a concept that is absolutely fundamental to dynamic psychotherapy. The physicist's words, 'Yes, it's awful being in hospital without your mother', were in effect a direct interpretation to the little girl of the *hidden feelings* that she was *defending herself* against. It was quite unnecessary to point out to her either the *mechanism of defence* or the *reason for* the defence. It would obviously have been absurd to have said something like: 'You are pushing your mother away [defence], in order to avoid the grief and anger about having been abandoned by her [hidden feelings], because you are afraid of being overwhelmed by them [anxiety]'. Yet this would have been the complete interpretation, which often *is* appropriate in psychotherapy, spelling out for the patient the three aspects of the mechanism going on inside her—*defence, anxiety*, and *hidden feeling*—the *triangle of conflict*, one or more aspects of which can be used to describe almost every interpretation that is made in dynamic psychotherapy.

There is also an important note on the *hidden feeling* that needs to be introduced here. In Roberta we have postulated that the hidden feeling contains two elements, grief and anger. Of these, anger may be described as an *impulse*, though grief cannot. Similarly, in the stories of the Anthropologist and the Cat, Upsetting the Sugar, and the Social Worker and her Father, the hidden feelings consisted of angry impulses; and in the story of the Franciscans the impulses were acquisitive and competitive. Moreover, as will appear later, the hidden feelings often consist of unacceptable sexual impulses. Thus, when appropriate, the word 'impulse' will often be substituted for 'hidden feeling', especially as it is more succinct. In fact the triangle of conflict is often taught as consisting of 'defence, anxiety and impulse', but this is not always correct, as the story of Roberta illustrates.

THE EFFECT ON THE ENVIRONMENT; VICIOUS CIRCLES; CONJOINT THERAPY

This story also leads to the final point of the present chapter. So far we have been entirely concerned with mechanisms *within a single person*, and have not considered either their effect on people outside, or the effect of this in turn on the person in whom the mechanisms are operating. The incident between the social worker and her father is not a good illustration, because her father was quite mature and insightful enough to know what was going on, and to cope with it by patient understanding and forbearance. But Roberta's mother was quite a different matter, as is shown by the situation that faced the physicist, with Roberta frozen in bed and her mother ignoring her at the other end of the ward. The mother may be forgiven for a feeling of bewildered resentment when she arrives full of anticipation at seeing her little girl again and finds herself rejected; and Roberta in turn may of course be forgiven if she begins to think her mother indifferent because she pays attention to the other parents instead of sitting by her bed; but the result may well be a vicious circle of resentment based on mutual and total misunderstanding of the situation, which is of course—on both sides—one of wounded love. I do not wish to suggest that this single incident in itself would have necessarily had any permanent effect—provided the relation between mother and daughter was good enough in the first place. But if the relation was already threatened in other ways, then the consequences might well be permanent, as the physicist himself had cause to know.

All this leads to the crucial point: as it happened, it was possible to undo the situation by an intervention aimed at one half of the vicious circle only. Yet at that moment *both* figures in the drama needed help; and this would certainly have been so if the vicious circle had been allowed to establish itself for any length of time. When a patient presents with a complaint of difficulty in relation to the marriage partner, this is almost always true; and then, although it may be possible and appropriate to help by treating one partner only, it may be far better to treat both; so that the treatment of choice may well not be individual therapy but some form of conjoint marital therapy.

9

J. O. WISDOM

Testing a Psycho-analytic Interpretation

FIELD-WORK IN MEDICINE AND PSYCHO-ANALYSIS

Psycho-analysis has made contributions to field-work that are extraordinarily extensive. They consist partly of discovering the bewildering variety of phenomena to be found in the neuroses and psychoses, and partly of discovering large numbers of linkages that hold with great regularity between these phenomena—e.g., between an inhibition and being afraid of the strength of one's desires. And this field-work has developed as a result of explicit ideas. A serious attempt to systematize psycho-analytic field-work has been made by compiling what is known as the Hampstead Index,* which is a valuable asset for teaching.

It is impossible to give an exhaustive textbook account of the results just as it is impossible in medicine, engineering, or chess. You may be able to teach physics to some extent without going into a laboratory; you cannot teach medicine without examining some patients. In medicine, a syndrome is a set of signs and symptoms characteristic of a disease. A textbook description of a syndrome is not enough to enable the student to recognize the variations of that syndrome when it turns up. Thus influenza does not present itself uniformly. A medical student learns to find his way amid the bewildering variety in a syndrome by means of a combination of textbook description, clinical observations pointed out to him tutorially, taking a history, following the course

---

*J. Bollard and J. Sandler, *The Hampstead Psychoanalytic Index* (New York: International Universities Press, 1965).—B. A. F.

Reprinted from *Ratio*, vol. 8, no. 1 (June 1966), pp. 57–76 (Oxford: Basil Blackwell). Reprinted by permission. Copyright © Institute of Psycho-Analysis.

of the complaint, and noting the effects of medicines given. No neat guide book of instructions is available here. An excellent analogue is to be found in chess. The enormous variety of chess openings has been disentangled in great detail and catalogued in a single work, *Modern Chess Openings*, but the game cannot be learnt by studying this remarkable collection. For one thing it is impossible to write down *all* the openings. The only way to learn chess is to play chess. Then some sort of intuitive mapping of the variations develops. Recognizing a disease is like recognizing a person or a particular make of car. Different people do it in different ways. Descriptions of marked features help a little though only a little. What is recognized seems to be a look characteristic of a disorder to a particular clinician.

It is important to stress that one of the firmest things in medicine, the syndrome, is rather slippery. First, one of the most characteristic signs constituting a syndrome may be absent. Second, a sign that does not go with the syndrome may be present. Third, a host of additional symptoms and signs could be correctly included in the syndrome but conventionally are not—mainly because they are less important, less frequent, or derivative rather than central. For instance, inability to close the eyelids and muscular tremors are not included in the syndrome of exophthalmic goitre. Like chess, this kind of variety cannot be written down in a textbook, even in principle. Moreover, research designed to check the clinical knowledge of physicians, e.g., to find out in what proportion of cases of migraine there is a one-sided headache, would never be able to catch up with clinical knowledge accruing from experience—at any rate without the help of a computer with the same imaginative powers as the human being. It is the same with neurosis. A textbook description of depression will include in the syndrome fewer than a dozen items. But a clinician could tell you all sorts of other symptoms to be expected fairly often—which may even guide him in his diagnosis—e.g., presenting a deceptive appearance of a bold face. Lakatos (1963–64) has shown that a similar difficulty can affect even mathematical proof.

Unless the theory of disease is grossly wrong, this elusiveness is not the fault of medicine; it is inherent in the nature of disease. It shows that a symptom by itself is no guide, without experience to show what weight to attach to it.

All this amounts to saying that medical and psychological clinical work, like chess playing, is an art, which is more than a skill. But it is an art that presupposes objective hypotheses. What I have been saying about the impossibility of writing down clinical knowledge and about its being a body of experience that cannot be completely articulated does not mean that clinical knowledge is a mere personal impression and that it cannot be challenged. Whenever there is any serious doubt, it must be challenged, and then the only recourse open to us is research, which consists of testing the hypothesis that is challenged. Thus if diabetes is diagnosed, this may be tested subsequently by investigating the blood. Again, if doubt arises about the efficacy of a drug, research into it is possible.

Is there a counterpart in psycho-analysis?

Psycho-analysis was originally characterized by the method of *free associa-tion*. This method was tried under the guidance of the idea that forgotten trau-matic episodes gave rise to neurosis, could be recalled by free association, and once recalled would lose their hold. Even though the conjecture was not wholly true, it held good sufficiently with some patients to elicit the most sur-prising reports. In this way knowledge of the phenomena of the field was vastly extended.

Superimposed on this method was another—present in a rudimentary form perhaps from the beginning—namely that of *interpretation*. Originally, inter-pretation took the form of reconstructing past forgotten situations—again un-der the guidance of the idea that if a scene the patient could not bear were thus reconstructed for him and faced by him in therapy, it would lose its stranglehold. Now, reconstruction like this—and even more interpretation as it is used now—presupposes all kinds of connections between symptoms and emotional experiences. The range would include such things as covering up jealousy with solicitousness, the sourness of grapes that are refused, or the giving of presents to gain a hold over someone—things that would be well un-derstood and portrayed by the more perceptive novelists and playwrights. Further, there would be the projections of the man who believes he is being followed, well known to psychiatrists of old. Then the range would include automatic and apparently meaningless actions, interference with which would provoke intense anxiety, or a man's terror of horses with no realization of his terror of his father, and a host of similar things unearthed by psycho-analysis and now known to all psychiatrists. (The range would further include stranger connections, disputed by some psychiatrists, such as the Oedipus complex, or infantile sexuality and its relation to adult forms, or the idea that a battle is felt to be raging between images within the mind. But discussion of these more recondite ideas must wait a little.)

Without a knowledge of these interconnections, the work of interpretation could not be done any more than a move in chess could be planned without a knowledge of the ways the pieces are inter-related in a game. But if some one of these links is in doubt, like say the relevance of a sign to the diagnosis of di-abetes or of schizophrenia, then the question of testing the linkage arises.

TESTING FIELD-WORK INTERPRETATIONS

How is this to be done? Can interpretations about preconscious attitudes be tested? Certainly no research has actually been conducted in it. To the clini-cian these things are a matter of experience like recognizing what a member of a committee may be up to. But, while this attitude may be sound enough in many instances, it is not sufficient where a real doubt enters. So there is a ba-sic problem here: how is a question like this to be settled?

At first sight it may seem hopeless to try to give an account of how we may settle a question about subtleties in people's minds when philosophers have been baffled about how to settle the simplest question about another person's feelings. It seems to me, however, that the reason for this is that philosophers supposed they had to sit back and observe people as they believe an astronomer passively observes the stars. Actually, an astronomer is not all that of a passive observer—he may introduce a spectroscope for instance. Now if, instead of observing people, we take some action, may we not perhaps test what is going on in their minds by their reaction to our action? Thus if you think that your colleague on a committee has a certain ulterior motive, and you think you know what it is, you can test for it: for example, you may suggest a course of action that would satisfy what he ostensibly asks for but clashes with what you think he wants, and you may find he picks holes in it; and then you may suggest a course that would do the reverse—satisfy what you think he wants but run counter to what he ostensibly asks for, and you may find him look gratified. Without embroidering this, it is plain that one can think of a way of testing for an attitude attributed to another person, and moreover do so in such a way that the conjecture can be shown to be false.

Such, I believe, is the basis of the way we all check our ideas of what is going on in those around us in our day-to-day activities. It has none of the tidy look of an experiment in a physics laboratory (as conceived by those who have never been inside one), but it satisfies the Popperian (1959) criterion for the testability of scientific statements.

The same procedure suffices to test a great number of the attitudes, feelings, ideas, and connections between them that form a part at least of the stock in trade of psycho-analysis in day-to-day work. It may be necessary to divine what is in a patient's mind when he refuses to tell or when it is something familiar to him but has not occurred to him at the moment. Such attitudes, feelings, or ideas are classed as preconscious (not unconscious), and it may sometimes be enough for the analyst to mention a thought and ask the patient if it is correct, but the main way of testing is as I have already indicated. If there is some barrier to eliciting the truth, the task resembles that of a diplomatist, who accepts as true some statements from his opposite number that are not likely to be suspect, but probes carefully to test conjectures about other ideas that he knows the other will not readily make available to him.

To summarize the position so far: I have tried to show that a great deal goes on under the heading of preconscious interpretation, which is in no worse a position as regards testing than the conjectures we make every day about our fellows. Psycho-analysis certainly involves huge numbers of what I may call 'home-truths', the dissembling side of human nature known especially to novelists, diplomatists, business people, and in some degree to everyone who spends part of his life outside an ivory tower. I have drawn attention to an overlooked area of psycho-analysis consisting of what I called 'field-work', mapping the ground of ordinary motives, e.g., finding out that men sometimes cover up jealousy with friendliness, the workings of ulterior motives that are known more or less to anyone who has witnessed the deliberations of an important committee. Psycho-analysts have no corner in the market of home-truths, but naturally have a more extensive and more detailed knowledge of them than most students of human nature, and they have doubtless added very greatly to such knowledge. This growth has attracted no attention from critics, partly because it is not systematically set out in books,[1] and partly because new additions are known and are added to the body of our unwritten knowledge, in the same way as men of the world find out more about the deceptions of their fellows.

TESTING UNCONSCIOUS INTERPRETATIONS

If this were all there were to psycho-analysis, there would be no controversy about it, and no psychiatric differences of opinion. Disagreement arises over explanations. In addition to home-truths that are 'preconscious' or accessible to anyone, there is a whole body of similar discernments that psycho-analysts regard as unconscious, not accessible to men to discover in the daily traffic of their lives. If the mapping of home-truths is the field-work of psycho-analysts, explaining them is the problem. And psycho-analysts find the explanation in unconscious clinical hypotheses. That is to say, feelings are ascribed to patients even though they are oblivious of them. The methodological problem then arises how interpretations of the unconscious are to be tested.[2]

Here it is useless to expect the patient to acquiesce; he is not in a position to do so—indeed if he should, something would have gone wrong. There is, by the way, even still a common enough idea that if the patient says 'Yes' the analyst regards his interpretation as confirmed and if he says 'No' this is because of 'resistance' to the treatment. Actually 'Yes' would be disconcerting, just as a diplomatist would be suspicious if he got a straight answer about a top secret, and 'No' would give no information on its own (Wisdom, 1962; cf. Freud, 1937). What, then, is left? There remains whatever the patient goes on to say after the interpretation. Can the analyst, then, test his interpretation by the diplomatist's method in just these cases where the thought ascribed to the patient is unconscious, e.g., incest or a wish to put part of his personality into someone else? Is this possible in the same way as with preconscious ideas and those we ascribe to our fellows in our daily lives? But here the methodological wood becomes denser because we do not, from our ordinary lives, know what signs to expect.

The most obvious example is the Oedipus complex, which, broadly speaking is that a man is unconsciously jealous of his father, regards him as a rival, and wants to eliminate him, in order to possess his mother incestuously. How is a hypothesis like this to be tested? It goes far beyond the category I have

---

[1] A recent book by Berne (1964) goes some way to meet this lack: Eric Berne, *The Games People Play*, New York, 1964.

[2] Some research on unconscious interconnections has been done by Ezriel, which will be discussed below. Research on a clinical hypothesis has also been carried out by Bowlby, but it does not, of course, apply to clinical interpretations.

called home-truths, but it is a hypothesis about people, their feelings, and their sentiments, i.e., it is about what actually goes on in patients' minds, and is not a remote or high-level theory. Thus it can concern clinical situations. But it would give a misleading picture of this part of psycho-analysis if certain complementary hypotheses were omitted. Thus, it is also a clinical hypothesis that a man is full of anxiety because of his parricidal wish, because of the punishment for it his father is expected to mete out. Then there is the further clinical hypothesis that, in order to escape this disaster, he adopts some defence against either his own parricidal wish or his incestuous desire or both; so that there will be no way of recognizing these desires in ordinary life comparable to the way home-truths can be recognized. And there is a further clinical hypothesis that certain of these defensive efforts combine to produce neurosis. These four hypotheses, perhaps with others of less importance, form one clinical theory. Nonetheless it is only the first of these, to do with parricide and incest, that constitutes the Oedipus complex. That a man may suffer because of its consequences is a further hypothesis. Clearly it is desirable to enquire into the main component hypothesis independently if possible, but the other contextual components have to be borne in mind. Can hypotheses like these be tested? This question is important in its own right, but also because on it hinges the question whether or not psycho-analysis is a science. For, whatever the status may be on the very abstract ideas to be found in it, like libido, psychical energy, or Thanatos, which perhaps constitute the core of the popular idea of the subject, the basic requirement for scientific status is that clinical hypotheses must, like those of any established science, be testable.

FAULTY METHODS

How, then, is a clinical hypothesis like the Oedipus to be tested? Certain too obvious methods suggest themselves—relying on intuitive insight or falling back on past experience.

It is, of course, just as important in psycho-analysis as it is in physics to have good insight. Hitting on a new clinical hypothesis is impossible without insight, just as in physics insight is essential for hitting on a new hypothesis, say to explain the magnetism of protons. But indispensable as insight is, it does not guarantee the truth of what it purports to reveal. I suppose the history of science is littered with the skeletons of insights that have turned out to be false. There are famous examples of this even in mathematics. There can be conflicting insights, as for instance over the nature of light, one being that it consists of corpuscles, the other of waves. But, even without such a conflict, an insight has, in the end, to be subjected to testing.

Nor can we fall back on the great traditional misrepresentation of scientific method, that a clinical hypothesis can be derived and established from past experience. Popper (1959) has made it clear that such is not the procedure of science, and his point has been interestingly elaborated in broadcasts by Medawar (1963) and Frisch (1963). But the point is strikingly plain where clinical hypotheses are concerned. There are still some logicians who hold that 'All swans are white' can be derived from observations of white swans, but it is impossible to infer the Oedipus complex in this way, because instances of a combination of parricidal and incestuous wishes are not to be found reported by neurotic or normal subjects, and do not emerge however long such a person free-associates. Indeed, if discoveries of this sort, which have led people to regard Freud as a genius, were so easily made, if all one had to do was listen to a patient free-associating until at last he produced these ideas, then it would have taken perseverance rather than genius to discover them. And it would be a relatively easy and uncontroversial matter to demonstrate them to the psychiatric world. But even psycho-analysts had difficulty at various times in accepting new clinical hypotheses made by their colleagues, even those hypotheses that later became part of the body of classical theory accepted by them all. Hence such hypotheses do not become obvious by simple observation. The view that discoveries might be obtained simply by waiting and listening would be the psycho-analytic equivalent of the traditional misdescription of scientific method that hypotheses are established by past experience. Acquiescence in this view is virtually the only way in which analysts have departed from Freud. For, although they mostly use his method, his clinical hypotheses, and his theoretical superstructure, it has not been usual to follow his mode of scientific reflection. Freud seems to have devoted an enormous amount of thought to trying to explain the puzzling elements in what his patients told him. In other words, he did not wait for answers to be presented to him; he seems to have made endless conjectures in an attempt to find explanations, and then sought to apply these and test them. This cast of mind comes out very clearly in his early work *Studies on Hysteria*, and evidence for it is also to be found in the fact that he sought to construct episodes that must have occurred in the past life of his patients—he did not *find* these, he constructed them, and then tried to check them (e.g., from independent witnesses or diaries or subsequent evidence from his patients that confirmed them).

We can now see that it is a methodological mistake to suppose that an interpretation can be correct only if it can be derived and established from preceding association.

THE GENERAL FRAMEWORK OF TESTING

What alternative procedure, then, might there be? Interestingly enough, the answer comes straight from analysts' own practice as found in published case-histories, and it has been mentioned by the well-known American analyst, Kubie (1952), though it has almost completely escaped notice in descriptive writing about the subject: study the patients' *response* to the interpretation. When an analyst reads a case report, it is true he looks at the associations leading up to the interpretation, for he can tell if that was the sort of interpretation he himself might have given, in the light of his experience of similar associations. But he would further look to the responses which *come after* the interpretation, and it is these that enable him to decide whether the interpretation was true or false. (The same holds good in training learners.) Now consider two possibilities. Suppose the preliminary associations make the interpretation seem very reasonable but the response is off the beam, then the interpretation will be regarded as at least partly false. Now suppose the preliminary associations do *not* make the interpretation seem reasonable to another analyst, he will nevertheless agree that the interpretation was correct if the response is definitely to the point.

Hence the practical position is that clinical interpretations are established or not by their consequences.[3] It is also a logical requirement.

To avoid misunderstanding it should be mentioned that this has nothing to do with whether the interpretation makes the patient better. A scientific test is concerned not with whether a desired change takes place, but with whether a change takes place that is to be expected or understood. So the broad principle involved is, after all, no different from what you would expect on Popper's methodology, and no different from what is involved when a member of a committee tests a conjecture about what is in a colleague's mind by making a proposal that will produce, not an admission, but a response that will disclose the truth.

THE BASIC PROBLEM

This, however, is only a beginning. How does one assess whether a patient's responses confirm or refute an interpretation or clinical hypothesis? That is the basic methodological problem. Take a situation in which the patient waxes indignant about the traffic he encountered on his way to visit a married woman he had designs upon—bad as it is, he remarks, perhaps it used to be more dangerous in the days of horses because even today, he says, he saw a horse snap at a man trying to control it. The meaning that would most probably be ascribed to this little scene with the horse by analysts is that it represents hostility from the patient's father or from the analyst. Further, the danger occurs in a context of possible adultery. So the analyst gives the Oedipus interpretation, and receives the reply from the patient that he has nothing against his father but has against his boss, who is loud and sharp tongued—still his bark is worse than his bite. This response provides a new disguised version of the interpretation—a man instead of a horse and biting replaced by barking. But emphasis has to be put on the disguise: in other words the response has itself to be interpreted before we can consider whether it confirms

---

[3]Certain psychological features of these methods are worth mentioning. The belief that intuition alone is sufficient stems from omnipotence of thought. The belief that the method of science is induction, which denies intuition any role, stems from a sense of lacking creativeness and is basically depressive. The belief that science works by means of bold ideas, i.e., intuitions, not in themselves sufficient but put to the test, stems from the creativeness of phantasy constrained by reality.

or refutes the interpretation being tested. And this may look like some sort of circular process, because it would hardly seem reasonable to test an interpretation by another one whose truth is just as much open to question.

The problem here is perhaps the most basic scientific or methodological problem in the entire subject. Whatever laboratory tests might be tried would establish only that people have Oedipus complexes, but a clinical test is indispensable to explain the patient's associations when they are given. So we are forced to consider the problem of testing one interpretation by another.

Let us consider the following as a possible criterion for testing: that an interpretation embodying a clinical hypothesis is corroborated if the response to it can be interpreted by means of the *same* clinical hypothesis. Thus the response about the barking boss would confirm part of the Oedipus interpretation if it in its turn could be interpreted by the Oedipus hypothesis. The broad idea is clear enough. If you were allowed (methodologically speaking) to interpret responses by means of any theory at all, then every response would confirm the one being tested (Wisdom, 1956). Freud (1937), by implication seems to have held this view.

More specific proposals have occasionally been made, but they all seem to presuppose this more general one; notable discussions have been given by Freud (1937), Isaacs (1939), Kubie (1952), Brenner (1955), Ezriel (1956), and Paul (1963).[4]

The very notion of interpreting an item implies that the item is a disguise. Thus in the associations leading to the Oedipus interpretation to do with the biting horse, there is the presupposition that the horse is functioning on behalf of the patient's father or is a disguised version of him. Underlying this is the hypothesis of *displacement*—the attitude towards the father is displaced on to the horse. Thus an interpretation presupposes a defence hypothesis. After all, the Oedipus hypothesis simply juxtaposes parricide and incest; it does not say that enmity towards a horse *is* parricide. The displacement hypothesis is needed for that (as a defence against the enormity of the idea). So, to turn the Oedipus hypothesis into an Oedipus interpretation, it is necessary to interpret displacements or other defences.

Likewise, when interpreting a response it is necessary to interpret a defence. There is, however, no reason why the defence in the response should be the same as the one in the prior associations.

A THEORY OF TESTING PROPOSED

Hence our criterion for testing would be, *that a response corroborates an interpretation embodying a hypothesis about clinical content provided it can be interpreted by means of the same hypothesis about clinical content even though with a different hypothesis of defence.*

---

[4]Fenichel (1939) denies the possibility of unconscious interpretation.

This complicates our problem, for it is not a case of testing solely the Oedipus hypothesis but of testing this along with some defence hypothesis. The simplest procedure now is to seek some independent test for defences. Displacement can be very simply examined experimentally under hypnosis, but it can also be studied in free association. Very little systematic research has been attempted here, but it could be done. Still, there is a vast body of *un*systematic knowledge garnered and *un*systematically tested over many years of instances of displacement, just as people have a wide unsystematic knowledge of where it is wise to count their change and where there is no need to do so.

The position now is this. Given that displacements do take place, an Oedipus interpretation is an assertion that certain associations are, e.g., father-displacements and that there is a triangular relationship between that patient and such displacements. Can our criterion now be applied? A specific form it could assume has in fact been the subject of research by Ezriel (1956), who has systematically attempted to show that in effect the same clinical content hypothesis applies to responses with a diminution of a certain defence, illustrated by the diminution of the physical distance felt by the patient to separate the explosive factors. Methodologically (though not therapeutically) the result would be equally satisfactory if the distance increased. However, such consequences yield only a sufficient condition for confirmation of an interpretation, not a necessary one. A necessary condition, though not the only one, would seem to be the reappearance in the response of the structure of the interpretation in some guise or other.

Now this leads to the question of how we can tell that a response refutes an interpretation. The obvious answer is that a response with a structure different from that of the interpretation refutes it.

A METHOD OF TESTING

None the less, if this is in order, my answer is hardly yet sufficiently elaborated. A further difficulty is that, if an interpretation that was given had in fact been held back, the response might have been in line with the unvoiced interpretation all the same, because continuous with the preceding associations.

To deal with this we should have to elaborate our criterion in terms of the effect of intervening. A broad answer is not too difficult: that the response should embody a predictable defence, i.e., the analyst should be able to know whether the response would express the preceding associations in a clearer form after the interpretation or whether a strong defence might be expected. He would have to be able to predict the form of defence likely to occur. But he would also have to be able to specify what defence would probably have occurred if he had made no active intervention, so as to see whether the flow of associations would be influenced by the actual giving of the interpretation. It should be possible to effect a more specific test by counting the proportion of predictions that are correct when interpretations are actually withheld and the proportion when they are given: from this one could tell the probability of influence of an interpretation.

It is, of course, vital to bear in mind that the procedure put forward applies in the first place only to interpretations to do with wishes where defences are not also interpreted. It could, however, be adapted to interpretations of defence.

With these qualifications in mind, it will be seen that there is such a thing as the clinical testing of clinical hypotheses, but that it is vastly different from the testing for home-truths that goes on in day-to-day life.

Moreover, on the present theory, a false interpretation is capable of being refuted. It therefore satisfies Popper's refutability criterion for science.

Unfortunately the possibility of refuting a false interpretation may be undermined by one special phenomenon—suggestion. How does this come about?

THE PROBLEM OF REFUTABILITY AND SUGGESTION

Almost as old as psycho-analysis itself is the charge that it acts by suggestion. It is well known that under hypnosis suggestions are obeyed: thus if a subject in a trance is told to stand on one leg he will do so; if he is given a post-hypnotic suggestion to brush his teeth after lunch, he will do so even though he is no longer in the trance and despite the strange time of day; if told he will be able to move his (hysterically) paralysed arm, he will be able to carry this out. Is it, then, in the same way that the psycho-analyst effects changes in patients, purely by suggestion? In other words, do the interpretations given by analysts merely implant suggestions, and is a change in a patient merely a suggestion-effect?

This is an interesting question. It has been less discussed of recent times than formerly. In the early days analysts were at considerable pains to point out that analysis is the exact opposite of suggestion. The chief ground for this was that analysis is based on insight while suggestion belies it. This answer is incomplete, however, for we should need to consider what proof there may be that an insight is true, i.e., that the sense of conviction of insight is not itself due to suggestion. Again, if an occasional patient can react as if to suggestion, how in principle can this be detected; for this is the complement of the question, how in principle can it be told that another patient is *not* reacting to suggestion? Again, if analytic therapy were suggestion, there would be no grounds for accepting the theory of psycho-analysis rather than some other. Part of the interest of the question lies in the challenge it presents to refute the suggestion view, which has never been adequately refuted; but the main point is that, unless this is done, analytic theory can have no claim to truth.

Critics down the decades have claimed that the suggestion-effect may always be present. Thus (i) it has long been argued that each type of psychotherapy leads to its own theoretical conclusions; it is implied that some of these are incompatible with each other, or at least that some are false; and the

consequence reached is that the psychotherapies work by implanting suggestions. Further (ii) it is argued that each type of therapy evokes associations
that fit the theories governing the type of therapy, which could only be a suggestion-effect. These criticisms amount to the same thing in the end,[5] but it
may be worth discussing them separately.

(i) The variation in the conclusions reached by various schools may,
however, be explained independently of suggestion. It is quite possible, indeed probable, that therapists mainly look only for *confirmations* of their
interpretations, overlooking the need to seek out *refutations*. Now it is vital
to distinguish between refutations that are present though not noticed and
the absence of refutations. If refutation is disregarded, Popper (1959) has
shown that confirmation of a hypothesis can in general be found *for any hypothesis* even though false; thus confirmation alone is valueless as support
for a hypothesis. Hence different hypotheses could all be confirmed simply
by seeking confirmations. Hence the phenomenon of different results could
be explained by faulty methodology on the part of therapists of the various
schools. It is conceivable that no discrepant conclusions would arise if therapists sought refutations rather than confirmations.

(ii) In the situation where the therapist gets associations that confirm
his theories, it looks even more strongly as though refutations have not
been sought. The associations are confirmatory but do not really strengthen
his theories unless they could have been refutations.

Where the therapist does not notice refutations that are present in the material presented by a patient but marks up *confirmations*, he takes his interpretation to be confirmed even though it is in fact false, i.e., he obtains
confirmation for a false hypothesis.[6] And this result would flow not from suggestion but from faulty methodology.

On the other hand, where no refutations are present, this might be the result of suggestion. For, if suggestion does occur, what it must do is to abolish
refutations that would otherwise be present. In such a situation confirmation
would flow from a suggestion-effect.

The therapist cannot be certain that a lack of refutation is real evidence for
an interpretation, unless there is some way of telling that it is free of suggestion.[7] And the presence of confirmations might arise either through the
methodology of confirmation which ignores refutation, or suggestion which
sabotages refutation; moreover no clear way of telling which is at work has yet
emerged.

---

[5]On the inductive methodology, (i) would concern conclusions arrived at inductively from a patient's associations, and (ii) would concern subsequent confirmation of conclusions; on the hypo-
thetics-deductive methodology, however, both are tests of hypotheses.

[6]As Mr. A. S. S. el Kaffash has pointed out to me, a therapist, both when he overlooks a negative
transference and when he notes it but treats it as resistance, may be overlooking the possibility of
refutations of his interpretation.

[7]Contrariwise, proof that an interpretation acted as a suggestion could be obtained if it could
somehow be shown to be false without being refuted by the patient.

Before trying to go further with this, let us inquire into the psychology of the situation.

The Psychology of Suggestion

Suppose an interpretation works by suggestion, what is it that is happening? To answer this, let us consider certain ways in which an interpretation might have an effect upon a patient. Possible ways are in virtue (i) of the sound of the interpretation, (ii) of the meaning or content of it irrespective of its truth or falsity, or (iii) of the content because it is in fact true of the patient and felt by him to be so.

(i) In certain states a patient may fail to attend to the meaning of what is said altogether, but may nevertheless respond to the analyst's act of speaking (when the uttering of something else would have the same effect), i.e., the patient is responding to the bare existence of a communication, in which the patient attributes to the analyst's remarks no more content than 'I am here, I accept you, and I am making contact with you'. This might be called 'communication of presence'. It might conceivably have an effect upon a patient that might be wrongly attributed to the content of the interpretation and therefore to the theory underlying it.

(ii) If the meaning or content of an interpretation brings about an effect irrespective of whether it is true or false, which is solely because the analyst has asserted that content, then we have the suggestion-effect. A further feature of the suggestion-effect comes to light here. The interpretation is accepted irrespective of whether it is *recognized* by the patient to be true (or false) of himself. But it is accepted by him as true: true not on the basis of *evidence* but of *authority*, true because somebody asserts it.

(iii) Truth of content involves recognition of evidence rather than authority, and therefore contrasts fundamentally with suggestion.

Which of these three possibilities is the mainspring of interpretations?

We may go some way towards answering this from a practical point of view by considering what sort of patient might come under the sway of the suggestion-effect. What would lead him to adopt a suggestion? He might do so, for instance, if he received a false interpretation and wanted to ingratiate himself with the therapist. Again he might do so to throw dust in the therapist's eyes, i.e., to prevent him from finding out where the real sore spots lay. Again he might accept the interpretation to avoid being terror-stricken at the idea that his therapist could possibly be wrong. In short there could be the (hysteric's) motive of control by ingratiation or the (more or less universal) motive of the safety of the false trail or the (infantile) motive of avoiding terror at helplessness—which are various facets of coping with dependence.

If these possibilities can be detected, then in their absence we should be on the road to the third one, that an important factor in the operation of an interpretation is its truth. Something can be done along these lines. The 'communication of presence' may sometimes be easy to recognize intuitively, but that is not enough: how could we exclude the possibility of a more concrete meaning being communicated to the patient? To this end a test can be invented: frame an 'interpretation' consisting of a meaningless string of words. (This might, of course, be therapeutically or ethically ruled out.) Then diminution of anxiety would be evidence of communication of presence alone. Again ingratiation, which may be intuitively recognized, can be tested by propounding an incompatible interpretation. The patient bent on ingratiation will swallow both, while one not so inclined will jib. The patient who is game to follow a red herring may be intuitively recognized by being overserious about it. This could be tested by going further along the false trail with an interpretation that ought to wound if the trail is genuine: if no resistance is offered, the trail is false. (Such a test could also be used for ingratiation.) Again, acceptance out of terror might be tested by making a stupid remark about the patient: he might then be expected to show mounting anxiety, yet to agree.

Supposing these possibilities of collusion are tested in a given patient and found to be absent, we have some practical grounds for being confident that the patient is not suggestible, and that the other interpretations given to him are not suggestion-implanting. Methodologically, however, this is incomplete. For there might be other ways, apart from ingratiation, false trails and avoidance of terror, not thought of so far, by which a patient could produce a suggestion-effect. So from a methodological point of view, stronger proof is needed. Moreover, the tests indicated presuppose various psycho-analytic hypotheses which are being scrutinized for a suggestion basis.

There is another facet of a wrong interpretation. Just now we have been considering classes of patients who might acquiesce in a wrong interpretation. What about patients who might revolt against a mistake (because of fear that their troubles would not be dealt with)? Such patients might be expected to make desperate efforts to get the therapist back on the rails (their efforts might very easily look like resistance—which of course they are, though not resistance to the truth). If they can be detected, they might seem to provide definite evidence against suggestion. Alas, this conclusion founders on the possibility of such a patient's being *contra-suggestible*. That is to say, if an interpretation somehow suggests to a patient that he likes something or other, he reacts by asserting that he dislikes it.

This idea has to be considered because it might be held that, where a patient does *not* acquiesce by ingratiation or following a false trail, his reactions, so far from being true, are merely *contra-suggestion-effects*.

Such a phenomenon would spring from the opposite source to that siring suggestion, namely annihilation of authority. It could reveal an insatiable wish to annoy the therapist and reduce him to pulp. The phenomenon could also spring from an overt refusal to allow the therapist to get near to the source of the patient's troubles. And it could presuppose that to accept an interpretation as true would be the patient's doom. Here evidence can play no part;

there is only a struggle between authorities: for the patient to accept an interpretation would be to lose his authority (without which he would see himself
as nothing). In general, a contra-suggestion-effect might be suspected where
a patient has a marked sense of omnipotence.

The first of these, the opposition-*motif*, could be tested by giving the
opposite interpretation, to see whether the patient would disagree at any
price, even the price of giving a response contradicting his previous one. The
second, to do with avoidance of sore spots, could be tested by giving an interpretation that would touch nothing sensitive, when no opposition would
normally be expected: here it would be opposed on principle. And the third,
to do with loss of authority, might be tested by the therapist's saying (if it
can be plausibly done) that the patient's contention was what he had really
meant—to see whether the patient would then have second thoughts about
his position.

But again the refutation of such contra-suggestion-effects is insufficient to
establish the truth of an interpretation.

Now supposing that in a given setting there is no suggestion-effect of the
kinds discussed, is the idea satisfactory of an interpretation producing an effect by reason of its being true? Psycho-analysts themselves—such authorities
as Freud (1912) and Strachey (1934)—have claimed that at this point suggestion plays some part. What is the meaning of such an admission, or claim, by
those who also oppose the charge that psycho-analytic therapy is suggestion?
Clearly 'suggestion' here has an altogether different meaning, but this has
never been adequately brought to light.

The occurrence of a true interpretation, which appeared by chance on a
news tape in front of the patient, would not do much; it needs also to be
uttered by the therapist. Thus the truth of an interpretation, while necessary,
is not sufficient to produce change. Also necessary is the utterance of it
by someone where there is a patient-therapist relationship. Certainly this
utterance may be called a 'suggestion' in so far as the authority of the therapist is invoked. But this authority is not a sufficient condition for implanting
a suggestion; for the authoritative interpretation has also to be true. The
whole difference between the charge of suggestion made by critics and the
claim of suggestion made by psycho-analysts is that suggestion in the ordinary sense is supposed to be at work to produce ideas in the patient that are
not already there, while suggestion in the sense used by Strachey is supposed
to be at work to evoke ideas in the patient that he already has. It is likely to
cause confusion, however, to speak of 'suggestion' in this sense, and I shall
avoid it.

ENACTIVITY AND TRUTH

Let us now look for a more decisive way of settling the matter whether or not
an interpretation works by suggestion. To do this, let us revert to the general
question of testing an interpretation by its effects. Earlier in this paper I have

put forward the theory that an interpretation of a motive is confirmed if it fits the patient's response to it, provided that in his response the defence used to disguise the motive is different from what it would have been without the interpretation. Now Seaborn Jones (1961),[8] discussing an earlier sketch of this view, has pointed out that, strictly speaking, this constitutes a theory not for testing the *truth* of the interpretation but for testing its power to bring about some change, i.e., it would be what Seaborn Jones called 'enactive'; for the response described would confirm that the interpretation had had some effect. And this could happen and yet the interpretation might actually be false. Seaborn Jones is therefore distinguishing sharply between the enactivity and the truth of an interpretation. It is a vital distinction.

The significant problem, then, concerns the discrimination between interpretations that are enactive and true and interpretations that are enactive and false.[9] The theory I have offered is a theory of enactivity, and thus amounts to an application of the methodology of refutability to purposive action. (Psychoanalysts are vitally concerned with enactivity: it bears on what they call 'technique'.) Our problem now is to find a way of telling whether an enactive interpretation is true or false.

PROPOSED SOLUTION

What would be the situation in which an interpretation would be false even though enactive?

To consider this we revert to the view I have already presented about the structure of an interpretation. It consists of (i) a hypothesis about the motives contained in the patient's associations; and (ii) a hypothesis about the defence he uses to *disguise* these motives. The interpretation is false if either of these is false. Now it is certainly false if the patient's response has a structure that has to be interpreted differently. But could it be false even if the interpretation does fit the motive of the response? What this comes to is the question: could the patient somehow (i) preserve the same motive in his response and yet (ii) concoct a defence in the form expected by the analyst that would not give a true picture of the workings of his mind? If this is possible, we should have an interpretation that was false but ostensibly enactive.

---

[8] Glyn Seaborn Jones was discussing the idea I put forward earlier (1956), but his point holds equally of the further development given above.

[9] The case of non-enactive interpretations has little interest, though there is a point worth noting. Suppose such an interpretation is true (it is perfectly possible to give a patient true interpretations that have absolutely no effect, as those learning to be psycho-therapists know only too well), but the analyst could not discover this at the time because of its lack of enactivity. Years later in the treatment of the patient the analyst might discover that his earlier useless interpretation had been in fact true. But this would probably depend on being able to test enactive interpretations. The likelihood is that it will be easier to test for their truth those interpretations that are enactive rather than those that have no effect.

This would be so if the patient had learnt from past experience to preserve the motive in his response and what sort of defence should be shown by it.[10] Here, I think, we have a statement of what the theory of the suggestion-effect, as it might be called, amounts to. It is worth stating, not only for its own sake and for the clarity gained, but also because it derives part of its power from remaining unarticulated.

An unarticulated theory is more or less immune to criticism. But now that we have a possible theory of the suggestion-effect before us, we can at once see an irreparable defect in it. The ordinary idea of suggestion, rooted in the context of hypnosis, is that the hypnotist tells a subject what to think and he thinks it, what to feel and he feels it, what to do, and he does it. Here the idea is in part the same: namely that the patient shall produce in his response the motive interpreted (suggested?) by the analyst. But it is in part very different: namely that the patient shall produce in his response a form of defence that is *not* suggested.

Could a patient, however, learn from past experience to preserve the motive in his response and learn what sort of defence should be shown by it? Even if such a feat were possible, it could not happen *early* in the treatment.

For example, there is on record an interpretation given to a schizophrenic patient within the first minutes of the first analytic session, which produced relief in him and a response of personal contact (recognisably similar to the response of a stranger, say, if you happen to mention a mutual friend, as contrasted, say, with a reference to the weather). The interpretation was enactive; and clearly so, because no other way has ever been found of making contact with psychotics.

After all, then, there is quite a simple answer to the question of suggestion. It consists of two points: (i) the theory of corroboration of an interpretation involves a predictable type of defence in a patient's response, which is not suggested; and (ii) the type of defence could not have been learnt in the early weeks of treatment. This answer implies that psycho-analytic interpretation does not, from its intrinsic nature, operate by suggestion.

THE FINAL TEST

We can, therefore, test a clinical interpretation by the method described earlier in this paper, provided we also ensure in the way now described that no suggestion-effect is present, so that the interpretation is refutable.

REFERENCES

Brenner, Charles (1955). Validation of psychoanalytic technique. *J. Am. Psychoanal. Assoc.* 3, ed. Marmor, reprinted in Paul (1963).

---

[10]A remote alternative would be if the patient had learnt to read the analyst's mind, i.e., what response the analyst expected. In this case the charge of suggestion would presuppose clairvoyance on the part of nearly all patients—an assumption that those who have levelled the charge of suggestion would be unwilling to make.

Ezriel, Henry (1956). Experimentation within the psycho-analytic Session. *Brit. J. Philos. Sc.* 7: 29f.

Fenichel, Otto (1945). *The Psychoanalytic Theory of Neurosis.* New York, 570.

Freud, S. (1925). *An Autobiographical Study. The Standard Edition* 20, 42–3.

Freud, S. (1937). Constructions in analysis. *The Standard Edition* 23.

Frisch, O. R. (1963). The magnetic proton. *The Listener*, Sept. 26, 459–60.

Isaacs, Susan (1939). Criteria for interpretation. *Inter. J. Psycho-Anal.* 20: 148.

Kubie, L. S. (1952). Problems and techniques of psychoanalytic validation and progress. In *Psychoanalysis as Science*, ed. Pumpian-Mindlin (1952), Stanford.

Lakatos, Imre (1963–4). Proofs and refutations. *Brit. J. Philos. Sc.* 14.

Medawar, P. B. (1963). Is the scientific paper a fraud? *The Listener*, Sept. 12, 377–8.

Paul, Louis (1963). *Psychoanalytic Clinical Interpretation.* New York, 264.

Popper, K. R. (1959). *The Logic of Scientific Discovery.* London.

Seaborn Jones, G. (1961). *Some Philosophical Implications of Psycho-Analysis.* Ph.D. Thesis, University of London.

Strachey, James (1934). The Nature of the therapeutic action of psycho-analysis. *Inter. J. Psycho-Anal.* 15, reprinted in Paul (1963).

Wisdom, J. O. (1956). Psycho-analytic technology. *Brit. J. Philos. Sc.* 7: 15–16, reprinted in Paul (1963), 155–7.

Wisdom, J. O. (1960). Some main mind-body problems. *Proc. Arist. Soc.* 60: 201–7.

Wisdom, J. O. (1962). Criteria for a psycho-analytic interpretation. *Proc. Arist. Soc.*, sup. vol. 36, 101–3.

10

BRIAN A. FARRELL

Can Psychoanalysis Be Refuted?

This paper examines the challenge that psychoanalytic theory cannot be refuted. It does so by considering the theory in its orthodox Freudian form, and in the main branches into which it can be divided—the theory of Instincts, of Development, of Psychic Structure, of Mental Economics or Defence, and of Symptom Formation. The essential character of the generalizations and concepts of these branches will just be indicated; and we shall ask of each branch whether it is possible to refute it. A considerable amount of scientific enquiry has been done into the concepts and generalizations of psychoanalysis. Relevant examples of these enquiries will be noted; and the question asked whether these scientific studies have in fact done anything to refute or support the various branches of psychoanalytic theory. The general upshot will be that the challenge is both important and a mistake.

INTRODUCTION

This question opens up a very large problem, and I shall only offer some thoughts on it in an abrupt and disjointed way. Because it is a large problem. I shall cut it down to more manageable size by restricting myself to psychoanalytic theory of the classical or orthodox Freudian sort. What we discover about this brand of psychoanalytic theory may not be without relevance to other brands, ancient, modern, and deviant.

Reprinted from *Inquiry* (Oslo: Norwegian University Press), vol. 1 (1961), pp. 16–36. Reprinted by permission.

Is it logically possible to refute this theory? The problem is well known. Analysts have been challenged to show that it is refutable,[1] and they have been slow to meet the challenge. Its importance lies in the fact that, if the theory cannot be refuted in principle, we will have good reason for saying that is not a "scientific" theory at all, but something more akin to "a myth" (as Popper suggests), or just a "wonderful representation" of the facts (as Wittgenstein apparently took it to be[2]).

THE PARTS OF PSYCHOANALYTIC THEORY

As soon as we take up the challenge, we notice one thing about the theory at once. It is not a unified theory—it does not contain certain fundamental, or primitive, concepts which appear in certain basic postulates, and from which the rest of the theory is developed. Hence it is not possible to refute "the theory" by testing directly any of its lowest level generalizations; nor is it possible to refute it by deducing an empirical consequence from any generalization, and indirectly testing it by directly testing the deduced consequence. But this limitation of psychoanalytic theory does not appear to matter. The fact that the theory is not unified, and hence not refutable as such—as a whole—does not mean that the constituent parts of the theory are not refutable. Psychoanalysis may be in the stage that our knowledge of the physical world was before the unification of Physics got under way last century. So it is misleading to frame the challenge in the one big question: can psychoanalytic theory be refuted? We must reformulate it and ask: can each of the different parts of psychoanalytic theory be refuted?

One of the traditional ways of dividing up the theory is as follows:

1. The theory of Instincts, or Dynamics;

2. The theory of Development;

3. The theory of Psychic Structure;

4. The theory of Mental Economics, or Defence;

5. The theory of Symptom Formation.

This traditional list of the parts of psychoanalytic theory may not be exhaustive; and it may give the quite mistaken impression that the various parts are unrelated to one another. But these five parts do jointly cover much of the ground usually regarded as covered by psychoanalytic theory. What we shall do, for brevity, is to examine some very few of the central or characteristic generalizations of each part of the theory. If we find that those from any one part are refutable, we shall have done something to show that this part, at

---

[1]Popper, K. R. (1957), in *British Philosophy in the Mid-Century*, C. A. Mace, ed. Allen and Unwin, London.

[2]Moore, G. E. (1955), "Wittgenstein's Lectures in 1930–33," *Mind* 64, no. 253.

least, of psychoanalytic theory is refutable. If we find the opposite, we shall have done something to show that the part concerned is not refutable.

The Theory of Instincts

This claims to discover and classify the basic drives of man. On Freud's *first* Instinct theory, as it is usually called, the basic drives fall into two types—the ego or self-preservative and the sexual. Consider two different ways in which it could be claimed that this generalization can be refuted.

(a) On Freud's view, an instinct or drive has a "source". This is a "somatic process", but "we do not know whether this process is regularly of a chemical nature or whether it may also correspond with the release of other, e.g., mechanical, forces."[3] Now when we do come to uncover relevant physiological processes, it is possible that we shall discover that whereas some of the ego instincts (e.g., thirst and hunger) have "a source", others (e.g., flight from danger) have not. Or, what is more likely perhaps, we shall discover that the whole notion of "a source" is far too naive to cover the complex facts about the bodily origins of instinctual activity.[4] If we discover either of these things we will succeed in forcing analysts to modify the theory. So, it could be said, it is possible in principle to refute this generalization of the Instinct theory.

(b) New clinical material may turn up which it is difficult to order in terms of the theory, and which suggests a different classification of instincts. It is well known that something like this is what actually happened. Freud found himself faced with the phenomenon of narcissism, as well as with the puzzle of masochism and a type of aggression that was apparently not a response to frustration. He decided that these phenomena constituted a good objection to his first theory of instincts. Accordingly he revised it and replaced it by what is known as the second theory. In this, the basic drives are grouped into the Death and the Life Instincts, the latter being subdivided into the self-preservative and the sex drives.

But though this material forced Freud to modify his first theory, is this an instance of refutation? There are two obvious objections to supposing that it is.

(i) The clinical material or data are obtained by the use of psychoanalytic method. This method is suspect on the ground that it helps *to manufacture* the data, unlike an accepted scientific method that merely uncovers them. In other words, the validity of psychoanalytic method has not yet been established. We do not know, therefore, what weight to attach to the claim that by means of it certain data have been discovered. Consequently, when Freud, or other analysts, apparently uncover material that conflicts

---

[3]Freud, S. (1915), "Instincts and their Vicissitudes," *Collected Papers*, vol. IV. Hogarth Press, London, 1925.

[4]Cf. Beach, F. A., "Instinctive Behaviour: Reproductive Activities," in *Handbook of Experimental Psychology*, S. S. Stevens, ed. Chapman and Hall, London, 1951.

with a generalization of the theory, we are uncertain whether we can count this material as a negative instance, and hence as refuting the generalization and the theory. The complications here are obviously immense.

(ii) But it is clear that, whatever be the truth about (i), the "discovery" of new, conflicting material by Freud, or any other analyst, does constitute *an* objection to his first Instinct theory, even if it is not a conclusive objection for the reason just mentioned under (i). Well, then, is it correct to say that the new material "refuted" Freud's first theory? We are inclined to say "Yes, it is", because the new material cannot be fitted into the theory. This led Freud and Freudians generally to agree that the first theory was unsatisfactory, even though most analysts did not accept Freud's second theory, or agree on what to accept instead. But we may be inclined to say "No, the new material has not refuted the first theory". If so, the reason behind our inclination may be that we are accustomed to talk of data as refuting a hypothesis, and not as exhibiting the inadequacy of a classificatory scheme.

It is now clear, however, that our difficulty hinges round the word "refute", and not round this part of psychoanalytic theory. In the context we are dealing with, the word "refute" functions as a tool of philosophical art, and the way we answer the question will depend partly on the way the word is used in our own special brand of the philosophy of science. Moreover, the fact that we hesitate over this case because we do not know whether to describe it as a case of "refutation"—this fact suggests that the ways in which generalizations are supported by data are more complex than we are led to suppose by the simple demand for refutation. For this reason alone, it may be quite misleading to demand *simpliciter* of a theory whether it can be refuted or not. Hence, even when we limit ourselves to a demand that the *parts* of psychoanalytic theory should be refutable, we may be making a demand that is misleading and more or less inappropriate.

THE THEORY OF DEVELOPMENT

I shall interpret this part of psychoanalytic theory widely to include the theory of character formation, as well as Freud's account of erotogenesis and sexuality. The essential characteristic of this part of the theory is that the generalizations it contains are universal and relatively straightforward in nature. This is understandable, since Freud is concerned here to give us the stages of mental growth and the antecedents of characters of different types. The natural way to express his "discoveries" here is to put them in universal form. I shall pick out, very arbitrarily, a few examples of his generalizations.

1. "A second pregenital phase is that of the sadistic-anal organization (of sexual life)."[5] Let us express part of this generalization in a more usual and convenient form. "All children go through an anal-sadistic stage." What this

[5]Freud, S., *Three Essays on the Theory of Sexuality*, Imago Publ. Co., London.

means, at least in part, is that all children go through a state when their chief sexual interest is anal pleasure.

Is this refutable? One hesitates because it is so vague. What is a "stage"? How does one decide that their interest in faeces is "sexual"? How does one discover that what a child is really interested in, in expelling its faeces, is anal pleasure? How does one set about determining the relative strengths of the oral, anal-sadistic and phallic interests? It is tempting to conclude that the generalization is *so* vague as to be irrefutable. But is there much point in falling for this temptation? For if we do fall for it, are we doing much more than advertising our personal decision to put a generalization with this degree of vagueness beyond the limits of the refutable? And is not such a decision a bit arbitrary in view of the fact that all sorts of empirical considerations obviously do have a bearing on the truth or falsity of this generalization? Would not a careful programme of Gesell-like observation on a large sample, from different home-training regimes, do *something* to support or upset the generalization? And can we not imagine a programme of investigation, the results of which could make us inclined to say that the generalization *had* been refuted? I think we can imagine such a programme.

Consider the other, related generalization: "All children go through an oral stage." As this activity is the manifestation of an instinct, it must have an aim; and, in accordance with the general theory of psychosexuality, this is the attainment of pleasurable, auto-erotic stimulation from the erogenous zone of the mouth. It is clear, therefore, that one way of testing this oral generalization is to try to discover whether infants have a drive to non-nutritional, or pleasure, sucking. Various workers have investigated this question. The general finding is that animals and infants do give good evidence of non-nutritional sucking, which goes to support Freud's generalization. However, it is possible to explain this sucking as an outcome of learning, in which case it would not be the manifestation of an instinct, sexual or otherwise, and Freud's generalization would be refuted.[6] It does not seem beyond the wit of man to devise further work to help to decide between these two alternatives. Indeed, this further work may have already been done—I am rather ignorant on these matters.

Now let us return to the generalization about the anal stage. What would help here is some work which would show whether infants and animals indulged in pleasure defecation; and if they did, whether this was an innate or learned drive. Clearly, there is nothing logically absurd about such a programme of investigation; and indeed it may not be beyond us at the present time to design an actual programme of this sort, if it has not already been done

---

[6]See, for example: Levy, D. M. (1934), "Experiments on the sucking reflex and social behaviour of dogs," *Amer. J. Orthopsychiat.* 4: 203–224; Roberts, E. (1944), "Thumb and finger sucking in relation to feeding in early infancy," *Amer. J. Dis. Child* 68:7–8; Halverson, H. M. (1938), "Infant sucking and Tensional behavior," *J. Genet. Psychol.* 53:365–430; Sears, R. R., and G. W. Wise (1950), "The relation of cup feeding in infancy to thumb-sucking and the oral drive," *Amer. J. Orthopsychiat.* 20:123–138.

and carried out. The important point, however, is that, if such a programme showed that the interest in anal pleasure was learned, we would be strongly inclined to say that Freud's generalization had been refuted. We would say this about it in spite of it being so depressingly vague.

Next let us look quickly at another generalization.

2. "All little girls have penis envy and wish to be boys."[7] It seems clear that the direct observation of little girls fails to support this generalization,[8] as most observant parents will agree. Orthodox analysts will probably reply that this negative evidence is not conclusive, because girls who do not show overt signs of penis envy have concealed it from view or repressed it. Their evidence for saying this stems from their use of psychoanalytic method in the analysis of adults and in play therapy with children. To assess the weight of this evidence we have to determine the validity of psychoanalytic method. In the absence of such an enquiry, the truth-value of the generalization will remain uncertain. But have we any grounds for asserting that it is not refutable *in principle?* Surely none whatever. Of course, it may be difficult to refute it in practice, and for reasons connected with the difficulty of doing satisfactory research in this field. But part of the business of scientific workers is to overcome the practical difficulties in their way. In any case, these difficulties constitute a fact about the sociology of psychoanalysis, not a fact about the logic of psychoanalytic theory.

I shall now glance at two generalizations from the psychoanalytic view of character formation. An essential part of the story about the Oral Character can be stated as follows.

3. "(i) All people can be placed on a continuum into two types—the self-assured optimists at one end and the insecure pessimists at the other; and (ii) the position of any one person on this continuum is determined by the gratification or frustration he experienced at the breast."[9]

Now this generalization asserts that there is a determining or causal connection between certain experiences at the breast and adult character; and in so doing presupposes that there is a correlation between these experiences and adult character. Goldman[10] discovered that people could be rated in the way the first part of the generalization alleges; and that there was a small but significant correlation between late weaning and optimism, on the one side, and early weaning and pessimism on the other. In short, she discovered that there was in fact a correlation of the sort presupposed by psychoanalytic theory. Suppose, however, that she had discovered something else—either that there was *no* correlation here at all, or that the correlation was the *reverse* of what she actually discovered. Her results would then have conflicted with

[7]Freud, S., op. cit.

[8]Valentine, C. W. (1942), *The Psychology of Early Childhood*, ch. 18, Methuen, London.

[9]Fenichel, O. (1945), *The Psychoanalytic Theory of Neurosis*, ch. 20, Kegan Paul, London.

[10]Goldman, F. (1948), "Breastfeeding and character formation," *J. Personality* 17:83–103; and (1950) "Breastfeeding and character formation: II. The etiology of the oral character in psychoanalytic theory," *J. Personality* 19:189–96.

generalization 3. Would this then have counted as a refutation of this generalization? Does it much matter what we would say here? It is quite clear that, whether we would call this a case of refutation or not, this generalization of psychoanalysis is open to empirical support and rebuttal.

An essential constituent of the psychoanalytic doctrine of the Anal Character is a generalization that can be expressed as follows:

4. "Fixation at the anal-erotic stage of instinctual development goes to produce or determine the 'anal character' traits of parsimoniousness, orderliness and obstinacy."[11]

This generalization implies a correlation between severe and rigid bowel training and the possession of these traits. Some studies have been made of this question, but, to my knowledge, the results have been inconclusive. It has not even been firmly established that there is such a cluster of traits as the anal character, let alone that such clusters, where they exist, are correlated with severe bowel training.[12] Some of us may be tempted perhaps to think that the uncertain status of this generalization is inevitable; and, if it is inevitable, then it is not refutable. But, as soon as one looks a little closer at it in its context in psychoanalytic theory, and in the relevant body of scientific work, it becomes clear that its present uncertain status neither entails nor implies that it is irrefutable. The temptation to think otherwise dissolves under the pressure of contextual fact.

The upshot about this part of psychoanalytic theory—the theory of Development—is that it is open in principle to scientific investigation, and that it is open to it in practice as much as the complexities and other difficulties of the field permit. It is worth noting that psychologists have not hesitated to investigate this part of psychoanalytic theory, even though they have recognised that their relatively crude methods may not be able to deal with the subtleties of the phenomena involved. We have to remember, however, that almost any negative finding—such as that over female penis envy—can be countered by analysts claiming that it is necessary to postulate such girlish envy in order to account for the material thrown up in analysis. The strength of this reply can only be resolved, presumably, by settling the validity of psychoanalytic method. All of which suggests that this part of psychoanalytic theory opens up a most interesting field for scientific research.

THE THEORY OF PSYCHIC STRUCTURE

This part of psychoanalytic theory is quite different in logical character from the two parts we have just glanced at. Its key words (e.g., id, ego, unconscious, etc.) appear to function in two different ways. They function as nouns, and they also function as adjectives, or in ways that are implicitly adjectival in

---

[11]Freud, S. (1908), "Character and Anal Erotism," *Collected Papers*, vol. 2 (1924), Hogarth Press, London; Fenichel, O. op. cit.

[12]Sears, R. R. (1936), "Experimental Studies of Projection: Attribution of traits," *J. Soc. Psychol.* 7:151–163. Blum, G. S. (1953), *Psychoanalytic Theories of Personality*, ch. 8, McGraw-Hill, New York.

character. As nouns, they go to make up a story that gives us "the topography of the mind"; as adjectives, they appear in expressions such as "ego functioning", "super-ego development", "unconscious fears", and so on.

Let us first consider their use as nouns—in other words, the psychoanalytic theory of mental topography. It is well known that Freud spoke of the mind as having parts (e.g., the Ego, the Unconscious), containing mental elements charged with energy which are held back by barriers, and so forth. What are we to make of this mystifying talk? Is it just a piece of reifying mythology? Freud himself suggested that we regard it as a *façon de parler*, to be rejected as soon as we find something better.[13] Perhaps a more fashionable way of regarding it today is to look on it as providing a model of mental functioning.

Suppose we do regard Freud's topographical talk in this light. At once we remove its dark and reifying aspects. For we are now only speaking of the mind *as if* it had parts, etc.; and in so doing we admit, more or less explicitly, that it does not really have them. However, it then follows that it is inappropriate to ask of this talk whether it is true or false. Hence it is also misleading to ask whether the statements that comprise it are true or false; and therefore misleading to ask whether they can be *shown* to be true or false—whether they can be supported or refuted. The concepts of truth and falsity, refutability and irrefutability do not apply in a straightforward way to the statements of his topographical theory.

It seems therefore as if the critics of psychoanalytic theory would be right if they picked on this part of the theory as being irrefutable. But how serious is this defect? Is it really the sort of irrefutability that the critics want to establish? I doubt whether it is serious, or the sort of defect that the critics are interested in. The fact that psychoanalytic theory uses a model makes it no worse, prima facie, than any other theory in science that uses one. If we are going to object to psychoanalytic theory *just* because it uses a model, then we should also have to object to any other theory in science that uses one. Which is absurd.

But though we cannot ask whether Freud's topographical talk is true and refutable, we can ask whether it is valuable or not. "How useful was and is it? Are there circumstances or developments in which it would cease to be useful and require modification?" The short answer to these large questions seems to be as follows. Analysts do need to talk in a shorthand way about the total functioning of the individual; and it just seems to be a fact that they find it convenient to do so in spatial terms. The particular model Freud provided was of enormous service to them at the time. Since he wrote, however, various things have led analysts to canvass alternative models more or less explicitly. Thus the work of Fairbairn and Klein[14] has led some analysts to speak of "the

<hr/>

[13]Freud, S. (1935), *An Autobiographical Study*, ch. III, Hogarth Press, London. In contrast Freud strongly repudiated Janet's view that "unconscious" as an adjective was just a *façon de parler*. See below, and Freud, op. cit. ch. III, and *Introductory Lectures on Psycho-analysis*, lectures 19 and 17, rev. 2nd ed. 1929, Allen and Unwin, London.

[14]Fairbarn, W. R. D. (1952), *Psychoanalytic Studies of the Personality*, Tavistock, London; Klein, M. *et al.* (1952), *Developments in Psycho-Analysis*, Hogarth, London.

internal objects that the infant incorporates", and to stress the importance of this and other related performances. A model constructed in accordance with these ideas would be rather different from Freud's. Again, the clinical experience of Laing[15] with schizophrenics has led him to stress that they lose their sense of self-identity, and that it is essential for us to grasp this fact to understand their condition. Clearly if we were to attempt to construct a model that used this idea, and that was general enough to cover the neuroses as well, we would produce one very different from Freud's. For his is suggested by his experience with the neuroses, and the Self does not figure in it. Here, then, it could be alleged, are two developments which show where Freud's model is somewhat unhelpful, and in need of modification. It is not difficult to think of further developments and circumstances that would suggest still other modifications of Freud's model.

But though this model had, and has, its uses, it is a *good* one? The answer is: certainly not! It is a very bad one—it has almost everything a model should not have. It produces the most misleading pictures about this part of psychoanalytic theory and about the theory as a whole. Indeed, it has been so misleading as to produce near apoplexy among some American students of behaviour.[16] When we look into it carefully, it crumbles under our scrutiny because it has not been worked out with sufficient care and precision. We cannot use the model to derive any predictions by reference to which it can be tested. In these respects it is quite different from the models currently employed by psychologists. If we wish to exhibit how inadequate it really is, we can do no better than compare and contrast it with some examples of models under current discussion in the psychological world.[17]

Now let us consider the adjectival use of the words such as "id" and "unconscious". When the words are used in this way, they do not function in model talk at all. This is evident from one fact alone, namely, that whereas Freud was prepared to regard their use in a model language as a *façon de parler*, and accordingly was prepared to sacrifice them in favour of any better alternative, he was not prepared to regard them in their adjectival use as mere ways of talking. On the contrary, in this use, he was convinced that they were indispensable, and for the reason that they expressed concepts that were valid, and hence went to form statements that were true.

Let us look at three examples of statements from the theory in which these words function as adjectives.

5. "An individual exhibits both ego and super-ego functioning." (This is an abbreviated version of a much longer story.)

---

[15]Laing, R. D. (1960), *The Divided Self*, Tavistock, London.

[16]See, for example, Skinner, B. F., "Critique of Psychoanalytic Concepts and Theories," in H. Feigl, and M. Scriven (1956), *Minnesota Studies in the Philosophy of Science*, vol. I, University of Minnesota Press, Minneapolis.

[17]For example, Deutsch, J. A. (1953), "A New Type of Behaviour Theory," *Brit. J. Psychol.* 44:304–17; and Broadbent, D. E. (1958), *Perception and Communication*, Pergamon Press, London.

6. "The super-ego is the heir of the Oedipus complex."[18] The use here of "super-ego" as a noun enables Freud to say with dramatic brevity that the development of super-ego functions culminates with the resolution of the Oedipus complex.

7. ". . . unconscious mental processes exist."[19]

Consider 5. This statement exhibits Freud's way of "dressing up" a truth of common sense. We all know that, for example, we do try to cope realistically with the world, that we do try to deal with threats to our security, and so on. We all know, too, that we are controlled by our consciences, and so forth. Freud dressed up these truths of common sense when he came to incorporate them within his general theory of mental functioning. Is statement 5 refutable? Presumably it is—but in the sort of way or ways characteristic of the generalizations of common sense. Thus, it is possible perhaps to imagine ourselves being shown that the two concepts—of ego and super-ego functions—are basically misguided and have no application at all. For it is possible that when we really have achieved a scientific understanding of the relevant phenomena, we shall discover that these concepts of ego and super-ego activity are so crude and naive that we have to reject them as inapplicable. Or we *could* object here and now and say that 5 is false because it overlooks a very important class of individuals, namely psychopaths. On one view of psychopathy, some psychopaths are people without super-ego development. If this view is correct, then 5 is false. But though we could say this, *would* we say it? I doubt it. For in producing this exception we bring out the importance of statement 5. Indeed, we bring out that we use 5 to explain this very exception to it, namely the class of psychopaths. Moreover, we do not withdraw our commonsensical generalization that, for example, "subject peoples resent their inferiority" by being told that some black servants in South Africa love their masters and do not resent their station in life. So, also, we do not withdraw the dressed-up, but commonsensical, generalization in 5 when we are presented with an exception. It is for these reasons that we would not use the class of psychopaths *as* an exception. The upshot, therefore, is that 5 is refutable, but that it is odd to raise the question of refutation about it—in the way that it is odd to raise this question about some of the generalizations of common sense.

Take 6. This is a straightforward generalization about development. We have commented on this type already. It is worth remembering that 6 has been challenged by Klein in the light of her evidence from play therapy.[20]

And 7. ". . . unconscious mental processes exist." This is a more complicated assertion. It resembles 5 in that it is saying something quite common-

[18]Freud, S. (1927), *The Ego and the Id*, Hogarth, London; and (1924) "The Passing of the Oedipus-Complex," *Collected Papers*, vol. II, ch. 23. Hogarth, London.

[19]Freud, S. (1929), *Introductory Lectures on Psycho-analysis*, rev. 2nd ed., Lecture 18, Allen and Unwin, London.

[20]Klein, M. (1933), "The Early Development of Conscience in the Child," in M. Klein (1948), *Contributions to Psychoanalysis*, Hogarth Press, London.

sensical. Unconscious wishes, etc., have been part of our common-sense knowledge of man since Aesop's report about the fox and the grapes. Where 7 is uncommonsensical is in the fact that Freud asserted it at all. He did this because he was concerned to maintain that a large number of certain *specific* unconscious mental processes were at work in us and with important results. (E.g., that unconscious Oedipal wishes occurred with important consequences for mental health later on in life.) In maintaining this view he flew flat in the face of common sense and of the science of his day. What is also uncommonsensical about 7 is the use to which he and others put it—namely in treatment. It was this whole new context in which 7 now functioned that made this commonsensical generalization so important and interesting. Because 7 is a common-sense generalization, it is refutable in the way that is characteristic of the generalizations of common sense. Just because of this, there is something odd about asking: "Is 7 refutable?", and we do not naturally raise this question. What we *do* ask quite naturally is whether a generalization about some *specific* unconscious process or state is true or not—for example, the generalization about unconscious Oedipal wishes. In asking such a question we presuppose that these generalizations about specific unconscious processes can be refuted in principle. We have discovered no reason so far for saying that this presupposition is false in any way that matters.

The Theory of Mental Economics

The character of this part of psychoanalytic theory is again very different from the other parts we have touched on. This part, in the orthodox view, is concerned to describe the ways in which the individual deals with the mental excitation to which he is subject and reduces it to an optimum level. Two of the essential features of this part of the theory seem to be as follows. (i) It contains certain concepts such as Repression, Regression, Projection, Identification, etc. (Quite often these words are also said to name Mechanisms of Defence.) (ii) These concepts do not appear typically in generalizations that are universal or statistical in form; but appear typically in generalizations with a form rather like this: "When so and so happens, the individual tends to, e.g., repress . . ." Thus, when Fenichel discusses these concepts he offers a number of scattered generalizations about them, and the key words in these generalizations are words such as "tend to", "may", "in general" (a non-numerical use), and "prevalent" (a non-numerical use).[21]

This part of psychoanalytic theory is confusing and obscure in various ways. There is no agreement on what set of concepts to include in this part of the theory. There is no one, generally used, formulation of these generalizations. To say that these concepts appear typically in generalizations that are "tendency statements" is to say something in need of further analysis.[22] Though

---

[21]Fenichel, O. op. cit., ch. 9.
[22]Farrell, B. A. (1949), "Causal Laws in Psychology," *Arist. Soc. Suppl.* 23; Braithwaite, R. B. (1953), *Scientific Explanation*, Cambridge.

the typical generalizations in which they appear may be of this form, some also appear in universal ones—especially those connected with the development of the person, and the ages and stages at which various mechanisms of defence are first or predominantly used. It is not at all clear how the different parts of this part of the theory fit together. It could be argued that they fit together very loosely, and that the connective "and" is about all that conjoins them. On top of all this, the concepts themselves are vague and obscure; and few analysts have ventured to help themselves and others by an exercise in clarification. Yet in spite of all this, the theory of Mental Economics or Defence is a critically important part of psychoanalytic theory. This becomes very apparent when psychoanalytic theory as a whole is applied to a given individual in the attempt to understand him and to develop clinical expectations about him. Indeed, some contemporary analysts might be tempted to say that much of the psychoanalytic theory we have already considered is rather dead wood and of uncertain value; but that the theory of Mental Economics is the part of psychoanalytic theory that is most alive and of growing importance.

Is this part of the theory open to refutation? In view of its confused and unsatisfactory state, anyone may be forgiven for thinking that the answer is obviously negative, and that we need pursue the matter no further. But let us glance at some generalizations.

8. "Where aggressive behaviour towards the external sources of frustration is prevented, this behaviour may be displaced."

Neal Miller constructed a situation experimentally between two rats in which, in the presence of a doll, aggressive behaviour against each other was rewarded. He then removed one rat, and the aggressive behaviour was then directed against the doll.[23] What is the relation between this finding and generalization 8? Suppose Miller's finding had been negative—that, e.g., the rat started to bite and apparently attack itself and not the doll. This would have forced us to ask various questions. For example, is this failure to obtain an analogue of displacement due to the vast differences between rats and humans? Or is it due to some defect in the design of the experiment? Or has the experimenter just misunderstood the concept of displacement in designing this experiment? We would have been forced to put these questions because this negative result would have been relevant to the truth of generalization 8. Suppose we had then investigated the problem in various different ways and turned up with negative results all along the line. We might then have found ourselves saying: "The only interpretation we can put on these results is to say that aggressive behaviour is not displaced. What we find is that the aggressive behaviour is apparently self-directed, where it is directed at all." It is quite conceivable that we should have discovered these negative results. If we had discovered them, they would have opposed the "may be displaced" of gener-

[23]Miller, N. E. (1948), "Theory and experiments relating psycho-analytic displacement to stimulus-response generalization," *J. Abnorm. (Soc.) Psychol.* 43:155–78.

alization 8 with the finding that the aggression "does not appear to be displaced at all". It is quite correct to say that such findings would have disconfirmed or failed to support the generalization 8 in some measure. Because of this, it is also correct to say that Neal Miller's actual findings lent the generalization some small measure of support.

9. "Boys tend to identify with their fathers in a more clear-cut and decisive way than do girls with their mothers."[24] Blum devised a projective test, using a series of cartoons or pictures about a dog Blacky, to investigate a number of psychoanalytic generalizations.[25] He discovered that there was a tendency of the sort asserted in 9. He also discovered, however, that females tend to have a motherly rather than a fatherly super-ego. This finding conflicts with psychoanalytic theory, if the latter be taken to include the generalization that both males and females tend to develop fatherly super-egos.[26] In other words, a tendency generalization of psychoanalytic theory is supported by finding the alleged tendency on enquiry, and it is not supported when the alleged tendency is not found but some conflicting tendency instead. It is apparent, however, to the discerning eye that fruitful work on identification may only be possible after further clarification of the concept itself. In recent years psychologists have turned their attention to this logical task on several of the concepts concerned, including that of identification.[27] This gain in clarity is one of the undoubted benefits that has accrued from the attempts of psychologists to investigate the generalizations of psychoanalysis.

10. "When an individual is subject to frustration, there is a tendency for him to regress to an earlier level of either libidinal or ego development."[28]

An oft-quoted investigation in this field is that of Barker, Dembo and Lewin.[29] These workers arranged a play situation in which children were subject to frustration and then showed what looked like considerable ego-regression. Like other studies of the concept of regression, this work raises quite acutely the question of how close is the experimentally produced analogue of regression to the regression that the analysts are really talking about. The less close the analogue, the less weight is to be attached to the experimental results, positive or negative; and conversely. To arrive at even a provisional decision about this question is a highly technical business; and the technicians are apt to be influenced in their judgements by various non-

[24]Freud, S. (1933), *New Introductory Lectures on Psycho-analysis*, ch. 33, Hogarth Press, London.

[25]Blum, G. S. (1949), "A study of the psychoanalytic theory of psycho-sexual development," *Genet. Psychol. Monogr.* 39:3–99.

[26]Fenichel, O., op. cit., ch. 6.

[27]Stoke, S. M. (1950), "An inquiry into the concept of identification," *J. Genet. Psychol.* 67:163–189; Gray, S. W., and R. Klaus (1956), "The assessment of parental identification," *Genet. Psychol. Monogr.* 54:87–114.

[28]Cf. Glover, E. (1949), *Psycho-analysis*, 2nd ed., Staples Press, London; Fenichel, O., op. cit., ch. 9.

[29]Barker, R., T. Dembo, and K. Lewin (1941), "Frustration and Regression: an experiment with young children," *Studies in Topological and Vector Psychology II. Univ. Iowa Stud. Child Welf.*, 18:1, 1–314.

rational considerations—such as their romantic or sceptical attitude to objective work in psychology, their readiness to work patiently to pick up the crumbs of scientific discoveries, and so forth.

11. "Unsatisfied wishes are the driving power behind phantasies; every separate phantasy contains the fulfilment of a wish, and improves on unsatisfactory reality."[30]

Suppose we give this statement a strong interpretation as a universal generalization. The kernel of it is that "All phantasies are wish fulfilling." We may be tempted to say two different things about this statement. That it is obviously true, being only a matter of common sense; and that it is obviously not the sort of thing we can investigate scientifically at all. But the fact is that not all people have believed it,[31] and it is open to scientific enquiry. Thus, Feshbach[32] argued that if a social situation were to arouse hostility in people, then the expression of their hostility in phantasy should reduce somewhat the hostility they felt towards this situation. On investigation Feshbach found this hypothesis was correct. It is natural to say that this finding supports generalization 11, and that if the contradictory finding had been made, it would have counted against the generalization. It is hardly necessary to say that, and why, Feshbach's work is not conclusive. The inconclusive outcome of a single experiment is a common feature of work in science, and not one restricted to psychology alone.

I have now run through a very inadequate sample of psychological enquiry in the field of Mental Economics or Defence. Do we *still* feel inclined to say that the generalizations in this part of psychoanalysis are irrefutable? Probably not. Obviously this inclination is a bit misplaced. Whatever may be wrong with this part of psychoanalytic theory—and it is evident that there is a great deal the matter with it—it is not its alleged irrefutability. When we look into the details here, the sharp dichotomy between what is refutable and what not ceases to be important and relevant.

THE THEORY OF SYMPTOM FORMATION

This part of psychoanalysis is concerned to tell us how the working of the mental system goes wrong. It includes statements of different sorts. It gives us a way of talking about neurotic conflict and symptom formation as a whole. It tells us about conditions that determine or contribute to the manifestation of mental disorder. It gives us descriptive accounts of the standard neurotic and character disorders, along with descriptions of the aetiology and psycho-

---

[30]Freud, S. (1908), "The relation of the poet to day-dreaming," in *Collected Papers*, vol. 4, Hogarth Press, London, 1948.

[31]McClelland, *et al.* (1949), "The projective expression of needs: IV. The effect of the need for achievement on thematic apperception," *J. Exp. Psychol.* 39:242–255.

[32]Feshbach, S. (1955), "The drive-reducing function of fantasy behaviour," *J. Abnorm. Soc. Psychol.* 50:3–11.

pathology of the typical cases of each type of disorder. Let us glance at some examples of statements of these different sorts.

12. "The neurotic conflict takes place between the ego and the id."[33]

Now this statement points to the way in which psychoanalytic theory is used to cover the facts of mental disorder. In this and many other related statements, Freud and others are applying their general scheme, or way of talking, to the pathological material. It follows, therefore, that it is not appropriate to plunge in at once and ask whether statement 12 is refutable. The appropriate question to ask is whether this statement represents the correct application of psychoanalytic theory to the pathological material. Is this the right way to talk about neurotic conflict inside psychoanalytic theory? It may seem that, to answer this question, we shall have to confine ourselves to a tortuous linguistic exercise inside psychoanalytic theory itself. But interestingly enough, this may not be the case, as the following discussion illustrates.

When we use psychoanalytic theory to describe neurotic conflict, a critical question that arises is: what role does the super-ego play in it? A few years ago Miller and Dollard argued[34] that the neurotic conflict is manifested when the super-ego in alliance with the ego becomes too strong for the id. On the other hand, Mowrer[35] argued that neurotic conflict was manifested when the id and the ego became jointly too strong for the super-ego. Eysenck has touched on this question in the course of factorial and objective studies of personality. He has suggested[36] that the disputants are concerned here to describe two different types of patients who fall along a personality dimension or continuum of Introversion and Extraversion. Miller and Dollard are describing in psychoanalytic terms the symptom pattern exhibited by introverted patients; Mowrer the symptom patterns exhibited by extraverted. We need not ask whether Eysenck's suggestion is correct and, if so, whether it is sufficient to resolve the argument. It is interesting to us because it brings out a connection between the psychoanalytic talk about ids and egos and psychological fact; and it shows that the logical tie is closer than we are apt to imagine.

13. "Anxiety (in the case of Anxiety Hysteria—B. A. F.) over being eaten or over being bitten may be a disguise for castration anxiety."[37]

This generalization springs from the analytic view that children who have had difficulties at the oral stage are more likely to exhibit castration anxiety. Hence when a person has castration anxiety this fact may come out in regressive form in symptoms of an oral kind. Now for 13 to be true, it must be true

[33]Fenichel, O., op cit., ch. 8.

[34]Dollard, J., and N. E. Miller (1950), *Personality and Psychotherapy*, McGraw-Hill, New York.

[35]Mowrer, O. H. (1953), *Psychotherapy: theory and research*, Ronald, New York.

[36]Eysenck, H. J. (1957), *The Dynamics of Anxiety and Hysteria*, Routledge and Kegan Paul, London.

[37]Fenichel, O., op. cit., ch. 11.

that disturbances in the oral stage are correlated with castration anxiety. Using the Blacky test, Blum found that there was a low positive correlation between the two.[38]

14. "A necessary condition for the production of male homosexuality is the fixation of erotic needs on the mother."

This is a summary of part of Freud's view on the matter.[39] It is worth noting that subsequent analytic experience with homosexuals has led analysts to modify this generalization by (roughly) restricting its validity to a certain type of homosexuality.[40]

Generalization 14 resembles a number of other generalizations in this part of the theory. These state that a certain condition is either a necessary or a contributory causal antecedent to the development of a certain mental disorder. Perhaps the best known of these is the generalization about maternal deprivation and its effects. The difficulties that have arisen in the attempts to investigate this generalization are typical of some of the difficulties facing scientific enquiry in this sea of subtle data.[41]

15. "(In Anxiety Hysteria—B. A. F.) the unconscious impulses belong to the genital incestuous phase of childhood (the Oedipus situation), and the punishment dread is genital castration or mutilation."[42]

There is a form of neurosis traditionally called "Anxiety Hysteria"; and generalization 15 is part of the orthodox account of the aetiology and psychopathology of this condition. Now it is a fact that not all analysts obtain this aetiology and pathology in all cases of anxiety hysteria. For example, Dicks has reported[43] a small sample of cases of this sort, some of which diverged more or less from the orthodox picture. He made the point that the classical cases of revived Oedipal conflicts "do undoubtedly occur", and these "led the Freudian school to a premature generalization which has of late been partly withdrawn". Of course, counter-evidence from psychoanalytic experience, such as Dicks has produced, raises the interesting and critical question: What supporting and what refuting force should we give to such evidence? Clearly Dicks' experience counts to some extent against generalization 15. But how much? This is a large question which takes us away—as we have already noted—into the whole unresolved issue about the validity of psychoanalytic method. However, in spite of this uncertainty it is still open to analysts and

[38]Blum, G. S., op. cit.

[39]Freud, S. (1910), "Leonardo da Vinci and a memory of his childhood," The Standard Edition of the complete psychological works of Sigmund Freud, vol. 11, ed. James Strachey, Hogarth Press, London, 1957.

[40]For a brief review of this question, see Wohl, R. R., and H. Trosman (1955), "A Retrospect of Freud's Leonardo, and Assessment of a Psychoanalytic Classic." Psychiatry 18:27–29.

[41]For a sceptical review by an outsider see Barbara Wootton (1959), Social Science and Social Pathology, ch. 4, Allen and Unwin, London.

[42]Glover, E., op. cit., ch. 10.

[43]Dicks, H. V. (1947), Clinical Studies in Psychopathology, 2nd ed., ch. 2, Edward Arnold, London.

others rationally to discuss and evaluate the force of the data that their own method produces.

Conclusion

Well, is it logically possible to refute psychoanalytic theory? Do we still feel moved to ask this question?

It is quite clear that the question poses an important and salutary challenge. It forces us to attend to the logical character of psychoanalytic theory. How far is this like and unlike a scientific theory? The question brings analysts to a full stop with a jolt, and obliges them to think about the presuppositions of their work, to take note of the weakness of the appeal to "psychoanalytic experience", to try to make their fuzzy discourse somewhat less fuzzy.

But this challenge is also very misguided. It suggests that there is a sharp line between the refutable and the irrefutable, which is quite misleading, both in general and when considering the nature of psychoanalysis. When one looks into the details of psychoanalytic discourse one finds it impossible generally to say whether a generalization is refutable or not, and the question does not really seem to matter. To ask whether psychoanalytic theory is refutable is also a bit silly in view of the fact that the scientific study of personality is so much concerned with the business of investigating the truth of the generalizations of the theory. Of course, one can *lay down* a tight set of criteria that have to be satisfied before a theory can count as refutable; and we can make these criteria such that psychoanalytic theory has then to be rejected as irrefutable. But what is the point of such legislation? Furthermore, to throw down the challenge of refutability reinforces the idea that psychoanalysis is just a wonderful representation of the facts—like some remarkable but fanciful picture. But it is clear that, in a very important way, the theory is a *very bad* representation of the facts, and not wonderful at all. The challenge of refutability also reinforces the idea that the whole story may be myth, rather like the pre-scientific myths of earlier days. But when one looks into the details of the discourse and sees the close connections between it and empirical fact, the mythical character of the story vanishes, and it becomes a theory that is an approximation to the truth. But, clearly, *no brief* characterization of psychoanalytic theory will do; it is far too complex and diversified for any short description to work. Still, if we *must* have a brief characterization then let us remember the origins and point of the discourse. Freud was forced to construct a story that purported to cover the whole or total field of fact he was meeting in his work. In being forced to construct a "total" narrative, he gave us, naturally enough, a very crude and provisional story. It is a remarkable story because of the novelty and importance of the suggestions it contains, and the range and genius it exhibits. But being a provisional story, it is a defective one. Obviously it is up to analysts and workers in cognate fields to try to improve the situation, and by the application of scientific methods to produce a better narrative. I hope that this paper has made it clear that an enterprise of this sort has been under way for some little time.

POSTSCRIPT (1992)

I now think that this paper has considerable limitations. Though it may succeed in showing that empirical considerations have a bearing on the parts of psychoanalysis, it does not examine and assess how well or badly analysis is actually attested by empirical fact. I refer to Freud's "topography of the mind," and this reference is confusing. For the word "topography" is used here in a wide sense, which covers both Freud's structural theory (which centers around id–ego–super-ego relations), and what is usually called his topographical theory, or point of view (which is prestructural, and which centers around unconscious and preconscious relations). Then, I am wrong in much of what I say, and do not say, about what I describe as Freud's theory of psychic structure. In this Freud is using a model of our mental functioning, which contains parts in their mutual relations; and these are not given a neurophysiological interpretation. It is quite sensible to ask whether the facts suggest we should postulate that we function in this sort of way; and whether this model and postulate represent correctly how we do function. In other words, and contrary to what I suggest, it is open to us to treat Freud's model in the same way as psychologists treat models in their own theories and inquiries. I am also wrong in omitting to explain how the parts of the model are mutually related. For Freud is concerned with the ways in which the psychic system of the individual works as a whole to deal with excitation from within and without, and thereby functions like a self-regulating system. Again, we can ask whether the facts do, or do not, support Freud's view of the ways in which we function as a whole.

11

MORRIS GINSBERG

Psycho-Analysis and Ethics

THE CONTRIBUTION OF Psycho-analysis to ethics may be considered from three points of view. We may enquire, in the first place, what light analytic theory throws on the natural history of morals, that is the ways in which moral rules and moral sentiments are formed and developed in the individual and the group. We may ask next whether Psycho-analysis can, from its own resources, provide the basis for an ethical theory or a set of standards or principles in the light of which existing moral codes can be criticized or evaluated. Finally, there is the question how far the insight into human nature acquired through the exploration of the unconscious elements in the human mind can help us in releasing the energies of man and removing the obstacles that hinder the realization of his ideals, whatever may be their ultimate source.

I propose to confine myself to the first and second of these questions. I do so not because I consider the third less important. On the contrary it may well be the most important. The reason for this self-imposed limitation is that a satisfactory treatment would necessitate a detailed study of case histories and should not properly be undertaken by anyone who, like myself, has no personal experience of analytic procedure. The problems raised in the first two questions are not always clearly distinguished by psycho-analytic writers and some would deny that there is such a thing as ethical theory other than the psychology of morals. Freud himself tells us that it is not the object of his investigations to provide an ethic, still less a *Weltanschauung*. Such activities,

*From Morris Ginsberg, *On the Diversity of Morals* (London: Heinemann Educational Books, 1956), chapter 5. Reprinted by permission of the publisher and executor of Morris Ginsberg.

he says, may be left to philosophers who avowedly "find it impossible to make
their journey through life without a Baedeker of that kind to tell them about
everything."[1] Professor Flugel, in his very thorough and searching examination of the ethical aspects of Psycho-analysis, distinguishes between questions
of origin and questions of validity, and he is of the opinion that the problem of
ultimate or intrinsic value is one for ethics and not psychology.* Despite
these disclaimers, however, the impression is conveyed, perhaps unwittingly,
that a fuller knowledge of the psychology of motivation will render philo-
sophic ethics unnecessary, and this despite the fact that assumptions
are made about the nature of value judgments which certainly require philosophical justification. Thus Freud has no hesitation in asserting, despite his
professed modesty in these matters, that value judgments are ultimately determined by desires and are in fact illusionary in character.[2] Similarly there
are many passages in Professor Flugel's book which suggest that he favours a
"naturalistic" view of moral judgments, as, for example, when he argues that
moral judgments are "orectic," i.e., expressions of feelings, desires or wishes,
and that reason is concerned with the means but not the ends of action. These
are views which, of course, have a respectable philosophical tradition. I do
not wish to prejudge the issue. But it is important to bear in mind that the
problems thus raised are philosophical rather than psychological and that
sooner or later they must be squarely faced as such.

Psychological theories of morals tend on the whole to be relativistic in outlook. For if moral judgments are considered to be expressions of desires or
emotions there will be a tendency to stress the fact that they vary from one individual or group to another. From this the conclusion is readily drawn that
they are not subject to rational tests, and, indeed, that the distinction between
true and false does not properly apply to them. It is interesting to note, however, that recently several attempts have been made by psycho-analysts to
move away from at least the more extreme forms of relativism. Thus Dr. Erich
Fromm tries to show that it is possible on empirical grounds to distinguish between "genuine" and "fictitious" ideals—"a difference as fundamental as that
between truth and falsehood," and that the test is not subjective attractiveness
but is to be found in the objective condition of mental life.[3] From another
point of view, Dr. Money-Kyrle tries to escape relativism by a redefinition of
the "normal" which he seeks to identify with the rational.† In both these cases
and in others the revulsion against relativism is to be traced to the impact of
Nazism which made ethical relativism emotionally untenable. The question

---

[1]*Inhibitions, Symptoms and Anxiety* (1926) *The Standard Edition* 20 (London: Hogarth Press,
1959), p. 29.

*J. C. Flugel, *Man, Morals and Society* (London: Duckworth, 1945)—B. A. F.

[2]*Civilization and Its Discontents* (1930) *The Standard Edition* 21 (London: Hogarth Press,
1961), p. 143.

[3]*Escape from Freedom* (New York: Farrar and Rinehart, 1941), p. 266. Published in England as
The Fear of Freedom (London: Kegan Paul, 1942).

†*Psychoanalysis and Politics*: A Contribution to the Psychology of Politics and Morals (London:
Duckworth, 1951).—B. A. F.

had to be faced whether it could really be the case that when Nazis say it is good and fitting to torture Jews and we say it is abominable the difference is one of personal taste only. The test of "adjustment to the environment" which would come naturally to a psycho-therapist clearly failed. As judged by this test, the Nazi could be as "good" as the democrat, so long as both were equally conditioned to fit into the environment favoured by their societies. Could it be that the real crime of the Nazis was their inefficiency, that is their failure to adopt the means likely to achieve the ends they set themselves? If this is rejected as morally repugnant, it would follow that moral judgments relate not merely to the means but also to the ends of action or else that the repudiation of the Nazi mode of life is emotional only and has no rational foundation. Questions of this sort troubled the minds of all who favoured ethical relativism. But they were felt with special acuteness by psycho-analysts, who realized that they had to re-examine their conception of what constitutes mental health, and that this could not be done without raising the problem of the validity of the criteria implicit in the ethical codes prevailing in different societies. The answers that have been given reveal a tacit reluctance to abandon ethical relativism combined with or qualified by a hope that objective or universal standards of the "normal" or the "healthy" can be derived from the data furnished by empirical psychology. In this respect the claims made by recent writers are bolder than anything to be found in Freud's work. With what success we have now to enquire.

A striking feature of Freud's treatment of morals is his preoccupation with the sense of guilt. In this respect he differs markedly from the philosophers, who with the exception of Plato and Kant give little attention to moral evil. For analogy we have to go to the doctrine of original sin, and it is interesting to note that theologians have themselves noted the affinity between their doctrine and Freud's. The theme forms the centre of Freud's *Totem and Tabu* where morality is represented as a reaction-formation against the evil inherent in man. As is well known, he connects it with the early Œdipus situation in the primal horde, the incestuous desires of the band of brothers, the murder of the father, the subsequent remorse and identification with him. Social organization and moral restrictions are all traced back to this sequence of events. The bond which holds the group together is complicity in a common crime; religion is rooted in the sense of guilt and the consequent remorse; and morality is "based partly on the necessities of society, and partly on the expiation which this sense of guilt demands."[4]

Freud's reconstruction of primeval society was based on the views of Atkinson and Lang and on Robertson Smith's interpretation of the totem feast, and

---

[4]*Totem and Taboo* (1913) *Standard Edition*, 13 (London: Hogarth Press, 1953).

as it is not now accepted by anthropologists, the matter need not here be pursued further.* Freud, however, never abandoned it, as is evident from one of his latest writings.[5] It retains its importance, I think, for two reasons. Firstly, it is taken by Freud as providing an explanation of "ambivalence," that is the coincidence of love and hate towards the same object, a concept essential to psycho-analytic theory. Secondly, it survives in Freud's deep-rooted belief in the existence of an inherited sense of guilt, transmitted in some way not further explained, through racial heredity. If this is taken seriously, it would involve the assumption of a group-mind, or a psyche of the mass as Freud calls it, in which mental processes occur analogous to those that occur in the mind of the individual, or else the possibility of the inheritance of acquired characters.

In the later writings the account that is given of the sense of guilt is not necessarily connected with these biological or anthropological theories and is compatible with the assumption that the individual starts his life as neither moral nor immoral but as amoral. The child acquires his morality from his environment. The formation of the "conscience" consists essentially in a process whereby the external authority of the father or of father-substitutes is transformed into an inner authority. It is described both by Freud and by his followers in terms of the distinctions they draw between the id, the ego, and the super-ego. Throughout, emphasis is laid on the negative or repressive aspects of morality, the "Thou shalt not" of the moral codes. This is no doubt partly due to the fact that in therapeutic treatment analysts are struck with the great severity of the conscience, often resulting in cruel self-humiliation and self-torture. To account for this, appeal is made to the part played by the aggressive tendencies in the formation of the super-ego. In incorporating the authority of the father into his own self the child also incorporates the aggression imputed to the father as the source of frustration, and, at the same time, the child turns the aggression which he feels towards the father, but which he has to repress, against himself. The conscience thus contains a double dose of aggression, the aggression of the father and that towards the father. To this redoubled aggression is attributed the rigour and severity of the conscience, often going beyond the actual severity of the father; it explains the fact that the individual can be harsher towards himself than his parents ever were. The tensions of the conscience are, on this view, due not merely to the discomfort of resisting the pressure of habits inculcated by the group, but result from the fact that every time we refrain from meeting frustration by aggression, the aggression is turned against ourselves. The tension is felt as the sense of guilt, in essentials the result of a struggle between the ego and the super-ego. It may

---

*A. Lang, *Myth, Ritual and Religion* (London: Longmans, 1885); W. Robertson Smith, *The Religion of the Semites* (Edinburgh: Adam and Charles Black, 1889); A. Lang, *Social Origins*, and J. J. Atkinson, *Primal Law*. Published as one volume. (London, New York, and Bombay: Longmans, 1903).—B. A. F.

[5]*Moses and Monotheism* (1939), *The Standard Edition* 33 (London: Hogarth Press, 1964).

be noted in passing that one of the functions of religion is to relieve this tension by the promise of salvation and inward peace.

Freud repudiates the charge frequently made against him that he ignores the more positive aspects of the moral life.

> It is no part of our intention [he says] to deny the nobility of human nature, nor have we ever done anything to disparage its value. On the contrary, I show you not only the evil wishes which are censored, but also the censorship which suppresses them and makes them unrecognizable. We dwell upon the evil in human beings with the greater emphasis only because others deny it, thereby making the mental life of mankind not indeed better, but incomprehensible. If we give up the one-sided ethical valuation then we are surer to find the truer formula for the relation of evil to good in human nature.[6]

It remains that the side of the moral life which is concerned with what is positively worth while receives scanty treatment. What there is, is couched in terms of the theory of sublimation, and the formation of the ego-ideal. Sublimation seems to be closely related to the process of identification, though in some of the later essays there are suggestions that it might be due also to the independent work of the ego, among whose functions is included that of introducing unity and harmony into the mental life. On the whole, however, what Freud has to say about the nature of ideals is brought within the framework of the theory of the libido. The love of ideals is in fact reduced to self-love or "narcissism." A portion of the libido is directed to ourselves, but some of it goes to ourselves not as we are but as we should like to be, in other words, to our ego-ideal. Now the ego-ideal is built up by identification with the father or father-substitute, and in the course of identification these are idealized, and we ascribe to them qualities which would make them worthy of our love. The root of the idealization, however, is narcissism or self-love. "The object serves as a substitute for some unattained ego-ideal of our own. We love it on account of the perfection which we have striven to search for in our own ego and which we should now like to procure in this roundabout way, as a means of satisfying our narcissism."[7] It will be seen that this leaves the problem of the root of idealism unresolved, since nothing further is said of the reasons which make us seek our own perfection. Furthermore, I find it difficult to believe that the love of ideals can be reduced to self-love. Why should there not be other things and qualities which are loved directly and for their own sake and not as parts of the self? Behind this assumption there seems to be a lingering attachment to the theory of psychological hedonism, the theory that desire is always for pleasure to the subject or self.

The value of the psycho-analytic contribution to the natural history of morals does not, I think, depend upon whether or not these particular theo-

---

[6]*Introductory Lectures to Psycho-Analysis* (1915–1916), parts 1 and 2, *The Standard Edition* 15 (London: Hogarth Press, 1961), p. 128.
[7]*Group Psychology and the Psychology of the Ego* (1921), *The Standard Edition* 18 (London: Hogarth Press, 1955), p. 74.

ries will prove acceptable. It is to be found to a far greater extent in the wealth of material which analytic experience has brought to light, showing the enormous part played by unconscious factors in the formation of the moral sentiments. No doubt the fact that in the censure which we direct against ourselves and against others, repressed impulses and desires find an outlet, has long been known.[8] Again self-deception and sophistication are processes which have been frequently described by novelists, and to some extent by moral psychologists, long before the days of Psycho-analysis. But no one has shown so clearly as the analysts how infinitely varied are the distortions to which the conscience is subject, or disclosed in greater detail the extent to which the processes may be concealed from the agent himself. Psycho-analysis has further thrown a flood of light on the fact that the knowledge of good is so frequently dissociated from the will to good, the fact so vividly described by St. Paul: "That which I do I allow not; for what I would, that I do not; but what I hate that I do . . . the good that I would I do not, but the evil which I would not, that I do."[9] Psycho-analysis can perhaps also help to explain the very remarkable variations in the emotional depth of the response to different types of offence against the moral code. The intensity with which we condemn "unnatural" lust, fraud, treachery, pride, cruelty, does not seem to be at all closely related to the degree of evil which the reflective conscience would find in each of these vices. Traditional moral psychology seems to have paid little attention to problems of this sort.[10]

The central weakness of Freudian moral psychology lies, I think, in its failure to deal adequately with the nature of moral obligation, and this in turn is due to the obscurity which surrounds the treatment of the relation between the cognitive and emotional components of the conscience. Obligation, it seems, consists in submission to authority, whether internal or external. The emotional basis is in either case fear, that is fear of punishment or of losing the love of those around us, or of our aggression towards those whom we love. The attitude towards ourselves when the moral sanctions have been internalized retains all the characteristics it had when the authority was external. Nothing is said of the possibility in the advanced levels of moral development of self-imposed rules, or of respect for principles of conduct rationally accepted as binding. The conscience, I would suggest, is a system of emotional dispositions or "sentiments," or rather a cluster of such sentiments of varying

---

[8]Professor Laird quotes in this connexion the following passages from *King Lear*: "Look with thine ears: see how yond justice rails upon yond simple thief. Hark in thine ear: change places; and, handy-dandy, which is the justice, which is the thief? . . ."

> "Thou rascally beadle, hold thy bloody hand!
> Why dost thou lash that whore? Strip thine own back;
> Thou hotly lust'st to use her in that kind
> For which thou whipp'st her . . ."

A Study in Moral Theory, p. 151. [London: Allen and Unwin, 1926.—B. A. F.]
[9]Romans vii, 15–19.
[10]Cf. A. E. Taylor, *The Faith of a Moralist,* p. 194. [London: Macmillan, 1930.—B. A. F.]

degrees of unity, which have gathered round our beliefs or judgments concerning right and wrong. The emotional components and the rational level of the judgments vary greatly in the different clusters or systems. There is not in fact one conscience, but an indefinite plurality of consciences, each with its own degree of emotional intensity and intellectual grasp. A man may be highly "conscientious" in his commercial dealings, but not in controlling his appetites; another may have rigid standards of sexual morality but very flexible ones in matters of business relations or professional morality. "I ought" may mean to one "my social circle expects this of me"; to another "God expects it of me"; to yet another "I expect it of myself." The degree of "internalization of authority" may differ widely from case to case in the same person and in different persons. The extent to which this internalization occurs can easily be exaggerated. For many individuals even in advanced societies a great deal of morality remains prudential and conventional. People like to believe that their conscience is their own, but in this they are easily deceived. Nevertheless the whole of morality is not "borrowed" morality. In morals as in other matters people do not live by taking in each others' washing. At some point we have to assume direct value judgments which are slowly clarified by experience and reflection. On this psycho-analytic theory seems to have very little to say.

Furthermore, the account given of the way in which the individual moves from a stage in which authority is external to that in which it becomes an inward monitor, is I think, open to objection. The transition is said to be effected through identification with the father, whereby his authority is incorporated into the self. It seems to me, however, that this process of internalization and individualization owes at least as much to our experience with equals with whom we have to establish a *modus vivendi*. It is through such experience that people come to make their own rules, and these may often be at variance with the rules that have come to them from superior authority. Another important factor is contact between different groups which brings to light conflicting moral standards between which the individual has to choose. In this context the psycho-analysts have tended to treat the family too much in isolation from the larger group, and this has led them to underestimate the part played by social factors in the moral life, and almost completely to ignore the forces, rational and other, making for change and development.

We have now to deal with the question whether psycho-analytic theory can provide the basis for a rational ethic. The morality so far discussed is super-ego morality. Its basis is the authority of the father or father-substitute internalized. If all the rules of morals come to us from without as commands, is there any rational method for choosing between them? We have seen that Freud himself nowhere claims to have worked out a rational ethic, yet in various places in his writings he holds out hopes for such an enterprise. In general, he has great faith in the power of rational inquiry. He dismisses subjectivist or relativist views of knowledge as "intellectual nihilism."[11] Though our knowledge of nature is affected by the structure of the mind, this does not make knowledge necessarily subjective, since the structure of the mind itself can be scientifically investigated, and the errors arising out of subjective factors allowed for. The theory of Psycho-analysis, so often accused of exaggerating the strength of the nonrational elements in human nature, rests in fact on the assumption that these are subject to rational control. The function of analysis is to extend the area of conscious control by bringing what was unconscious into consciousness, to ensure, as we are told, that "where id was there shall ego be." The ultimate ideal is the "primacy of reason" and on the moral side, "the brotherhood of man and the reduction of suffering."[12] An ethic of this sort, it is suggested, requires another foundation than that of religion.[13] Only hints are given, however, where such a foundation is to be sought for. It is suggested, for example, that a scientific ethic might play a therapeutic role analogous to that which the physician plays in dealing with neuroses in the individual. The analyst frequently finds that he has to do battle with the individual's conscience, which is often excessively severe and makes demands which he cannot possibly fulfil and which threaten his happiness. What Freud calls the "cultural super-ego" as represented, for example, in the ethical injunctions of the higher religions, calls for similar therapy. They set up standards too high for human nature and are therefore easily defeated by those who take a more realistic view. Thus the command to love your neighbour as yourself is no defence against human aggressiveness. "Such a grandiose inflation of love only lowers its value and cannot remove the evil." It is not clear, however, by what principles such an examination of idealistic codes is to be guided. The analogy with individual therapy breaks down. In dealing with the individual, the analyst assumes a "normal" environment and considers behaviour as neurotic which is in conflict with it. No such standard is available for societies, since there exists no scientific, comparative study of the pathology of civilizations, and we therefore cannot tell what is normal and what pathological.

Despite the lack of comparative data Freud has ventured on a general statement of the role of repression in the history of culture. Our civilization, he argued already in his early papers, is in the main founded on the suppression of instincts.[14] The theme is developed more fully in his sombre essay on

---

[11]"New Introductory Lectures on Psychoanalysis" (1933), *The Standard Edition* 22 (London: Hogarth Press, 1964), p. 224.

[12]*The Future of an Illusion* (1927), *The Standard Edition* 21 (London: Hogarth Press, 1961), p. 93.

[13]"New Introductory Lectures," p. 215. [See note 11—B. A. F.]

[14]*"Civilized" Sexual Morality and Modern Nervousness* (1908), *Collected Papers*, II, *The Standard Edition* 9 (London: Hogarth Press, 1959).

the Malaise of Culture.[15] Both the libidinal and the aggressive tendencies have to be repressed if civilization is to flourish. Sexual energy has to be diverted from its original object to make possible the formation of wider groups and to keep them together. This is one of the reasons for the rules and regulations by which all known societies seek to control the sexual relations of their members. Another reason is to be found in the fact that love is needed to control hate. The aggressive impulses which, in Freud's view, are an ineradicable and primary element in human nature, could destroy mankind if left to work themselves out. To control them, aim-inhibited sexual energy has had to be used. The process involves the building up of the super-ego by the aid of which aggression is turned inwards and prevented from expressing itself directly. Following this line of thought Freud might have said with Buddha that "hatred does not cease by hatred; by love alone is hate destroyed." Freud, however, does not share the hope held out by the spiritual religions of the ultimate triumph of love. Eros is pitted against Thanatos and the antagonism between them will in all probability never be overcome.

In urging that the growth of civilization depends on the control or repression of fundamental instinctive drives Freud is saying what, in their different ways, the moralists of all ages have said. From the point of view of ethical theory the important problem is whether it is possible to elicit from his teaching any principles for determining the limits of this inevitable repression or any standards for estimating the loss and gain involved. As regards "civilized" sexual morality his discussion in the early papers at least is tentative and inconclusive. It is possible, he allows, to maintain that the cultural gains derived from sexual restraint outweigh its manifestly injurious results. But he finds himself unable to balance gain and loss with any precision. And he ends by saying that as judged by individual happiness it is very doubtful whether the sacrifices demanded can be justified—so long, at least, as we are "still so insufficiently purged of hedonism as to include a certain degree of individual happiness among the aims of our cultural development."[16] As regards the effect of sexual restraint on cultural activities, Freud's conclusions are equally tentative. He does not, of course, claim to have undertaken any comparative study of moral codes from this point of view. But on the basis of his own personal impressions he believes that "the relation between possible sublimation and indispensable sexual activity naturally varies very much in different persons, and indeed with the various kinds of occupation." He does not support the view that "sexual abstinence helps to shape energetic self-reliant men of action, or original thinkers, bold pioneers and reformers; far more often it produces 'good' weaklings who later become lost in the crowd that tend to follow

---

[15]*Das Unbehagen in der Kultur*, 1930. English translation, *Civilization and its Discontents*, The *Standard Edition* 21 (London: Hogarth Press, 1961).
[16]*"Civilized" Sexual Morality and Modern Nervousness*, p. 99. [See note 14.—B. A. F.]

painfully the initiative of strong characters."[17] In the end it emerges that while Freud is convinced that the code of sexual morality in Western societies urgently needs to be reformed, he is not prepared as a physician to come forward with definite proposals. This was not to be expected. But the discussion throws light on the sort of ethical theory that Freud might have developed, had he chosen to pursue the matter further. It is clear that the ethical criteria to which he appeals in criticizing existing moral codes are individual happiness and cultural advance. Furthermore, he realizes that we have not the knowledge that would be necessary for any accurate application of these criteria, and he is obviously disturbed by the fact that gains in one direction are often countered by loss in the other.

In the later writings the problem thus raised reappears in another form. Freud finds that there is a certain antagonism between the growth of culture and the development of the individual. The antagonism results, in the first place, from the struggle between Eros and Thanatos. The aim of cultural development is the unification of all mankind. This can only be achieved by a repression of aggression. But every time we control our aggression, it turns against the self. The result is an increasing tension between the ego and the super-ego which is felt as a sense of guilt. It seems to be assumed that the larger the group, the greater the difficulty of achieving libidinal unity and the greater the cost in human happiness. The progress of mankind can only be achieved at the expense of an intensification of the sense of guilt "until perhaps it may swell to a magnitude that individuals can hardly support."[18] No wonder that Freud thought the sense of guilt constituted the most important problem in the evolution of culture.

In the second place, there is, according to Freud, not only this irreconcilable conflict between the life and death instincts but a fissure within the libido itself, which from the ethical point of view is at least as important. The growth of the individual is shaped by the pleasure principle, that is, by the desire of the individual for his own happiness. No doubt he can only attain this through membership in a community. But this condition is sometimes represented by Freud as a sort of unfortunate necessity, as something he would be

[17]Dr. J. D. Unwin has produced an elaborate argument to show that in primitive societies there is a definite relation between sexual continence and degree of cultural advance (*Sex and Culture*, [London: Allen and Unwin.—B.A.F.] 1934). But the criteria which he uses both for cultural condition and sexual regulation are very vague and the evidence he adduces is not sufficient to justify a generalization so far-reaching. (Cf. my review of this book in *Nature*, Vol. CXXXV, p. 205, 1935.) Westermarck, [E. Westermarck, *The History of Human Marriage*, vol. 1, ch. 4 (London: Macmillan, 1921).—B. A. F.] who made a very comprehensive survey of the available information, concludes that there is no relation between the toleration of unchastity and the degree of culture, and that on the contrary chastity is more respected in the lowest tribes than in the higher ones. In *The Material Culture and Social Institutions of the Simpler Peoples* (1915), L. T. Hobhouse, G. C. Wheeler and the present writer [London: Chapman and Hall—B. A. F.] found that the evidence was not sufficient to establish a universal association between sexual regulation and cultural grade as judged by economic criteria.

[18]*Civilization and its Discontents*, p. 116. [See note 2.—B. A. F.]

libido fissure

better without. For culture, as we have seen, is necessarily restrictive of the individual; it demands instinctual renunciation. There is thus, as Freud says,[19] dissension in the camp of the libido itself, a struggle between the striving for happiness and the impulse towards union with others. Freud asserts that this contest will ultimately be resolved in the case of the individual and perhaps also in the future of civilization. But unfortunately the theme is not further developed.

The ethical theory that Freud's discussion suggests is one of enlightened self-interest, that is self-interest purged of unconscious distortions, fears and anxieties not rooted in the objective situation. What such self-interest would require can only emerge after therapeutic analysis both of the individuals and societies. But it is difficult to believe that psychology will ever by itself solve the fundamental problems of human relations, or in the Freudian terminology, the problem of the right apportionment of libidinal attachment as between self and other "objects." A theory of ethics which rests on the assumption that in dealing justly with others the individual can after all secure his own happiness has all the air of an "illusion" which, from the Freudian point of view, should be relegated to the infantile stages of the development of morality.

It is, I think, remarkable that while Freud and his followers have so much to say about love, they pay hardly any attention to justice. The only reference I can find is in Freud's *Group Psychology and the Psychology of the Ego.** "Social justice," we are told, "means that we deny ourselves many things so that others may have to do without them as well, or what is the same thing, may not be able to ask for them." The demand for equality among the members of a group is said to be rooted in the jealousy aroused against those who would monopolize the love of the leader, just as their sense of community rests on their common renunciation of his exclusive love. This reduction of humanity and justice to envy and jealousy is somewhat mitigated by his interpretation of Eros as a force working for unity and harmony. But the two sides of his theory, ultimately due to the vagueness and ambiguity of the concept of the libido, are nowhere satisfactorily brought into relation, and on the whole the "egoistic" trend in his thought predominates. It is difficult to see how such a conception of human nature can ever provide the basis for a rational ethic.

Justice

The most important problems of ethics centre round the theory of justice and in dealing with it Psycho-analysis is, I think, at its weakest. I see no reason, from the purely psychological side, for accepting the Freudian view of the origins of the sense of justice. Neither in the history of the individual or of civilization can this be shown to be rooted predominantly in the desire that no one shall fare better than ourselves. It owes at least as much to the power of sympathy, that is the power of entering in imagination into the situation of another and seeing it as though it were our own. Above all there is a rational ele-

[19]Ibid, p. 136.
*See note 7.—B. A. F.

ment in it which the Freudian analysis completely ignores. The core of justice is the demand for equality and this is based at bottom on the rejection of arbitrariness, the recognition that individuals ought not to be treated differently unless a reasonable ground can be given for so treating them. I can see no ground for regarding this demand as merely emotional. If I say that "one man's good is of as much intrinsic worth as the like good of another," I certainly do not mean that "the emotion which I experience in knowing that one man is benefited or injured is the same as that which I should experience in the case of any other." This latter statement would be manifestly untrue in many instances but the recognition of its falsity has no bearing on the truth or falsity of my recognition of the principle of equality as binding on me. The difficulties in the theory of equality begin to emerge when we try to think out the grounds which justify differential treatment. On these again psychology may throw some light, but in the end value judgments have to be made, which, though ineffectual if lacking in emotional warmth, do not depend for their validity on the strength of the emotional response.

In sum, the issue that psycho-analytic theories of ethics have to face is that with which all naturalistic ethics are confronted. The problem is whether moral judgments express desires, strivings or emotions, or whether they go beyond what is actually desired to what *ought* to be desired. It seems to me that psycho-analysts suffer from what might be called an "ought phobia." They show too great an anxiety to explain the "ought" away, and they tend to pass from the indicative to the imperative mood without realizing the implications of the transition. Thus, for example, Professor Flugel in his very illuminating study of the psychological basis of morals is in search of an ethic purged of anger and aggression and one that would make its appeal to reason. Yet reason is, in his view, concerned with means and not with ends, which in the last resort are set by "orexis" or desire. The moral criterion which is finally adopted, however, clearly goes beyond what individuals actually desire to what they ought to desire, or, if you like, to what they would desire if they were rational. This criterion is the free and spontaneous expression of the instincts in so far as this is compatible with harmony not only in the individual but in society. Is this ideal then "orectic" or cognitive? Again when we are told that increasing sociality and increasing individualization are complementary aspects of moral evolution, is this a statement of fact or of what ought to be fact? We have seen that according to Freud the conflict between individual and social development is far from being resolved, and Professor Flugel also points out that the compromise which has to be effected between socialization and individualization remains one of the most acute problems of modern democracy.[20] To set up social harmony as an ideal is to describe a form of life held to be desirable, not one which in fact is necessarily desired. If the test is to be found in what people actually desire, the impulses making for discord

[20]*Man, Morals and Society*, p. 253. [See asterisked note on p. 121.—B. A. F.]

may prove more powerful, or no less powerful, than those making for harmony. Despite a good deal that is attractive in Professor Flugel's exposition I feel that in the end he leaves undefined the relation between the striving and the cognitive elements in the moral judgment. He says that in a scientific handling of human relations "we must substitute a cognitive and psychological approach for an emotional and a moral one."[21] But this, I think, would be not to explain morality, but to explain it away.

I turn now to the views of Erich Fromm, which in important respects involve a departure from Freudian theory. In the first place, his conception of human nature is not as individualistic, or asocial, as he takes Freud's to be. He has a different conception of both the love and hate elements in the human mind. Man is fundamentally social in that he needs to be related to others, to escape aloneness, to belong or to be needed. Destructiveness on the other hand is the result of a baulking of vitality, not an inherent or primary need to hurt or destroy. In the second place, he distinguishes more radically than the Freudians between what he calls an "authoritarian" conscience and a "humanistic" conscience. The former is the voice of an internalized external authority, the super-ego of Freudian theory. The latter is not "the internalized voice of an authority we are eager to please and are afraid of displeasing; it is our own voice, present in every human being and independent of external rewards and sanctions."[22] It is the "expression of our true selves," "the reaction of our total personality to its proper functioning or disfunctioning." It bids us develop fully and harmoniously, that is "to realize ourselves, to become what we potentially are."

Here we are back full circle to theories long familiar to philosophers, but now claiming to be derived from empirical psychology. While there is a great deal that is very helpful in Fromm's analysis of the conditions of harmonious development, he does not seem to me to succeed any better than the Freudians in making the transition from what is or may be to what ought to be. To say that we should aim at becoming what we potentially are is not illuminating, since we are potentially evil as well as good and what we need is a criterion for distinguishing between them. The appeal to the "real" or "true" self is purely verbal, since the real self is not the self as it is but as it ought to be. Furthermore, the formula of self-realization leaves out of consideration the central problem of ethics—that of the relation between self and others. In the end, it is not any form of self-fulfilment that is desirable, but only that which is compatible with the fulfilment of others. Clearly such an end goes far beyond what any particular individuals actually desire, and it may require them to abandon or sacrifice a good deal of what they so desire. The philosophical problem of the principles of justice thus remains. It seems to me that writers

---

[21]*Man, Morals and Society*, p. 255.
[22]*Man for Himself*, p. 158. [London: Routledge and Kegan Paul, 1948—B. A. F.]

like Fromm and Karen Horney are too optimistic in assuming that these can be discovered by "listening to ourselves." What we may thus hear may not be very enlightening. The conditions of social harmony have to be discovered; they will not follow automatically from the striving towards self-realization, even if each individual is "true to himself."

It follows, I think, from the above survey that the attempts that have been made to derive an ethical theory from Psycho-analysis have not so far proved successful. Psycho-analysis, it seems to me, is not necessarily committed to any particular theory, and is compatible with very different theories of the logical character of moral judgments. Its business as a therapy is to break down the barriers between the unconscious and the conscious levels of the mind and in this way to expand the area of conscious control. But it is not to be assumed that when an individual has become more fully aware of the impulses by which he has been influenced he will necessarily have discovered the right principles of conduct. That would only follow on the assumption of a natural moral sense which needs only to be freed from the obstructions to which it has been subjected to be enabled to see at once what is right and what is wrong in human relations. Psychoanalysts are of course as entitled as anyone else to subscribe to a naturalistic theory of morals, but I cannot see that such a theory derives special support from the teaching of Psycho-analysis.

The predilection shown by psycho-analytic writers for the view that moral judgments are "orectic," that is expressions of desire or striving, is, I think, traceable to two sources. Firstly psycho-analysts have never freed themselves from the doctrine of psychological hedonism, despite the criticisms directed against it by moral philosophers. They tend to interpret Freud's "pleasure principle" as implying that impulses have for their sole object the pursuit of pleasure and the avoidance of pain. From psychological hedonism they pass in a manner familiar in the history of philosophy to ethical hedonism, in other words from the assertion that men seek pleasure or happiness to the assertion that happiness is their good. The appeal to the "real self" also lends itself to a species of naturalism amounting to the assertion that the good is what satisfies the self or what would satisfy it, if it knew its "true" nature.

In the second place, I suggest that the predilection for the view that moral judgments are rooted in desire or striving may be a sort of defensive reaction against the authoritarian element in morals. In their flight from the "ought" psycho-analysts overlook the distinction between moral obligation and self-coercion. This is encouraged by the fact that the moral law is often regarded as a sort of command. But strictly the relation of command-obedience is inter-personal, and it is only by analogy that it is extended to the self. A man cannot really "obey" himself or such an abstraction as a general principle. It is no doubt the case that moral judgments claim to possess authority, but this is only another way of saying that they claim to be true. It is psychologically con-

venient to speak of recalcitrant impulse struggling against reason or of conflicts between impulses. But all this has little bearing on the problem of the
logical validity of moral judgments. Constraint and validity are not interchangeable terms.

On the empirical side Psycho-analysis can, I think, make important contributions to the study of morality mainly in two directions. It can help, in the
first place, by building up what might be called a comparative moral pathology. It would be of the greatest interest to the moralist to know what moral
changes are brought about by analysis in, say, a Muhammadan, a Buddhist, or
a Communist living in their own setting. The analysis of representatives of
these creeds in other than their own environment is another matter, the issues
being complicated by the influence on the individual of conflicting moral
codes. Data of this sort would provide valuable material for the study of the
causes making for variation in moral codes and they would facilitate the task
of their critical evaluation.

In the second place, Psycho-analysis can contribute towards the clarification of moral experience by ridding it of the magical elements that have
gathered around it and purging it of fear and anger. An example of what I have
in mind is to be found in the persistent influence of the emotional demand for
retribution on the criminal law and on the philosophical theories of the ethical
basis of punishment. The movement in recent psycho-analytic writings towards a "humanist" ethics is clearly in this direction. But though an ethic
based on love is vastly superior to one based on obedience, it will not suffice
to solve the complex problems of human relations, even in small groups, and
still less in the "great society." The demands of love generate conflicts of their
own. There are fissures, as Freud saw, within the libido itself. To overcome
them we need more than goodwill. Neither in theory nor in practice can love
replace justice.

12

JOHN HOSPERS

What Means This Freedom?

I AM IN agreement to a very large extent with the conclusions of Professor Edwards' paper,* and am happy in these days of "soft determinism" to hear the other view so forcefully and fearlessly stated. As a preparation for developing my own views on the subject, I want to mention a factor that I think is of enormous importance and relevance: namely, unconscious motivation. There are many actions—not those of an insane person (however the term "insane" be defined), nor of a person ignorant of the effects of his action, nor ignorant of some relevant fact about the situation, nor in any obvious way mentally deranged—for which human beings in general and the courts in particular are inclined to hold the doer responsible, and for which, I would say, he should not be held responsible. The deed may be planned, it may be carried out in cold calculation, it may spring from the agent's character and be continuous with the rest of his behavior, and it may be perfectly true that he could have done differently *if* he had wanted to; nonetheless his behavior was brought about by unconscious conflicts developed in infancy, over which he had no control and of which (without training in psychiatry) he does not even have knowledge. He may even *think* he knows why he acted as he did, he may *think* he has conscious control over his actions, he may even *think* he is fully responsible for them; but he is not. Psychiatric casebooks provide hundreds of examples. The law and common sense, though puzzled sometimes by such

From *Determinism and Freedom in the Age of Modern Science*, edited by Sidney Hook (New York: New York University Press, 1958), pp. 126–142. Reprinted by permission.
*"Hard and Soft Determinism," in the same volume as the paper by Hospers.—B. A. F.

cases, are gradually becoming aware that they exist; but at this early stage countless tragic blunders still occur because neither the law nor the public in general is aware of the genesis of criminal actions. The mother blames her daughter for choosing the wrong men as candidates for husbands; but though the daughter thinks she is choosing freely and spends a considerable amount of time "deciding" among them, the identification with her sick father, resulting from Oedipal fantasies in early childhood, prevents her from caring for any but sick men, twenty or thirty years older than herself. Blaming her is beside the point: she cannot help it, and she cannot change it. Countless criminal acts are thought out in great detail; yet the participants are (without their own knowledge) acting out fantasies, fears, and defenses from early childhood, over whose coming and going they have no conscious control.

Now, I am not saying that none of these persons should be in jails or asylums. Often society must be protected against them. Nor am I saying that people should cease the practices of blaming and praising, punishing and rewarding; in general these devices are justified by the results—although very often they have practically no effect; the deeds are done from inner compulsion, which is not lessened when the threat of punishment is great. I am only saying that frequently persons we think responsible are not properly to be called so; we mistakenly think them responsible because we assume they are like those in whom no unconscious drive (toward this type of behavior) is present, and that their behavior can be changed by reasoning, exhorting, or threatening.

I

I have said that these persons are not responsible. But what is the criterion for responsibility? Under precisely what conditions is a person to be held morally responsible for an action? Disregarding here those conditions that have to do with a person's *ignorance* of the situation or the effects of his action, let us concentrate on those having to do with his "inner state." There are several criteria that might be suggested:

1. The first idea that comes to mind is that responsibility is determined by the presence or absence of *premeditation*—the opposite of "premeditated" being, presumably, "unthinking" or "impulsive." But this will not do—both because some acts are not premeditated but responsible, and because some are premeditated and not responsible.

Many acts we call responsible can be as unthinking or impulsive as you please. If you rush across the street to help the victim of an automobile collision, you are (at least so we would ordinarily say) acting responsibly, but you did not do so out of premeditation; you saw the accident, you didn't think, you rushed to the scene without hesitation. It was like a reflex action. But you acted responsibly: unlike the knee jerk, the act was the result of past training and past thought about situations of this kind; that is why you ran to help instead of ignoring the incident or running away. When something done originally from conviction or training becomes habitual, it becomes *like* a reflex action. As Aristotle said, virtue should become second nature through habit: a virtuous act should be performed *as if* by instinct; this, far from detracting from its moral worth, testifies to one's mastery of the desired type of behavior; one does not have to make a moral effort each time it is repeated.

There are also premeditated acts for which, I would say, the person is not responsible. Premeditation, especially when it is so exaggerated as to issue in no action at all, can be the result of neurotic disturbance or what we sometimes call an emotional "block," which the person inherits from long-past situations. In Hamlet's revenge on his uncle (I use this example because it is familiar to all of us), there was no lack, but rather a surfeit, of premeditation; his actions were so exquisitely premeditated as to make Freud and Dr. Ernest Jones look more closely to find out what lay behind them.* The very premeditation camouflaged unconscious motives of which Hamlet himself was not aware. I think this is an important point, since it seems that the courts often assume that premeditation is a criterion of responsibility. If failure to kill his uncle had been considered a crime, every court in the land would have convicted Hamlet. Again: a woman's decision to stay with her husband in spite of endless "mental cruelty" is, if she is the victim of an unconscious masochistic "will to punishment," one for which she is not responsible; she is the victim and not the agent, no matter how profound her conviction that she is the agent; she is caught in a masochistic web (of complicated genesis) dating back to babyhood, perhaps a repetition of a comparable situation involving her own parents, a repetition-compulsion that, as Freud said, goes "beyond the pleasure principle." Again: a criminal whose crime was carefully planned step by step is usually considered responsible, but as we shall see in later examples, the overwhelming impulse toward it, stemming from an unusually humiliating ego defeat in early childhood, was as compulsive as any can be.

2. Shall we say, then, that a person is not responsible for his act unless he can *defend it with reasons?* I am afraid that this criterion is no better than the previous one. First, intellectuals are usually better at giving reasons than nonintellectuals, and according to this criterion would be more responsible than persons acting from moral conviction not implemented by reasoning; yet it is very doubtful whether we should want to say that the latter are the more responsible. Second, the giving of reasons itself may be suspect. The reasons may be rationalizations camouflaging unconscious motives of which the agent knows nothing. Hamlet gave many reasons for not doing what he felt it was his duty to do: the time was not right, his uncle's soul might go to heaven, etc. His various "reasons" contradicted one another, and if an overpowering compulsion had not been present, the highly intellectual Hamlet would not have been taken in for a moment by these rationalizations. The real reason, the

---

*S. Freud, *The Interpretation of Dreams* (1900), *The Standard Edition* 4 (London: Hogarth Press, 1953), pp. 264–266; E. Jones, *Hamlet and Oedipus* (London: Gollancz, 1949).—B. A. F.

Oedipal conflict that made his uncle's crime the accomplishment of his own deepest desire, binding their fates into one and paralyzing him into inaction, was unconscious and of course unknown to him. One's intelligence and reasoning power do not enable one to escape from unconsciously motivated behavior; it only gives one greater facility in rationalizing that behavior; one's intelligence is simply used in the interests of the neurosis—it is pressed into service to justify with reasons what one does quite independently of the reasons.

If these two criteria are inadequate, let us seek others.

3. Shall we say that a person is responsible for his action unless it is the *result of unconscious forces* of which he knows nothing? Many psychoanalysts would probably accept this criterion. If it is not largely reflected in the language of responsibility as ordinarily used, this may be due to ignorance of fact: most people do not know that there are such things as unconscious motives and unconscious conflicts causing human beings to act. But it may be that if they did, perhaps they would refrain from holding persons responsible for certain actions.

I do not wish here to quarrel with this criterion of responsibility. I only want to point out the fact that if this criterion is employed a far greater number of actions will be excluded from the domain of responsibility than we might at first suppose. Whether we are neat or untidy, whether we are selfish or unselfish, whether we provoke scenes or avoid them, even whether we can exert our powers of will to change our behavior—all these may, and often do, have their source in our unconscious life.

4. Shall we say that a person is responsible for his act unless it is *compelled?* Here we are reminded of Aristotle's assertion (*Nicomachean Ethics*, Book III) that a person is responsible for his act except for reasons of either ignorance or compulsion. Ignorance is not part of our problem here (unless it is unconsciously induced ignorance of facts previously remembered and selectively forgotten—in which case the forgetting is again compulsive), but compulsion is. How will compulsion do as a criterion? The difficulty is to state just what it means. When we say an act is compelled in a psychological sense, our language is metaphorical—which is not to say that there is no point in it or that, properly interpreted, it is not true. Our actions are compelled in a literal sense if someone has us in chains or is controlling our bodily movements. When we say that the storm compelled us to jettison the cargo of the ship (Aristotle's example), we have a less literal sense of compulsion, for at least it is open to us to go down with the ship. When psychoanalysts say that a man was compelled by unconscious conflicts to wash his hands constantly, this is also not a literal use of "compel"; for nobody forced his hands under the tap. Still, it is a typical example of what psychologists call *compulsive* behavior: it has unconscious causes inaccessible to introspection, and moreover nothing can change it—it is as inevitable for him to do it as it would be if someone were forcing his hands under the tap. In this it is exactly like the action of a powerful external force; it is just as little within one's conscious control.

In its area of application this interpretation of responsibility comes to much the same as the previous one. And this area is very great indeed. For if we cannot be held responsible for the infantile situations (in which we were after all passive victims), then neither, it would seem, can we be held responsible for compulsive actions occurring in adulthood that are inevitable consequences of those infantile situations. And, psychiatrists and psychoanalysts tell us, actions fulfilling this description are characteristic of all people some of the time and some people most of the time. Their occurrence, once the infantile events have taken place, is inevitable, just as the explosion is inevitable once the fuse has been lighted; there is simply more "delayed action" in the psychological explosions than there is in the physical ones.

(I have not used the word "inevitable" here to mean "causally determined," for according to such a definition every event would be inevitable if one accepted the causal principle in some form or other; and probably nobody except certain philosophers uses "inevitable" in this sense. Rather, I use "inevitable" in its ordinary sense of "cannot be avoided." To the extent, therefore, that adult neurotic manifestations *can* be avoided, once the infantile patterns have become set, the assertion that they are inevitable is not true.)

5. There is still another criterion, which I prefer to the previous ones, by which a man's responsibility for an act can be measured: the degree to which that act can (or could have been) *changed by the use of reasons*. Suppose that the man who washes his hands constantly does so, he says, for hygienic reasons, believing that if he doesn't do so he will be poisoned by germs. We now convince him, on the best medical authority, that his belief is groundless. Now, the test of his responsibility is whether the changed belief will result in changed behavior. If it does not, as with the compulsive hand washer, he is not acting responsibly, but if it does, he is. It is not the *use* of reasons, but their *efficacy in changing behavior*, that is being made the criterion of responsibility. And clearly in neurotic cases no such change occurs; in fact, this is often made the defining characteristic of neurotic behavior: it is unchangeable by any rational considerations.

II

I have suggested these criteria to distinguish actions for which we can call the agent responsible from those for which we cannot. Even persons with extensive knowledge of psychiatry do not, I think, use any one of these criteria to the exclusion of the others; a conjunction of two or more may be used at once. But however they may be combined or selected in actual application, I believe we can make the distinction along some such lines as we have suggested.

But is there not still another possible meaning of "responsibility" that we have not yet mentioned? Even after we have made all the above distinctions, there remains a question in our minds whether we are, in the final analysis, *responsible for any of our actions at all.* The issue may be put this way: How can anyone be responsible for his actions, since they grow out of his character, which is shaped and molded and made what it is by influences—some hereditary, but most of them stemming from early parental environment—that were not of his own making or choosing? This question, I believe, still troubles many people who would agree to all the distinctions we have just made but still have the feeling that "this isn't all." They have the uneasy suspicion that there is a more ultimate sense, a "deeper" sense, in which we are *not* responsible for our actions, since we are not responsible for the character out of which those actions spring. This, of course, is the sense Professor Edwards was describing.

Let us take as an example a criminal who, let us say, strangled several persons and is himself now condemned to die in the electric chair. Jury and public alike hold him fully responsible (at least they utter the words "he is responsible"), for the murders were planned down to the minutest detail, and the defendant tells the jury exactly how he planned them. But now we find out how it all came about; we learn of parents who rejected him from babyhood, of the childhood spent in one foster home after another, where it was always plain to him that he was not wanted; of the constantly frustrated early desire for affection, the hard shell of nonchalance and bitterness that he assumed to cover the painful and humiliating fact of being unwanted, and his subsequent attempts to heal these wounds to his shattered ego through defensive aggression.

> The criminal is the most passive person in this world, helpless as a baby in his motorically inexpressible fury. Not only does he try to wreak revenge on the mother of the earliest period of his babyhood; his criminality is based on the inner feeling of being incapable of making the mother even feel that the child seeks revenge on her. The situation is that of a dwarf trying to annoy a giant who superciliously refuses to see these attempts. . . . Because of his inner feeling of being a dwarf, the criminotic uses, so to speak, dynamite. Of that the giant must take cognizance. True, the "revenge" harms the avenger. He may be legally executed. However, the primary inner aim of forcing the giant to acknowledge the dwarf's fury is fulfilled.[1]

The poor victim is not conscious of the inner forces that exact from him this ghastly toll; he battles, he schemes, he revels in pseudo-aggression, he is miserable, but he does not know what works within him to produce these catastrophic acts of crime. His aggressive actions are the wriggling of a worm on a fisherman's hook. And if this is so, it seems difficult to say any longer, "He is responsible." Rather, we shall put him behind bars for the protection of society, but we shall no longer flatter our feeling of moral superiority by calling him personally responsible for what he did.

Let us suppose it were established that a man commits murder only if, sometime during the previous week, he has eaten a certain combination of

---

[1] Edmund Bergler, *The Basic Neurosis* (New York: Grune and Stratton, 1949), p. 305.

foods—say, tuna fish salad at a meal also including peas, mushroom soup, and blueberry pie. What if we were to track down the factors common to all murders committed in this country during the last twenty years and found this factor present in all of them, and only in them? The example is of course empirically absurd; but may it not be that there is *some* combination of factors that regularly leads to homicide, factors such as are described in general terms in the above quotation? (Indeed the situation in the quotation is less fortunate than in our hypothetical example, for it is easy to avoid certain foods once we have been warned about them, but the situation of the infant is thrust on him; something has already happened to him once and for all, before he knows it has happened.) When such specific factors are discovered, won't they make it clear that it is foolish and pointless, as well as immoral, to hold human beings responsible for crimes? Or, if one prefers biological to psychological factors, suppose a neurologist is called in to testify at a murder trial and produces X-ray pictures of the brain of the criminal; anyone can see, he argues, that the *sella turcica* was already calcified at the age of nineteen; it should be a flexible bone, growing, enabling the gland to grow.[2] All the defendant's disorders might have resulted from this early calcification. Now, this particular explanation may be empirically false; but who can say that no such factors, far more complex, to be sure, exist?

When we know such things as these, we no longer feel so much tempted to say that the criminal is responsible for his crime; and we tend also (do we not?) to excuse him—not legally (we still confine him to prison) but morally; we no longer call him a monster or hold him personally responsible for what he did. Moreover, we do this in general, not merely in the case of crime: "You must excuse Grandmother for being irritable; she's really quite ill and is suffering some pain all the time." Or: "The dog always bites children after she's had a litter of pups; you can't blame her for it: she's not feeling well, and besides she naturally wants to defend them." Or: "She's nervous and jumpy, but do excuse her: she has a severe glandular disturbance."

Let us note that the more *thoroughly* and *in detail* we know the causal factors leading a person to behave as he does, the more we tend to exempt him from responsibility. When we know nothing of the man except what we see him do, we say he is an ungrateful cad who expects much of other people and does nothing in return, and we are usually indignant. When we learn that his parents were the same way and, having no guilt feelings about this mode of behavior themselves, brought him up to be greedy and avaricious, we see that we could hardly expect him to have developed moral feelings in this direction. When we learn, in addition, that he is not aware of being ungrateful or selfish, but unconsciously represses the memory of events unfavorable to himself, we feel that the situation is unfortunate but "not really his fault." When we know that this behavior of his, which makes others angry, occurs more

---

[2]Meyer Levin, *Compulsion* (New York: Simon and Schuster, 1956), p. 403. [The gland referred to here is the hypophysis or pituitary.—B. A. F.]

constantly when he feels tense or insecure, and that he now feels tense and insecure, and that relief from pressure will diminish it, then we tend to "feel sorry for the poor guy" and say he's more to be pitied than censured. We no longer want to say that he is personally responsible; we might rather blame nature or his parents for having given him an unfortunate constitution or temperament.

> In recent years a new form of punishment has been imposed on middle-aged and elderly parents. Their children, now in their twenties, thirties or even forties, present them with a modern grievance: "My analysis proves that *you* are responsible for my neurosis." Overawed by these authoritative statements, the poor tired parents fall easy victims to the newest variations on the scapegoat theory.
>
> In my opinion, this senseless cruelty—which disinters educational sins which had been buried for decades, and uses them as the basis for accusations which the victims cannot answer—is unjustified. Yes "the truth loves to be centrally located" (Melville), and few parents—since they are human—have been perfect. But granting their mistakes, they acted as *their* neurotic difficulties forced them to act. To turn the tables and declare the children not guilty because of the *impersonal* nature of their own neuroses, while at the same time the parents are *personally* blamed, is worse than illogical; it is profoundly unjust.[3]

And so, it would now appear, neither of the parties is responsible: "they acted as their neurotic difficulties forced them to act." The patients are not responsible for their neurotic manifestations, but then neither are the parents responsible for theirs; and so, of course, for their parents in turn, and theirs before them. It is the twentieth-century version of the family curse, the curse on the House of Atreus.

"But," a critic complains, "it's immoral to exonerate people indiscriminately in this way. I might have thought it fit to excuse somebody because he was born on the other side of the tracks, if I didn't know so many bank presidents who were also born on the other side of the tracks." Now, I submit that the most immoral thing in this situation is the critic's caricature of the conditions of the excuse. Nobody is excused merely because he was born on the other side of the tracks. But if he was born on the other side of the tracks *and* was a highly narcissistic infant to begin with *and* was repudiated or neglected by his parents *and* . . . (here we list a finite number of conditions), and if this complex of factors is *regularly* followed by certain behavior traits in adulthood, and moreover *unavoidably* so—that is, they occur no matter what he or anyone else tries to do—then we excuse him morally and say he is not responsible for his deed. If he is not responsible for A, a series of events occurring in his babyhood, then neither is he responsible for B, a series of things he does in adulthood, provided that B inevitably—that is, unavoidably—follows upon the occurrence of A. And according to psychiatrists and psychoanalysts, this often happens.

---

[3]Edmund Bergler, *The Superego* (New York: Grune and Stratton, 1952), p. 320.

But one may still object that so far we have talked only about neurotic behavior. Isn't nonneurotic or normal or not unconsciously motivated (or whatever you want to call it) behavior still within the area of responsibility? There
are reasons for answering "No" even here, for the normal person no more than
the neurotic one has caused his own character, which makes him what he is.
Granted that neurotics are not responsible for their behavior (that part of it
which we call neurotic) because it stems from undigested infantile conflicts
that they had no part in bringing about, and that are external to them just as
surely as if their behavior had been forced on them by a malevolent deity
(which is indeed one theory on the subject); but the so-called normal person is
equally the product of causes in which his volition took no part. And if, unlike
the neurotic's, his behavior is changeable by rational considerations, and if he
has the will power to overcome the effects of an unfortunate early environment, this again is no credit to him; he is just lucky. If energy is available to
him in a form in which it can be mobilized for constructive purposes, this is no
credit to him, for this too is part of his psychic legacy. Those of us who can dis-
cipline ourselves and develop habits of concentration of purpose tend to
blame those who cannot, and call them lazy and weak-willed; but what we fail
to see is that they literally *cannot* do what we expect: if their psyches were
structured like ours, they could, but as they are burdened with a tyrannical
super-ego (to use psychoanalytic jargon for the moment), and a weak defense-
less ego whose energies are constantly consumed in fighting endless charges
of the superego, they simply cannot do it, and it is irrational to expect it of
them. We cannot with justification blame them for their inability, any more
than we can congratulate ourselves for our ability. This lesson is hard to learn,
for we constantly and naively assume that other people are constructed as we
ourselves are.

For example: A child raised under slum conditions, whose parents are socially ambitious and envy families with money, but who nevertheless squan-
der the little they have on drink, may simply be unable in later life to mobilize
a drive sufficient to overcome these early conditions. Common sense would
expect that he would develop the virtue of thrift; he would make quite sure
that he would never again endure the grinding poverty he had experienced as
a child. But in fact it is not so: the exact conditions are too complex to be
specified in detail here, but when certain conditions are fulfilled (concerning
the subject's early life), he will always thereafter be a spendthrift, and no rational considerations will be able to change this. He will listen to the rational
considerations and see the force of these, but they will not be able to change
him, even if he tries; he cannot change his wasteful habits any more than he
can lift the Empire State Building with his bare hands. We moralize and plead
with him to be thrifty, but we do not see how strong, how utterly overpowering, and how constantly with him, is the opposite drive, which is so easily
manageable with us. But he is possessed by the all-consuming, all-encompass-
ing urge to make the world see that he belongs, that he has arrived, that he is
just as well off as anyone else, that the awful humiliations were not real, that

they never actually occurred, for isn't he now able to spend and spend? The humiliation must be blotted out; and conspicuous, flashy, expensive, and wasteful buying will do this; it shows the world what the world must know! True, it is only for the moment; true, it is in the end self-defeating, for wasteful consumption is the best way to bring poverty back again; but the person with an overpowering drive to mend a lesion to his narcissism cannot resist the avalanche of that drive with his puny rational consideration. A man with his back against the wall and a gun at his throat doesn't think of what may happen ten years hence. (Consciously, of course, he knows nothing of this drive; all that appears to consciousness is its shattering effects; he knows only that he must keep on spending—not why—and that he is unable to resist.) He hasn't in him the psychic capacity, the energy to stem the tide of a drive that at that moment is all-powerful. We, seated comfortably away from this flood, sit in judgment on him and blame him and exhort him and criticize him; but he, carried along by the flood, cannot do otherwise than he does. He may fight with all the strength of which he is capable, but it is not enough. And we, who are rational enough at least to exonerate a man in a situation of "overpowering impulse" when we recognize it to be one, do not even recognize this as an example of it; and so, in addition to being swept away in the flood that childhood conditions rendered inevitable, he must also endure our lectures, our criticisms, and our moral excoriation.

But, one will say, he could have overcome his spendthrift tendencies; some people do. Quite true: some people do. They are lucky. They have it in them to overcome early deficiencies by exerting great effort, and they are capable of exerting the effort. Some of us, luckier still, can overcome them with but little effort; and a few, the luckiest, haven't the deficiencies to overcome. It's all a matter of luck. The least lucky are those who can't overcome them, even with great effort, and those who haven't the ability to exert the effort.

But, one persists, it isn't a matter simply of luck; it *is* a matter of effort. Very well then, it's a matter of effort; without exerting the effort you may not overcome the deficiency. But whether or not you are the kind of person who has it in him to exert the effort is a matter of luck.

All this is well known to psychoanalysts. They can predict, from minimal cues that most of us don't notice, whether a person is going to turn out to be lucky or not. "The analyst," they say, "must be able to use the residue of the patient's unconscious guilt so as to remove the symptom or character trait that creates the guilt. The guilt must not only be present, but *available* for use, *mobilizable*. If it is used up (absorbed) in criminal activity, or in an excessive amount of self-damaging tendencies, then it cannot be used for therapeutic purposes, and the prognosis is negative." Not all philosophers will relish the analyst's way of putting the matter, but at least as a physician he can soon detect whether the patient is lucky or unlucky—and he knows that whichever it is, it *isn't the patient's fault*. The patient's conscious volition cannot remedy the deficiency. Even whether he will co-operate with the analyst is really out of the patient's hands: if he continually projects the denying-mother fantasy on the analyst and unconsciously identifies him always with the cruel, harsh forbidder of the nursery, thus frustrating any attempt at impersonal observation, the sessions are useless; yet if it happens that way, he can't help that either. That fatal projection is not under his control; whether it occurs or not depends on how his unconscious identifications have developed since his infancy. He can try, yes—but the ability to try enough for the therapy to have effect is also beyond his control; the capacity to try more than just so much is either there or it isn't—and either way "it's in the lap of the gods."

The position, then, is this: if we *can* overcome the effects of early environment, the ability to do so is itself a product of the early environment. We did not give ourselves this ability; and if we lack it we cannot be blamed for not having it. Sometimes, to be sure, moral exhortation brings out an ability that is there but not being used, and in this lies its *occasional* utility; but very often its use is pointless, because the ability is not there. The only thing that can overcome a desire, as Spinoza said, is a stronger contrary desire; and many times there simply is no wherewithal for producing a stronger contrary desire. Those of us who do have the wherewithal are lucky.

There is one possible practical advantage in remembering this. It may prevent us (unless we are compulsive blamers) from indulging in righteous indignation and committing the sin of spiritual pride, thanking God that we are not as this publican here. And it will protect from our useless moralizings those who are least equipped by nature for enduring them. As with responsibility, so with deserts. Someone commits a crime and is punished by the state; "he deserved it," we say self-righteously—as if we were moral and he immoral, when in fact we are lucky and he is unlucky—forgetting that there, but for the grace of God and a fortunate early environment, go we. Or, as Clarence Darrow said in his speech for the defense in the Loeb-Leopold case:

> I do not believe that people are in jail because they deserve to be. . . . I know what causes the emotional life. . . . I know it is practically left out of some. Without it they cannot act with the rest. They cannot feel the moral shocks which safeguard others. Is [this man] to blame that his machine is imperfect? Who is to blame? I do not know. I have never in my life been interested so much in fixing blame as I have in relieving people from blame. I am not wise enough to fix it.[4]

III

I want to make it quite clear that I have not been arguing for determinism. Though I find it difficult to give any sense to the term "indeterminism," because I do not know what it would be like to come across an uncaused event, let us grant indeterminists everything they want, at least in words—influences that suggest but do not constrain, a measure of acausality in an otherwise rigidly causal order, and so on—whatever these phrases may mean. With

[4]Levin, op. cit., pp. 439–40, 469.

all this granted, exactly the same situation faces the indeterminist and the determinist; all we have been saying would still hold true. "Are our powers innate or acquired?"

> Suppose the powers are declared innate; then the villain may sensibly ask whether he is responsible for what he was born with. A negative reply is inevitable. Are they then acquired? Then the ability to acquire them—was *that* innate? or acquired? It is innate? Very well then. . . .[5]

The same fact remains—that we did not cause our characters, that the influences that made us what we are are influences over which we had no control and of whose very existence we had no knowledge at the time. This fact remains for "determinism" and "indeterminism" alike. And it is this fact to which I would appeal, not the specific tenets of traditional forms of "determinism," which seem to me, when analyzed, empirically empty.

"But," it may be asked, "isn't it your view that nothing ultimately *could* be other than it is? And isn't this deterministic? And isn't it deterministic if you say that human beings could never act otherwise than they do, and that their desires and temperaments could not, when you consider their antecedent conditions, be other than they are?"

I reply that all these charges rest on confusions.

1. To say that nothing *could* be other than it is, is, taken literally, nonsense; and if taken as a way of saying something else, misleading and confusing. If you say, "I can't do it," this invites the question, "No? Not even if you want to?" "Can" and "could" are power words, used in the context of human action; when applied to nature they are merely anthropomorphic. "Could" has no application to nature—unless, of course, it is uttered in a theological context: one might say that God *could* have made things different. But with regard to inanimate nature "could" has no meaning. Or perhaps it is intended to mean that the order of nature is in some sense *necessary*. But in that case the sense of "necessary" must be specified. I know what "necessary" means when we are talking about propositions, but not when we are talking about the sequence of events in nature.

2. What of the charge that we could never have acted otherwise than we did? This, I submit, is simply not true. Here the exponents of Hume-Mill-Schlick-Ayer "soft determinism" are quite right. I could have gone to the opera today instead of coming here; that is, if certain conditions had been different, I should have gone. I could have done many other things instead of what I did, if some condition or other had been different, specifically if my desire had been different. I repeat that "could" is a power word, and "I could have done this" means approximately "I *should* have done this *if* I had wanted to." In this sense, all of us could often have done otherwise than we did. I would not want to say that I should have done differently even if *all* the condi-

[5]W. I. Matson, "The Irrelevance of Free-will to Moral Responsibility," *Mind*, LXV (October 1956), p. 495.

tions leading up to my action had been the same (this is generally not what we mean by "could" anyway); but to assert that I could have is empty, for if I *did* act different from the time before, we would automatically say that one or more of the conditions were different, whether we had independent evidence for this or not, thus rendering the assertion immune to empirical refutation. (Once again, the vacuousness of "determinism.")

3. Well, then, could we ever have, not acted, but *desired* otherwise than we did desire? This gets us once again to the heart of the matter we were discussing in the previous section. Russell said, "We can do as we please but we can't please as we please." But I am persuaded that even this statement conceals a fatal mistake. Let us follow the same analysis through. "I could have done *X*" means "I should have done *X* if I had wanted to." "I could have wanted *X*" by the same analysis would mean "I should have wanted *X* if I had wanted to"—which seems to make no sense at all. (What does Russell want? To please as he doesn't please?)

What does this show? It shows, I think, that the only meaningful context of "can" and "could have" is that of *action*. "Could have acted differently" makes sense; "could have desired differently," as we have just seen, does not. Because a word or phrase makes good sense in one context, let us not assume that it does so in another.

I conclude, then, with the following suggestion: that we operate on two levels of moral discourse, which we shouldn't confuse; one (let's call it the upper level) is that of actions; the other (the lower, or deeper, level) is that of the springs of action. Most moral talk occurs on the upper level. It is on this level that the Hume-Mill-Schlick-Ayer analysis of freedom fully applies. As we have just seen, "can" and "could" acquire their meaning on this level; so, I suspect, does "freedom." So does the distinction between compulsive and noncompulsive behavior, and among the senses of "responsibility," discussed in the first section of this paper, according to which we are responsible for some things and not for others. All these distinctions are perfectly valid on this level (or in this dimension) of moral discourse; and it is, after all, the usual one—we are practical beings interested in changing the course of human behavior, so it is natural enough that 99 percent of our moral talk occurs here.

But when we descend to what I have called the lower level of moral discourse, as we occasionally do in thoughtful moments when there is no immediate need for action, then we must admit that we are ultimately the kind of persons we are because of conditions occurring outside us, over which we had no control. But while this is true, we should beware of extending the moral terminology we used on the other level to this one also. "Could" and "can," as we have seen, no longer have meaning here. "Right" and "wrong," which apply only to actions, have no meaning here either. I suspect that the same is true of "responsibility," for now that we have recalled often forgotten facts about our being the product of outside forces, we must ask in all seriousness what would be added by saying that we are not *responsible* for our own characters and temperaments. What would it mean even? Has it a significant opposite? What would it be like to be responsible for one's own character? What possible situation is describable by this phrase? Instead of saying that it is *false* that we are responsible for our own characters, I should prefer to say that the utterance is meaningless—meaningless in the sense that it describes no possible situation, though it *seems* to because the word "responsible" is the same one we used on the upper level, where it marks a real distinction. If this is so, the result is that *moral* terms—at least the terms "could have" and "responsible"—simply drop out on the lower level. What remains, shorn now of moral terminology, is the point we tried to bring out in Part II: whether or not we have personality disturbances, whether or not we have the ability to overcome deficiencies of early environment, is like the answer to the question whether or not we shall be struck down by a dread disease: "it's all a matter of luck." It is important to keep this in mind, for people almost always forget it, with consequences in human intolerance and unnecessary suffering that are incalculable.

13

JONATHAN GLOVER

Freud, Morality and Responsibility

AT TIMES IT seems as if Freud made no impact on moral attitudes. For in the moral pronouncements of bishops and headmasters, or in letters to the newspapers about 'permissiveness', the appropriate post-Freudian note of self-doubt is not often heard. The sense that human acts are often more complicated than they seem, the awareness of the ambiguities of our own motives when moralizing or denouncing, are arguably as rare as ever. Yet it may be mistaken to suppose that Freud has had no influence here. Causal links in such matters are notoriously hard to establish, but there is often to be found in our culture a variety of moral scepticism which is perhaps partly traceable to psychoanalytic thinking. It is often said or implied that argument about right and wrong is pointless, since our conduct is determined always by factors other than our professed moral beliefs. It is also sometimes suggested that morality is a kind of fraud by which people are duped into behaving in socially convenient ways. Another form of moral scepticism suggests that holding people responsible for what they do is a practice that will fade away as old superstitions are replaced by a 'scientific' view of man.

Even if it is hard to be sure how widespread such scepticism is, or how much it is influenced by Freud, it is worth asking to what extent, if any, Freud's theories provide a justification for changes of moral attitude. Three aspects of Freud's thought are relevant here: his own account of the origin of

From *Freud, the Man, His World, His Influence*, edited by Jonathan Miller (London: Weidenfeld and Nicolson, 1972), chapter 11. Reprinted by permission.

conscience and morality, his determinism, and his claims about unconscious motivation.

Freud holds a Hobbesian view of man, who is seen, not as a social animal, but as one whose dangerous instincts must be restrained. One crucial restraining factor is morality. In *The Future of an Illusion*,* Freud discusses the prohibition of murder.

> It is manifestly in the interest of man's communal existence, which would not otherwise be practicable, that civilization has laid down the commandment that one shall not kill the neighbour whom one hates, who is in one's way, or whose property one covets. . . . Insecurity of life, an equal danger for all, now unites men in one society, which forbids the individual to kill. . . . We do not, however, tell others of this rational basis for the murder prohibition; we declare, on the contrary, that God is its author.

If the social function of morality is a Hobbesian one, how does it work? Why do people take notice of what morality commands or forbids? Here Freud's account is entirely original. There is a psychological process which consists in 'many developments, repressions, sublimations and reaction-formations by means of which a child with a quite other innate endowment grows into what we call a normal man, the bearer, and in part the victim, of the civilization that has been so painfully acquired'. The key to this process is the Oedipus phase, when the young boy sees his father as a rival for his mother, and has to repress his own unsatisfiable desires.

Freud describes this in *The Ego and the Id*:†

> Clearly the repression of the Oedipus complex was no easy task. The child's parents, and especially his father, were perceived as the obstacle to a realization of his Oedipus wishes, so his infantile ego fortified itself for the carrying out of the repression by erecting this same obstacle within itself. It borrowed strength to do this, so to speak, from the father, and this loan was an extraordinarily momentous act. The superego retains the character of the father, while the more powerful the Oedipus complex was and the more rapidly it succumbed to repression . . . the stricter will be the domination of the superego over the ego later on—in the form of conscience or perhaps of an unconscious sense of guilt.

He goes on to refer to the superego's 'compulsive character which manifests itself in the form of a categorical imperative'.

Some of the difficulties of this account of conscience are well known. The existence of the Oedipus phase itself is a matter of dispute. Even if the Oedipus phase does exist it is unclear what would count as testing the claim that conscience is the outcome of repressing the Oedipus desires. Apart from these doubts about the postulated psychological mechanism, there are also fa-

---

The Standard Edition 21 (1927) (London: Hogarth Press, 1961).—B. A. F.
†*The Standard Edition* 19 (1932) (London: Hogarth Press, 1961).—B. A. F.

miliar problems of defending both the functionalist account of morality and
the large Hobbesian generalizations about innate human nature with which
its Freudian form is interwoven. How do we know what men who somehow
escaped all current forms of socialization would be like? Are all moral beliefs
socially useful in the way the prohibition on murder is? But these are doubts
rather than refutations. The point is not that Freud is wrong, but that there
are not clearly established answers. We cannot yet go beyond agnosticism on
these matters.

In response to these commonplace objections, it may be said that in the
study of man little is clearly established, and that the Freudian account of
morality has, at least in part, a certain intuitive plausibility. Our parents give
us commands when we are young and the 'commands' of conscience may be
shadows of these. We imitate our parents in many ways, and giving commands to ourselves may be one such way. And from where do the commands
of conscience get their authority? May it not be that we obey them because, if
we do not, we will feel guilty? And is it not likely that this guilt is the result of
childhood conditioning?

All this does have some plausibility, even if being plausible is not the same
as being true. But even if the account is true as far as it goes, it is important to
see that it will not do as an explanation of the whole of morality. It can only be
taken for that if a narrow and crude view of morality is presupposed. If morality is thought of as a series of arbitrary commands, backed up by the sanction
of guilt feelings, then perhaps a Freudian account will be all that is required.
But this view of morality will at best only fit people whose moral thinking is itself simple and crude, and in particular who altogether exclude reasoning
from their morality.

There certainly are people whose morality consists in an arbitrary list of
commands, which are thought of as having an authority that is obscure but un-
challengeable. (Freud's own use of the Kantian term 'categorical imperative'
suggests that he thought of morality in terms of authoritative internal commands.) But more reflective people often start to reason about ethics. Should I
be a pacifist? What would be a just distribution of income? Can I justify abor-
tion without also justifying infanticide? Moral questions are often hard to answer: we do not have a set of inner commands which always tell us what to do.
And thinking about such questions does not consist in a kind of intent listening, in the hope that the inner voice will speak loudly enough for us to hear its
commands. Nor does it consist in inspecting what makes us feel guilty. In a
sophisticated morality, it may be considered wrong to be swayed by feelings
of guilt in cases where we know these feelings to be the result of conditioning
in values we reject. Guilt feelings are often harder to give up than the beliefs
that go with them: the atheist who had a heavy childhood conditioning in religion may be unable to escape irrational guilt feelings when he spends Sunday
morning in bed instead of in church.

A fuller account of morality than that presupposed by Freud would allow
for people standing back from the childhood set of commands and guilt feelings, and modifying their beliefs in the light of experience, reasoning and

imagination. We may see the consequences of our beliefs (as when the supporter of a war visits a hospital for wounded children), find those consequences unacceptable, and set about modifying our beliefs. Or we may find our beliefs about right and wrong to be inconsistent or arbitrary (as most people's are about the ethics of killing) or that they presuppose factual beliefs that we no longer hold. Developed moral thought is not a static state of imprisonment within social norms imposed by childhood, but a process of interaction between general beliefs and particular responses. In the light of our responses to new experiences, we modify our stock of general moral beliefs. But equally, in the light of our general beliefs we may sometimes reject some of our particular responses as crude or perhaps sentimental. There is no reason why this process should leave us accepting the assumptions either of our upbringing or of our society.

But, despite the possibility of a moral autonomy and sophistication unrecognized by Freud, it may well be that the primitive system of commands and guilt feelings is the necessary basis out of which a developed morality must grow. It may be that, without the social pressures and internalization of parental commands Freud describes, no moral attitudes would develop, and we would all be like psychopaths. It is not clear that this is so. Again, we know virtually nothing with certainty here, but the speculation once more has some plausibility. It may also be that an explanation such as Freud's of the social function of this embryonic morality is correct. Yet, even if all this were true, no grounds would be given for the moral scepticism sometimes thought to be based on Freud's account of the superego. The claim that this account shows morality to be a fraud practised by society, and a way of imposing conformity to norms not of one's own choice, tacitly presupposes that all moral thinking can be reduced to the embryonic morality discussed by Freud. So crude a reductionism is tempting only to the degree it is not made explicit.

It may be said that Freudian theory has, or should have, modified our attitudes because of the support it gives to a determinist view of man. We do not have to think Freud's view of morality adequate, but we may be more impressed by the powerful case he made for psychological causal mechanisms underlying behaviour previously thought mysterious or the product of a somehow uncaused will. If explanations of at least some persuasiveness can be provided in terms of psychological mechanisms for slips of the tongue, dreams, jokes and various neurotic disorders, it is then more convincing to suggest that the human mind is one vast and complex mechanism. This is a presupposition of the psychoanalytic view of people, and is also a presupposition of many of those who are either sceptical about morality in general, or in particular about our moral responsibility for what we do.

The mere fact that Freud's approach to people was a determinist one need not detain us long. For Freud was by no means the first person in history to take such a view, and the status of determinism in his work is unclear. It is not certain whether Freud thought his work had provided evidence for the truth of determinism, or whether he merely adopted a kind of methodological determinism, resolving never to give up the search for causes of behaviour.

But if, for the sake of argument, we assume that Freud's explanations add to the plausibility of determinism, we are not forced by this increased plausibility to regard people as less likely to be acting freely or less responsible for their actions. This is because the truth of determinism is not by itself sufficient to show that no one ever acts freely. I often have both the ability and the opportunity to do things I do not in fact do. I could have gone to the zoo today, although I did not. The reason I did not was because I did not want to go, not because I was unable to do so. And this remains true even if my lack of enthusiasm for the zoo turns out to be causally explicable. In thinking of human acts, we contrast motivation on the one hand with abilities on the other. If I had sufficient motive for doing something but did not do it, I must have lacked the ability or opportunity. If I had the ability and opportunity but did not do it, I must have lacked the desire. Lack of freedom, and hence nonresponsibility, comes from limited opportunities or abilities. Where I knowingly do something normally considered bad, the question of whether I am to blame for it is largely a question of whether I did it because I wanted to do it, or whether I did it, despite not wanting to do it, as a result of inability to do otherwise.

There are special cases, where I do what I want but am still unfree. These are cases of desires I cannot help having or cannot resist. Drug addicts, alcoholics, compulsive hand-washers and others have such desires. But the reason that such people are not acting freely has nothing to do with any general thesis of determinism. It is not *any* causal explanation that shows that a desire is unavoidable or irresistible. There must be reason to think that the person could not give up or resist the desire if he wanted to do so. The compulsive hand-washer cannot give up his desire to wash even if he wants to do so. Other desires are more easily mastered. Freedom is a matter of degree, so any drawing of boundaries here is a rather blurred affair. But there remains a substantial difference between acts which I would have altered if given some incentive to do so, and acts I would not have altered however much I wanted to do so. This difference, between freedom and unfreedom, is not obliterated by the fact that both acts may be causally determined.

The basis for saying that freedom and responsibility are not undermined by determinism is the distinction between two sorts of causal explanation of why a person does one thing rather than another. It may be that he wants to do the other act but cannot, or it may be that he performs this act because he wants to, although he is able to do the other thing. In the first case he cannot help the outcome, while in the second case he can. We identify people with their desires, rather than with their abilities or opportunities. Moral praise and blame can appropriately be applied to a person's desires and motives, but not to his abilities and opportunities. (This is subject to two qualifications: some desires or motives are ones a person wants to give up but cannot, while some limitations on our abilities and opportunities are the result of our own previous decisions, for which we can be blamed or praised.)

But if holding people responsible is based on making moral judgements in terms of their motives and desires, it is clear that motives or desires which are unconscious pose a special problem. It seems a serious moral criticism of someone to say that his actions are always motivated by self-interest and that all his desires are selfish. But are we equally, or at all, justified in disapproving of someone whose desires and motives, while just as selfish, are unconscious? For, surely, if he does not identify with these desires, and does not even know of their existence, it is odd for us to identify him with them? Should our attitudes to him be based on our attitude to desires and motives he might repudiate if he became aware of them?

Freud himself never directly confronts the problem of responsibility for actions that are unconsciously motivated. But he does discuss the links between his account of the unconscious and responsibility in the content of a note about the curious problem of *Moral Responsibility for the Context of Dreams*.* His remarks there about the unconscious impulses that determine our dreams seem to rest on considerations that could apply equally to any unconscious desires.

Freud confidently says: 'Obviously one must hold oneself responsible for the evil impulses of one's dreams. What else is one to do with them?' The fatuity of the rhetorical question does not increase the obviousness of the view it is intended to support. But Freud partly recovers after this unpromising start, and puts forward some arguments that are worth quoting in full.

His first argument is that I am not entitled to identify myself with only the conscious part of my mind. He says:

> Unless the content of the dream (rightly understood) is inspired by alien spirits, it is a part of my own being. If I seek to classify the impulses that are present in me according to social standards into good and bad, I must assume responsibility for both sorts; and if, in defence, I say that what is unknown, unconscious and repressed in me is not my ego then I shall not be basing my position upon psychoanalysis, I shall not have accepted its conclusions—and I shall perhaps be taught better by the criticisms of my fellow-men, by the disturbances in my actions and the confusion of my feelings. I shall perhaps learn that what I am disavowing not only 'is' in me but sometimes 'acts' from out of me as well.

What exactly is Freud rejecting here? We are normally willing to regard some desires as alien to the person who has them. We do not hold the alcoholic responsible for drinking because we believe that he is neither capable of resisting his desire to drink nor of giving up the desire. He may well wish he did not have any desire to drink. We are prepared to regard the possession of an

*The Standard Edition 19 (1925) p. 131ff. (London: Hogarth Press, 1961).—B. A. F.

unwanted desire that a person cannot eliminate or resist as a form of incapacity, and not to hold him responsible for what he does as a result. (We may hold him responsible for becoming an alcoholic, but that is another matter.) The view which Freud is arguing against is that we should regard unconscious desires as alien to a person in a similar way.

Freud's argument is not clear. He says that if I adopt the view he rejects 'I shall not be basing my position upon psychoanalysis'. But what does this mean? If we decide that actions coming from some kinds of motive are not blameworthy, this is a moral decision of ours. The only way in which it could be undermined by any psychoanalytic findings would be if it depended on some factual assumption that turned out to be false. What is this assumption, and what is the evidence that it is false? The only clue Freud gives is his remark that 'what I am disavowing not only "is" in me but sometimes "acts" from out of me as well'. This seems to mean no more than that I do have the unconscious motive, and that it does influence my behaviour. But the alcoholic also does have his desire to drink, and it does influence his behaviour. Freud does not show that the decision to treat unconscious motives as similar to the unwanted but inescapable desires of the alcoholic is based on any false beliefs.

Freud has a second argument for saying that we are responsible for unconsciously motivated acts. This is his claim that acceptance of such responsibility is psychologically inescapable. He says: 'Moreover, if I were to give way to my moral pride and tried to decree that for purposes of moral valuation I might disregard the evil in the id and need not make my ego responsible for it, what use would that be to me? Experience shows me that I nevertheless *do* take that responsibility, that I am somehow compelled to do so.'

This argument depends on the belief that feeling guilty about something is the same as believing oneself to be blameworthy. But we have seen that it is possible to think one's own guilt feelings irrational, as in the case of the atheist with reflex guilt feelings about not going to church. If it is true that we feel guilty about acts even when we see that they were unconsciously motivated, it still seems an open question whether or not we ought to regard such feelings as rational. And, if we came to think them irrational, might we not perhaps find that these feelings of guilt started to fade away? Freud says about my accepting responsibility that experience shows me that I am somehow compelled to do so. But without trying to give up such guilt feelings, we cannot be sure that the feeling of compulsion is not an illusion.

The argument is also unsatisfactory in treating questions of responsibility as though they only concerned whether or not we ought to blame ourselves for what we do. No consideration is given to the question of what attitudes we ought to adopt towards other people who act out of possibly disreputable unconscious motives. Even if it were true that someone could not help feeling guilty about something, this would not establish that others were entitled to blame him. It is the avoidability of a bad act that makes blame reasonable, not the unavoidability of guilt feelings afterwards.

If we cannot accept that Freud's own remarks settle the question of responsibility for what is unconsciously motivated, is there any other way of approaching the problem? In outlining an alternative approach, one may start by asking what difference it should make to a person's decision how to act if he knows of the possibility of unconscious motivation. For it is arguable that knowledge of one's own motives is less relevant to such decisions than it is often taken to be.

Consider someone wondering whether he ought to give some money to Oxfam. He may well suspect that if he gives the money his motives may be less purely unselfish than they seem at the conscious level. Is it not possible that his most powerful motives are below the level of consciousness? Perhaps he wants to feel a glow of virtue, and to act in a way that flatters his picture of himself. Or it may be that he wants to avoid the feelings of guilt induced by reading the Oxfam advertisement and then doing nothing about it. Suppose, on the other hand, he decides not to send any money. At the conscious level his reasons may be those of a radical political kind. He may think that Oxfam does more harm than good by easing the conscience of the rich, and thus being a substitute for more effective action at government level. But, even here, he may suspect that powerful unconscious motives are at work. May the political case against Oxfam perhaps be functioning as a rationalization for an unconscious determination to preserve his own standard of living?

In a case like this, the motives involved in either course of action may be suspect. But there seems no reason why this should lead to any kind of paralysis. There is something unattractively self-absorbed about treating the purity of one's own motives as a prime consideration when deciding what to do. This is part of the case for saying that decisions about right and wrong ought to be based on the consequences of the acts being considered, with questions of motivation left largely on one side. If giving money to Oxfam leaves the world a slightly better place than not going so, one should give the money. This holds even if one suspects that one's motives for giving are, whether at a conscious or unconscious level, a bit dubious.

But this needs some qualification. If our motives are unconscious, they may well distort our view of the likely consequences of what we do. Perhaps self-deception about our motives is in itself not of great moral importance, but where it is linked with self-deception about the facts of our situation it becomes more relevant. Consider a question related to the one about giving to Oxfam. Should a country like Britain give more aid to economically poorer countries? Some people argue either that such aid is always a concealed form of exploitation, or else that the most effective way of improving the lot of people in backward countries is for advanced ones to forget aid and concentrate on increasing their own prosperity. I have not the knowledge to assess with any certainty the truth of such views. But it is reasonable to say that beliefs so obviously convenient to so many of us ought to have their credentials very thoroughly examined before being accepted.

This point can be generalized. Knowledge of the possibility of unconscious factors distorting our view of our situation places on us a special duty of sceptical scrutiny. This duty is not primarily to examine our own motives, but is rather a duty to look with special care at our grounds for holding factual beliefs that are suspiciously convenient to us.

We can now return to the problem of whether or not we are justified in holding other people responsible for acts that are unconsciously motivated. The various excuses that absolve people from responsibility for what they do can broadly be classified, as they were by Aristotle, under the headings of ignorance or compulsion. I am not blameworthy when I do not know certain crucial facts about what I am doing, nor am I blameworthy when I am compelled to act, either by external pressures or by irresistible desires. Both of these factors, ignorance and compulsion, function as excuses only where they are not themselves the result of my own relevantly blameworthy act or omission. If I fire a gun in a busy street without bothering to look and see if anyone is in the line of fire, my ignorance does not excuse me from blame for killing someone. And irresistible impulses are not an excuse if they result from my deliberately taking a drug knowing it would have that effect.

To what extent do unconscious motives involve either compulsion or ignorance? It does not seem likely that all unconscious motives are irresistible. Addicts, whose impulses sometimes really are irresistible, are not open to any normal degree of persuasion to act differently. But there seems no reason why unconscious motivation should always be as powerful as this. Perhaps a man's unconscious motive for buying his cigarettes at a certain shop is that he finds a girl who works there attractive. Although the whole thing is unconscious, it may still be that he finds her only so mildly attractive that he could be persuaded to go to another shop by being told that it gave double green shield stamps.

Perhaps unconscious motives are more often irresistible than conscious ones, though even this would not be easy to prove. But if they do not always involve compulsion, do they always involve excusable ignorance? We have seen that unconscious motivation can involve ignorance, not only of one's motives, but also of relevant facts of one's situation. We may 'overlook' what unconsciously we do not wish to know. I have argued here that knowledge of one's own motives is normally not centrally relevant to the right and wrongs of a decision how to act. It follows from this that ignorance of one's motives will normally not be sufficient to clear one of the charge of knowingly doing wrong. So any claim that people never ought to be held responsible for unconsciously motivated actions will have to depend on the view that unconscious desires always cause a relevant and excusable ignorance of some other kind.

The assertion that whenever I do not know my own motives there is always something else I also do not know seems a sweeping one. And even in cases where unconscious motivation clearly does distort someone's way of seeing things, it is not clear that this distortion is always excusable. It has been argued here that we have a sp :cial duty to resist such distortions in cases where there is a possibility that suspiciously convenient beliefs are self-interested rationalizations. Some kinds of self-deception are not excusable ignorance, but a kind of semi-deliberate negligence.

It may be said that this sort of criticism can only be made in cases where motives are not really unconscious. There is a duty to resist our view of things being distorted by selfish motives which we suspect may be present. But many people suppose that motives whose presence may be suspected by the person who has them are not genuinely unconscious.

This seems to be based on an over-dramatic view of unconscious motivation. Some of the most convincing cases of unconscious motives occur with post-hypnotic suggestion. The person under hypnosis may be told to take his shoes off an hour after recovering normal consciousness, and also be told to forget the whole episode of being hypnotized. When the time comes he will remove his shoes, perhaps explaining to anyone present that his feet hurt. This kind of case is dramatic partly because, without knowledge of the post-hypnotic suggestion, no one would suspect any unconscious forces to be at work.

But there is no reason to think that most unconscious motives are as deeply inaccessible as this. Where external observers have good evidence for ascribing such motives to someone this evidence is usually available to himself. His behaviour falls into a pattern that does not fit his officially declared goals but does fit the postulated unconscious aims. Such cases are far more common than those where the external observer has access to a dramatic episode such as the post-hypnotic suggestion. And, in these more common cases, the pattern into which his behaviour falls should be visible to the agent himself, if he cares to look for it.

It is sometimes thought that during the process of psychoanalysis, many motives as deeply inaccessible as those supplied by post-hypnotic suggestion are discovered. But the difficulty here is to see what sort of inaccessible evidence such 'discoveries' could be based on. If the unconscious motives cannot be suspected from the patterns of conduct of the person who has them, what counts as testing the claim that they exist? The fact that the patient comes to accept his analyst's interpretation is not enough, for this may be the result of a kind of indoctrination. The fact that the patient feels helped by his psychoanalysis is not enough, for being given a coherent view of oneself, even if a false one, could still be beneficial. The truth of the analyst's claims about motivation can only be judged by how plausibly they fit the patient's habitual patterns of behaviour. And this evidence is available to the patient himself, independently of his psychoanalysis.

If we are sceptical about the evidence for inaccessible unconscious motives, outside such special contexts as post-hypnotic suggestion, we will be less inclined to take the view that people cannot help it when their view of their situation is distorted in ways described by Freud. For, if most of our unconscious motives can at least be suspected when we take the trouble to think about the matter, we ought to be fairly successful in noticing self-deception if we keep a look out for it. And it has been argued here that at least where its influence may have an important effect on our actions, self-deception is something which we ought to try to detect.

14

SIGMUND FREUD AND OSKAR PFISTER

Correspondence

Berggasse 19,
Vienna IX,
9.2.1909

Dear Dr Pfister,

The permanent success of psycho-analysis certainly depends on the coincidence of two issues: the obtaining of satisfaction by the release of tension, and sublimation of the sheer instinctual drive. If we generally succeed only with the former, that is to be attributed to a great extent to the human raw material—human beings who have been suffering severely for a long time and expect no moral elevation from the physician, and are often inferior material. In your case they are young persons faced with conflicts of recent date, who are personally drawn towards you and are ready for sublimation, and to sublimation in its most comfortable form, namely the religious. They do not suspect that success with them comes about in your case primarily by the same route as it does with us, by way of erotic transference to yourself. But you are in the fortunate position of being able to lead them to God and bringing about what in this one respect was the happy state of earlier times when religious faith stifled the neuroses. For us this way of disposing of the matter does not exist. Our public, no matter of what racial origin, is irreligious, we are generally thoroughly irreligious ourselves and, as the other ways of sublimation which *we* substitute for religion are too difficult for most patients, our

The numbered footnotes that are not in brackets are by the editors of the letters, Heinrich Meng and Ernst L. Freud.—B. A. F.

From *Psychoanalysis and Faith: The Letters of Sigmund Freud and Oskar Pfister*, edited by Heinrich Meng and Ernst L. Freud, Translated by Eric Mosbacher. Copyright © 1963 by Basic Books, Inc., Publishers, New York. Reprinted by permission of the publisher, with acknowledgment to Sigmund Freud Copyrights and The Hogarth Press.

treatment generally results in the seeking out of satisfaction. On top of this there is the fact that we are unable to see anything forbidden or sinful in sexual satisfaction, but regard it as a valuable part of human experience. You are aware that for us the term 'sex' includes what you in your pastoral work call love, and is certainly not restricted to the crude pleasure of the senses. Thus our patients have to find in humanity what we are unable to promise them from above and are unable to supply them with ourselves. Things are therefore much more difficult for us, and in the resolution of the transference many of our successes come to grief.

In itself psycho-analysis is neither religious nor non-religious, but an impartial tool which both priest and layman can use in the service of the sufferer. I am very much struck by the fact that it never occurred to me how extraordinarily helpful the psycho-analytic method might be in pastoral work, but that is surely accounted for by the remoteness from me, as a wicked pagan, of the whole system of ideas.

Let me express the hope that your interest will not fade if the first phase of striking successes gives way to the familiar second phase in which the difficulties tend to obtrude. After overcoming the latter one attains a feeling of quiet confidence.

Yours with grateful thanks,
Freud

Bergasse 19,
Vienna IX,
18.3.1909

Dear Dr Pfister,

Perhaps I cannot better express my thanks for your latest paper[1] in the *Evangelische Freiheit* than by asking you to accept some observations that occurred to me while reading it.

I realised that your situation and public laid you under the necessity of withholding or censoring a great deal. That is always as painful to the author as it is to the understanding reader. The censor cuts into the flesh; what he cuts out is always 'the best thing', as the mocker Heine remarks. At one point, I think, you could have been more outspoken for, after all, ecclesiastical authority cannot object to the human phantasy's taking charge of the messages which it has no hesitation in so obtrusively proclaiming.

In the first dream 'the young lady *jumped into the lake*, I wanted to go after her, but *she kept herself above the water . . . she was immediately* quite dry'.

Dreams with this content, as you certainly have long been aware, are birth dreams. Children come from the water, fetched by the stork. The bit of biological reality behind this is familiar to us all, hence the impulse to give children this piece of information. Thus emerging from the water is equivalent to giving birth. (As a consequence of the indissoluble connection between death and sexuality a poor woman who wishes to commit suicide can do so

---

[1]O. Pfister, "Ein Fall von Psychoanalytischer Seelsorge und Seelenheilung" *Evangelische Freiheit,* 1909, Nos. 3–5.

only by means of a symbolic performance of a sexual phantasy. She goes into the water, i.e., gives birth, or flings herself from a height, i.e., drops,[2] or takes poison, i.e., becomes pregnant. Poisoning as a consequence of morning sickness is equivalent to pregnancy.)

Because of the ease by which things are represented by their opposite, the symbolisms of child-bearing and being born are often exchanged. In the well-known exposure myths of Sargon of Agade, Moses, Romulus, etc., putting the child out in a basket or in the water means the same; both mean being born. (See in this connection Vol. 5 of *Angewandten*[3] due to appear shortly, Rank's[4] *The Myth of the Birth of the Hero*. Box is *box*,[5] casket, genitals, womb—which takes us to the flood myths.)

In the dream he wanted to hurry to the aid of the young lady who jumped into the water, but she remained afloat and emerged by herself. As this young lady was the Madonna, this incident means he wished to help her to give birth, i.e., to have a child, but she gave birth without male intervention, remained a virgin. Hence the next reference. She immediately became quite dry, in other words the conception was immaculate. The hesitation at the end of the dream, the doubt about her, can only reflect the dreamer's doubt about the Catholic doctrine which he would like to accept, about the possibility of the immaculate conception and virgin birth.

Our predecessors in psycho-analysis, the Catholic fathers, did not of course work on the principle of paying a mere minimum of attention to sexual matters, but very explicitly asked for full details. I believe that the truth lies in between, but much nearer the Catholic practice than your proposition.

Your work should soon yield a typical result, as the general lines of religious thinking are laid down in advance in the family. God is equivalent to father, the Madonna is the mother, and the patient himself is no other than Christ. . . .

> *Yours,*
> *Freud*

> *Berggasse 19,*
> *Vienna IX,*
> *9.10.1918*

Dear Dr Pfister,

I have now read through your little book[6] and I can well believe the pleasure with which you wrote it. It has a gladdening warmth and demonstrates all the fine qualities which we so value in you; your enthusiasm, your integrity, and love of humanity, your courage and candour, your understanding and also—your optimism.

It will undoubtedly render us good service, if we are to mention such practical considerations; as you know, we generally pay little regard to them.

---

[2]The German *niederkommen*, 'to descend', also means (of a woman) 'to be confined'.
[3]*Schriften zur Angewandten Seelenkunde*, Deuticke, Leipzig and Vienna, 1909.
[4]Otto Rank, psycho-analyst, 1886–1939.
[5]Word in English in the original.
[6]Presumably O. Pfister, *Was bietet die Psychoanalyse dem Erzieher?* Leipzig, 1917 (*Psycho-Analysis in the Service of Education*, Henry Kimpton, London, 1922).

Well, praise can always be brief, but criticism has to be more long-winded. One thing I dislike is your objection to my 'sexual theory and my ethics'. The latter I grant you; ethics are remote from me, and you are a minister of religion. I do not break my head very much about good and evil, but I have found little that is 'good' about human beings on the whole. In my experience most of them are trash, no matter whether they publicly subscribe to this or that ethical doctrine or to none at all. That is something that you cannot say aloud, or perhaps even think, though your experiences of life can hardly have been different from mine. If we are to talk of ethics, I subscribe to a high ideal from which most of the human beings I have come across depart most lamentably.

As for the possibility of sublimation to religion, therapeutically I can only envy you. But the beauty of religion certainly does not belong to psycho-analysis. It is natural that at this point in therapy our ways should part, and so it can remain. Incidentally, why was it that none of all the pious ever discovered psycho-analysis? Why did it have to wait for a completely godless Jew?

> With cordial greetings from
> Your old friend
> Freud

PFISTER TO FREUD

> Zürich,
> 29.10.1918

. . . Finally you ask why psycho-analysis was not discovered by any of the pious, but by an atheist Jew. The answer obviously is that piety is not the same as genius for discovery and that most of the pious did not have it in them to make such discoveries. Moreover, in the first place you are no Jew, which to me, in view of my unbounded admiration for Amos, Isaiah, Jeremiah, and the author of Job and Ecclesiastes, is a matter of profound regret, and in the second place you are not godless, for he who lives the truth lives in God, and he who strives for the freeing of love 'dwelleth in God' (First Epistle of John, iv, 16). If you raised to your consciousness and fully felt your place in the great design, which to me is as necessary as the synthesis of the notes is to a Beethoven symphony, I should say of you: A better Christian there never was. . . .

PFISTER TO FREUD

> Zürich,
> 3.4.1992

Dear Professor Freud,

I am taking the liberty of making just one short observation about the book[7] I am sending you to-day. It represents an advance, in so far as I have

---

[7]O. Pfister, *Die Liebe des Kindes und ihre Fehlentwicklungen*, Bircher, Berne, 1922 (*Love in Children and its Aberrations*, Allen and Unwin, London, 1924).

finally overcome a great many confusions to which I had succumbed because of Jung and Adler. So, to my great pleasure, I can say without doubt or reservation that I have now seen the correctness of your views even in areas where for a long time I had no experience of my own. In matters of ethics, religion, and philosophy there remain differences between us which neither you nor I regard as a gulf. In my new work, which is the first volume of a monograph on the development and aberrations of love, I address myself to parents and teachers, because my faith in the pundits has notably shrunk. My primary aim is to help to overcome distress, and this is better done by pointing out to people the way to the psycho-analyst than by battling with the serried ranks of thick-headed psychologists and educationists. But it is incredibly difficult to write simply and at the same time cover the ground thoroughly. I took a great deal of trouble to combine the two objectives in this book, I do not know if I have succeeded. . . .

Berggasse 19,
Vienna IX,
6.4.1922

Dear Dr Pfister,

Thank you for your latest book, which arrived to-day, after your letter. All I know of it so far is from opening the parcel, but I suspect that it will be my favourite among the creatures of your mind and, in spite of Jesus Christ and occasional obeisances to anagogics, the closest to my own way of thinking. Complete objectivity requires a person who takes less pleasure in life than you do; you insist on finding something edifying in it. True, it is only in old age that one is converted to the grim heavenly pair λόγοζ χαὶ αυάγχη.*

With cordial greetings and thanks,
Yours,
Freud

PFISTER TO FREUD

Zürich,
1.4.1926

. . . I am taking the opportunity of sending you a just published book about a fashionable Indian miracle worker. You will perhaps be surprised at my taking so much trouble about a sterile subject, and I am even more surprised

---

*Ewen Bowie (of Corpus Christi College) reminds me that "λόγος" has a wide range of meanings. Here presumably it translates as "reason." He also pointed out to me that the last word should read ἀνάγκη. That is, the second letter should be nu, and not upsilon. The whole expression then translates as "reason and necessity."

Christopher Taylor (of Corpus Christi College) suggests that possibly Freud had in mind a fragment of the atomist Leucippus in the fifth century B.C. Taylor writes to me as follows: "The fragment of Leucippus (Diels-Kranz, *Die Fragmente der Vorsokratiker* 68 B 2) runs: 'Ouden chrēma matēn ginetai, alla panta ek logou te kai hup anangkēs.' [Nothing happens at random, but everything from a rational principle and by necessity.]"—B.A.F.

myself. I wrote an article denouncing the stupid belief people had in the fakir's superhuman claims, with the result that I was attacked, not just as if, like Luther, I had laid hands on the sacred person of the Pope, but as if I had made a bad smell in the Holy of Holies. Now these gentry have got their deserts. The saint is exposed like a prima donna extricated from a stinkbutt and the outcry his fanatical admirers are making is enough to make the devil sick. The freer Protestant circles are delighted at my disclosures. I wanted to strike a blow at superstition, stupidity and goggle-eyed self-abasement, but one should really spend one's time less unprofitably. One makes no real headway against the stink, and the worse the stink the more quickly do worth-while people seek fresh air. I assure you therefore that it is with the greater pleasure that I am returning to the analysis which predominates in the last part of my book. . . .

> *Berggasse 19,*
> *Vienna IX,*
> *11.4.1926*

Dear Dr Pfister,

I like to think of this letter's travelling to Sicily, which is prohibited to me.

I now lie down for an hour every day with a hot water bottle and am using the leisure to read the book about the Christian fakir[8] which your son brought. (I should have liked to have talked to him, but I am now supposed to take a great deal of rest and not see visitors.) The book amused me more than it pleased me. For myself I was glad that I have no religion and therefore do not find myself in the cleft stick which you cannot avoid. So far as you were concerned, I was sorry that you had to busy yourself with such (let us call it) muck. No doubt it will do good in some circles, or you would not have done it. All the same, it is a pity that even you could not be completely honest. You could not possibly count it a virtue of the psychopath that he made such fine speeches, the patterns for which have for a long time been available to all. But that seems to be the whole of his merit.

> *Yours,*
> *Freud*

PFISTER TO FREUD

> *Zürich,*
> *10.9.1926*

Dear Professor Freud,

I read through your kind gift[9] at one sitting and with great admiration. You have never before written in such a readily comprehensible fashion, yet everything springs from the depths. As one of your first lay pupils, the book gave me unspeakable pleasure. Only *one* lacuna struck me. You mention educational cases, but not the enormous number of adults who are not ill in the medical sense but are nevertheless in extreme need of analysis; I am thinking

---

[8] O. Pfister, *Die Legende Sundar Singhs*, Berne and Leipzig, 1926.
[9] *The Question of Lay Analysis* (1926). [*The Standard Edition* 20 (London: Hogarth Press, 1959)—B. A. F.]

of alcoholics, people with warped lives, those whose love life has gone astray, frustrated artists, etc. As all these come into the field of the cure of souls, I have a great deal to do with them, and I earnestly appeal to you to cast a benevolent glance at the analytic cure of souls, which is, after all, another of your children. Undoubtedly the cure of souls will one day be a recognised non-ecclesiastical and even non-religious calling. If only men can be made good and happy, with religion or without it, the Lord will assuredly smile approvingly at the work. . . .

It is a great grief to me that the theologians are so backward and wanting. I have now been at work for eighteen years. The educationists have accepted a great deal, and I hear on all sides that analysis is engaging more and more of their interest. But the theologians are too involved in stupid squabbles about principles to care very much about the mental well-being of the laity—or their own. All the same, it has not been all in vain. I am writing an article on Sigmund Freud for the big encyclopaedia *Die Religion in Geschichte und Gegenwart.* . . .

Semmering,
14.9.1926

Dear Dr Pfister,

I am glad that on the whole you like my pamphlet. But do not judge it as an objective, scientific piece; it is a piece of polemics written for a special occasion. Otherwise I should certainly not have omitted the application of analysis to the cure of souls. I considered doing so, but in Catholic Austria the idea of a 'churchman's' working with analysis is totally inconceivable, and I did not wish further to complicate the issue. Besides, my argument would not have benefited; the answer would have been that, if these spiritual gentlemen wished to use analysis, that was no affair of ours, they should apply for permission to their bishop. I am well aware that Catholic analysis exists in Germany, but it would hardly be possible in Austria.

In regard to your remark about the latency period, let me say that the setting aside of sexuality is often only partial, with the result that a certain amount of activity is maintained. That is very frequent, and there are also plenty of cases with which one would never have hit on the idea of a latency period at all. When one considers the events of the early period, a relative residue of sexual activity is nearly always to be detected. The opposite objection, that in savages there is no latency period, the consequence of which would be that the latter was not innate but a product of civilisation, seems to me to be interesting. I do not believe it to be correct, but the question can be settled only by new and extensive investigations (Malinowski).[10]

I know that your jubilee in the church is imminent. Allow me, though prematurely, to be one of those who will congratulate you.

With cordial greetings,
Yours,
Freud

[10]Bronislaw Malinowski (1881–1942), British anthropologist.

Berggasse 19,
Vienna IX,
16.10.1927

Dear Dr Pfister,

Thanks to your letters, I have been following with intelligible interest your triumphal progress through the Scandinavian countries. The very gratifying result must largely be attributed to your personality, because the resistance to analysis of these Scandinavians is particularly deep-rooted.

In the next few weeks a pamphlet of mine[11] will be appearing which has a great deal to do with you. I had been wanting to write it for a long time, and postponed it out of regard for you, but the impulse became too strong. The subject-matter—as you will easily guess—is my completely negative attitude to religion, in any form and however attenuated, and, though there can be nothing new to you in this, I feared, and still fear, that such a public profession of my attitude will be painful to you. When you have read it you must let me know what measure of toleration and understanding you are able to preserve for the hopeless pagan.

Always your cordially devoted
Freud

PFISTER TO FREUD

Zürich,
21.10.1927

. . . As for your anti-religious pamphlet, there is nothing new to me in your rejection of religion. I look forward to it with pleasurable anticipation. A powerful-minded opponent of religion is certainly of more service to it than a thousand useless supporters. In music, philosophy, and religion I go different ways from you. I have been unable to imagine that a public profession of what you believe could be painful to me; I have always believed that every man should state his honest opinion aloud and plainly. You have always been tolerant towards me, and am I to be intolerant of your atheism? If I frankly air my differences from you, you will certainly not take it amiss. Meanwhile my attitude is one of eager curiosity.

PFISTER TO FREUD

Zürich,
24.11.27

Dear Professor Freud,

If I express my sincere thanks for the warmth of your dedication, please do not regard it merely as a conventional reaction to a friendly gift. That you care for me a little gives me uncommon pleasure and makes me almost a little proud. As for what I think of your work, it is exactly as I foresaw. If anything surprised me, it is that I was so little surprised. You have the right to expect

---

[11]*The Future of an Illusion, The Standard Edition* 21 [London: Hogarth Press, 1961—B. A. F.].

complete frankness from me, and you know that neither my attitude to you nor my pleasure in psycho-analysis is in the slightest degree diminished by your rejection of religion. I have always emphasised that psycho-analysis is the most fruitful part of psychology, but is not the whole of the science of the mind, and still less a philosophy of life and the world. You are certainly of the same view.

I cannot have things out with you properly on the subject of religion because you completely reject philosophy, approach art in a way that differs from mine, and regard morality as something self-evident. I can understand an important natural scientist like Driesch,[12] who went over to philosophy after a long and successful career in experimental research, much better than one who merely abides by the data. 'Pure' experience is in my view a fiction in any event, and if we look at the history of the sciences we see how doubtful is the reality hidden behind our so-called experience. And even this mixture of illusion and truth that we call 'experience' we acquire only with the aid of trans-empirical assumptions. Conceptions such as causality, the aether, the atom, etc., are certainly saturated with much bigger contradictions than those of the theologians, and you know better than I do how natural laws have been uprooted by present-day physics. In my view there can be no such thing as a pure empiricist, and a man who sticks rigidly to the data is like a heart specialist who ignores the organism as a whole and its invisible laws, divisions of function, etc. Thus I have to find a place for the unconscious in mental life as a whole, and for the latter in society, the universe, and its trans-empirical realities. For this in the first place I require a theory of perception. If error is liable to creep into this, the same in your own opinion applies to you.

What you say about the contradictions of religious and theological thought you yourself describe as a repetition, a repetition psycho-analytically developed in depth, of long familiar ideas. But what surprises me is that you pay no regard to the voices of those defenders of religion who bring out those contradictions just as sharply and resolve them in a higher philosophical-religious context. Let me mention von Eucken, *Der Wahrheitsgehalt der Religion*, first edition, p. 274ff. Also Brunstäd, *Die Idee der Religion*, p. 256ff., concerns himself with conflicting values, and it is significant that deeply intelligent men have gone over from philosophy to theology. My friend Albert Schweitzer, the distinguished philosopher, professor of theology, organ virtuoso, etc., thinks just as pessimistically as you do about the optimistic-ethical interpretation of the world (*Kultur und Ethik*, Introduction, p. xiii); but in his view that is only the beginning of the real problem, and he does not shut himself off from insight into the philosophy of life of those without a philosophy of life. (*Verfall und Wiederaufbau der Kultur*, p. 53.)

Your substitute for religion is basically the idea of the eighteenth-century Enlightenment in proud modern guise. I must confess that, with all my pleasure in the advance of science and technique, I do not believe in the ade-

---

[12]Hans Driesch (1867–1941), Professor of Philosophy in Cologne and later Leipzig.

quacy and sufficiency of that solution of the problem of life. It is very doubtful whether, taking everything into account, scientific progress has made
men happier or better. According to the statistics, there are more criminals
among scholars than in the intellectual middle class, and the hopes that were
set on universal education have turned out to be illusory. Nietzsche summed
up your position in the words:

> The reader will have realised my purport; namely that there is
> always a metaphysical belief on which our belief in science rests—
> that we observers of to-day, atheists and anti-metaphysicians as we
> are, still draw our fire from the blaze lit by a belief thousands of
> years old, the Christian belief, which was also that of Plato, that
> God is truth and that the truth is divine. . . . But supposing that this
> grew less and less believable and nothing divine was left, save er-
> ror, blindness, lies?

I do not properly understand your outlook on life. It is impossible that
what you reject as the end of an illusion and value as the sole truth can be all.
A world without temples, the fine arts, poetry, religion, would in my view be
a devil's island to which men could have been banished, not by blind chance,
but only by Satan. In that case your pessimism about the wickedness of
mankind would be much too mild; you would have to follow it through to its
logical conclusion. If it were part of psycho-analytic treatment to present that
despoiled universe to our patients as the truth, I should well understand it if
the poor devils preferred remaining shut up in their illness to entering that
dreadful icy desolation.

Have you as much tolerance for this frank profession of faith as I have for
your long-familiar heresies? I hold it as a piece of good fortune that you had
to deprive yourself of so much in order to do such tremendous work in your
science (with which your faith or lack of faith has nothing whatever to do).
But allow me to add two questions. Would you agree to my dealing with your
views in *Imago*?* Perhaps I might be able to offer a little aid to many who
now, according to your own expectation, run the risk of rejecting the whole
of psycho-analysis, and thus I might be doing a service to the psycho-analytic
movement. . . .

Thus there remains between us the great difference that I practise analysis within a plan of life which you indulgently regard as servitude to my calling, while I regard this philosophy of life, not only as a powerful aid to
treatment (in the case of most people), but also as the logical consequence of
a philosophy that goes beyond naturalism and positivism, is well based on
moral and social hygiene, and is in accordance with the nature of mankind
and the world. In all this it is the patient's business to what extent he will
strike out on a road in harmony with his social and individual characteristics,
and the amount of aid he requires to find what is the right road for him depends on himself alone.

*A journal founded by Freud in 1911 for the publication of papers by analysts.—B. A. F.

Well, I have come to the end of a long letter. In writing it I have had your picture in front of me, listening to what I said with indulgence and friend-liness. I hope that speaking out like this has only strengthened our friend-ship. It has, has it not?

With cordial greetings,
Yours,
Pfister

Berggasse 19,
Vienna IX,
26.11.1927

Dear Dr Pfister,

You were quite right, there was no room for any surprises; you were pre-pared for what I had to say, and I for your disagreement. I might have been tempted to point out that the argument you are using is: This must be wrong because accepting it as the truth it would be too unpleasant, and that the difficulties of my position do nothing to strengthen yours. But that would not forward the argument, and would be only a repetition, because it is already in the little book, so I prefer to go on to your two questions, both of which are of practical importance.

To the best of my belief, we have already made up our minds on one of them. I attach importance to your publishing your criticism—in *Imago*, if you like—and I hope that in it you will specifically draw attention to our undisturbed friendship and your unshaken loyalty to analysis. Your second question involves issues which perhaps had better be separated out. Let us be quite clear on the point that the views expressed in my book form no part of analytic theory. They are my personal views, which coin-cide with those of many non-analysts and pre-analysts, but there are cer-tainly many excellent analysts who do not share them. If I drew on analysis for certain arguments—in reality only one argument—that need deter no-one from using the non-partisan method of analysis for arguing the oppo-site view. That too is mentioned in the little book. If it were argued that that was not so easy, for the practice of analysis necessarily led to the abandon-ment of religion, the reply would be that that was no less true of any other science.

The other issue, that of influencing analytic therapy by granting or re-fusing an illusory emotional satisfaction is, strictly speaking, irrelevant, be-cause, however warm-heartedly the analyst may behave, he cannot set himself up in the analysand's mind as a substitute for God and providence. If your authority complains about the dry tracing back of his aspirations to the father-son relationship, it must be pointed out to him that the analyst cannot satisfy this aspiration, but must leave it to the analysand either to overcome it after the explanation has been given to him or to satisfy it in a religious or any other sublimated fashion. The analyst can of course make a bad technical mistake if he creates the impression of belittling this emotional demand, or calls on everyone to overcome a piece of infantilism which only a few are ca-pable of overcoming.

The whole question is of great importance and requires a cool all-round assessment. Whether you will undertake it in connection with your criticism of the *Illusion* is a matter on which I do not want to influence you.

With cordial greetings,
Yours,
Freud

P.S. As you quoted statements by a number of important men on our problem, you will certainly be interested in what Bleuler wrote to me:

> I promptly devoured your *Future of an Illusion* and enjoyed it. Starting from quite different standpoints one comes to the identical conclusion, but your argument is not only particularly elegant, it of course goes to the heart of the matter. There is only one point on which I cannot agree with you. In your book civilisation and morality merge into a single concept, or at any rate the boundaries between them are largely obliterated. I cannot help making a sharp distinction between the two.

PFISTER TO FREUD

Zürich,
20.2.28

Dear Professor Freud,

This is the third week I have been in bed, and I am very annoyed that no-one has purloined and made off with my phlebitis. I have been using the rest chiefly to write my friendly criticism of you. I have been doing so with the greater pleasure because in it I do battle for a cause that is dear to me with an opponent who is the same. There is not much danger of your turning up for baptism or of my descending from the pulpit, but among the points that bring us closer to each other there are some which are very important, and when I reflect that you are much better and deeper than your disbelief, and that I am much worse and more superficial than my faith, I conclude that the abyss between us cannot yawn so grimly. While I wrote I saw your picture smiling indulgently at me, but all the same I felt in a very glad mood. I very much hope that you will not take amiss what I have to say; I even hope that in spite of my friendly attack on you you will derive a tiny little bit of pleasure from it.

I am sending you the manuscript to give you the opportunity of letting me know if anything strikes you as unsuitable for publication, or if you think I have done you an injustice on any point.

Our difference derives chiefly from the fact that you grew up in proximity to pathological forms of religion and regard these as 'religion', while I had the good fortune of being able to turn to a free form of religion which to you seems to be an emptying of Christianity of its content, while I regard it as the core and substance of evangelism. . . .

Berggasse 19,
Vienna IX,
24.2.1928

Dear Dr Pfister,

It is very unfair of fate to send you to your bed with phlebitis. Your active way of life, your mountain-climbing, should have assured your circulation better than that. But when is fate not unfair?

That provides the transition to your reply to me. It has already gone to the editorial office. It was very necessary that my *Illusion* should be answered from within our own circle, and it is very satisfactory that it should be done in such a worthy and friendly fashion.

What the effect on me was of what you have to say you have no need to ask. What is to be expected if one is judge in one's own cause? Some of your arguments seem to me to be poetical effusion, others, such as the enumeration of great minds who have believed in God, too cheap. It is unreasonable to expect science to produce a system of ethics—ethics are a kind of highway code for traffic among mankind—and the fact that in physics atoms which were yesterday assumed to be square are now assumed to be round is exploited with unjustified tendentiousness by all who are hungry for faith; so long as physics extends our dominion over nature, these changes ought to be a matter of complete indifference to you. And finally—let me be impolite for once—how the devil do you reconcile all that we experience and have to expect in this world with your assumption of a moral world order? I am curious about that, but you have no need to reply.

But enough of all such profundities. I regress to the unspeakably stupid but universal assumption of the omnipotence of thoughts and wish you a speedy recovery and resurrection.

Cordially,
Yours,
Freud

PFISTER TO FREUD

Zürich,
16.11.1928

. . . I have been very impressed at the attitude of the International Society's journal in the debate on *The Future of an Illusion*. Such non-partisanship is very creditable. If our opponents always tell us that analysts are pettier and more spiteful, more intolerant and more fanatical, than the unanalysed, this debate refutes them. To me the tussle with you has been stimulating and helpful. Let me again thank you cordially for your kindness. . . .

Berggasse 19,
Vienna IX,
25.11.1928

Dear Dr Pfister,

In your otherwise delightful letter there is one point I cavil at, namely your finding something surprising and gratifying in the attitude of the International Journal (editor and staff) on the subject of the *Illusion*.[13] Such 'toler-ance' is no merit.

In both works which have recently reached me from the publishing house, one of which contains a reprint of your *Discussion*,[14] I note with satisfaction what a long way we are able to go together in analysis. The rift, not in ana-lytic, but in scientific thinking which one comes on when the subject of God and Christ is touched on I accept as one of the logically untenable but psy-chologically only too intelligible irrationalities of life. In general I attach no value to the 'imitation of Christ'. In contrast to utterances as psychologically profound as 'Thy sins are forgiven thee; arise and walk' there are a large number of others which are conditioned exclusively by the time, psychologi-cally impossible, useless for our lives. Besides, the above statement calls for analysis. If the sick man had asked: 'How knowest thou that my sins are for-given?' the answer could only have been: 'I, the Son of God, forgive thee'. In other words, a call for unlimited transference. And now, just suppose I said to a patient: 'I, Professor Sigmund Freud, forgive thee thy sins'. What a fool I should make of myself. To the former case the principle applies that analysis is not satisfied with success produced by suggestion, but investigates the ori-gin of and justification for the transference.

I do not know if you have detected the secret link between the *Lay Analy-sis* and the *Illusion*. In the former I wish to protect analysis from the doctors and in the latter from the priests. I should like to hand it over to a profession which does not yet exist, a profession of *lay* curers of souls who need not be doctors and should not be priests.

Cordially,
Your old friend,
Freud

PFISTER TO FREUD

Zürich,
9.2.29

. . . Please allow me to return to your remark that the analysts you would like to see should not be priests. It seems to me that analysis as such must be a purely 'lay' affair. By its very nature it is essentially private and directly yields no higher values. In innumerable cases I have done nothing but this negative work, without ever mentioning a word about religion. The Good Samaritan also preached no sermons, and it would be tasteless to have a suc-cessful treatment paid for in retrospect by religious obligations. Just as Protestantism abolished the difference between laity and clergy, so must the cure of souls be laicised and secularised. Even the most bigoted must admit that the love of God is not limited by the whiff of incense.

However, it seems to me that not only children but adults very frequently have an inner need of positive values of a spiritual nature, of ethics and a phi-

[13]O. Pfister, *Die Illusion einer Zukunft*, Imago, 1928.
[14]Title not identifiable.

losophy of life, and these, as Hartmann[15] has recently so elegantly demonstrated, psycho-analysis cannot supply. Indeed, there are many who need ethical considerations, which they are not willing to modify merely by way of the transference, in order to be able to cope with their pathogenic moral conflicts. If no priest should analyse, neither should any Christian or any religious or morally deep-thinking individual, and you yourself emphasise that analysis is independent of philosophy of life. Disbelief is after all nothing but a negative belief. I do not believe that psycho-analysis eliminates art, philosophy, religion, but that it helps to purify and refine them. Forgive a long-standing enthusiast for art and humanitarianism and an old servant of God. Your marvellous life's work and your goodness and gentleness, which are somehow an incarnation of the meaning of existence, lead me to the deepest springs of life. I am not content to do scientific research on their banks, but have to drink and draw strength from them. Goethe's *Wenn ihr's nicht fühlt, ihr könnt es nicht erjagen*[16] is still valid, and will always be. At school my cleverest master used to say that music was a pitiful row. I did not try to convert him, but took refuge in Beethoven and Schubert. At heart you serve exactly the same purpose as I, and act 'as if' there were a purpose and meaning in life and the universe, and I with my feeble powers can only fit your brilliant analytical discoveries and healing powers into that gap. Do you really wish to exclude from analytical work a 'priesthood' understood in this sense? I do not believe that that is what you mean. . . .

> *Berggasse 19,*
> *Vienna IX,*
> *16.2.1929*

Dear Dr Pfister,

My remark that the analysts of my phantasy of the future should not be priests does not sound very tolerant, I admit. But you must consider that I was referring to a very distant future. For the present I put up with doctors, so why not priests too? You are quite right to point out that analysis leads to no new philosophy of life, but it has no need to, for it rests on the general scientific outlook, with which the religious outlook is incompatible. For the point of view of the latter it is immaterial whether Christ, Buddha, or Confucius is regarded as the ideal of human conduct and held up as an example to imitate. Its essence is the pious illusion of providence and a moral world order, which are in conflict with reason. But priests will remain bound to stand for them. It is of course possible to take advantage of the human right to be irrational and go some way with analysis and then stop, rather on the pattern of Charles Darwin, who used to go regularly to church on Sundays. I cannot honestly see that any difficulties are created by patients' demands for ethical values; ethics are not based on an external world order but on the inescapable exigencies of human cohabitation. I do not believe that I behave as if there were 'one life, one meaning in life,' that was an excessively friendly

---

[15]Dr Heinz Hartmann, formerly of Vienna, now of New York [a well-known psychoanalyst.— B. A. F.]

[16]'If you cannot feel it, you will never lay hold of it.'

thought on your part, and it always reminds me of the monk who insisted on regarding Nathan as a thoroughly good Christian. I am a long way from being Nathan, but of course I cannot help remaining 'good' towards you.

Cordially yours,
Freud

Berggasse 19,
Vienna IX,
23.2.1929

Dear Dr Pfister,

I know how lonely you must feel now that such a long period of life together has been cut short,[17] and in all friendship and sympathy I clasp your hand.

Yours,
Freud

---

[17]The reference is to the death of Pfister's first wife.

15

SIGMUND FREUD

The Question of a Weltanschauung

LADIES AND GENTLEMEN,—At our last meeting we were occupied with little everyday concerns—putting our own modest house in order, as it were. I propose that we should now take a bold leap and venture upon answering a question which is constantly being asked in other quarters: does psycho-analysis lead to a particular *Weltanschauung*[1] and, if so, to which?

'*Weltanschauung*' is, I am afraid, a specifically German concept, the translation of which into foreign languages might well raise difficulties. If I try to give you a definition of it, it is bound to seem clumsy to you. In my opinion, then a *Weltanschauung* is an intellectual construction which solves all the problems of our existence uniformly on the basis of one overriding hypothesis, which, accordingly, leaves no question unanswered and in which every-

The footnotes in brackets in this chapter are by the editor of *The Standard Edition*.—B. A. F.

Reprinted from *New Introductory Lectures on Psychoanalysis* by Sigmund Freud, Translated from the German and Edited by James Strachey. By permission of W. W. Norton & Company, Inc. Copyright © 1965, 1964 by James Strachey. Copyright 1933 by Sigmund Freud. Copyright renewed 1961 by W. J. H. Sprott.

From *The Standard Edition of the Complete Psychological Works of Sigmund Freud*, Vol. XXII, Edited and translated by James Strachey. Reprinted by permission of Sigmund Freud Copyrights Ltd., The Institute of Psycho-Analysis, and The Hogarth Press. Published by Basic Books Inc., by arrangement with The Hogarth Press and The Institute of Psycho-Analysis, London. Reprinted by permission.

[1][This word might be translated 'A View of the Universe', but Freud himself explains its meaning in the second paragraph below. As it appears more than thirty times in the course of this lecture, the simplest plan seems to be to leave it in German; and in any case it has almost naturalized itself in our language. Freud had already approached the topic of this lecture in a passage at the end of Chapter II of *Inhibitions, Symptoms and Anxiety* (1926d).]

thing that interests us finds its fixed place. It will easily be understood that the possession of a *Weltanschauung* of this kind is among the ideal wishes of human beings. Believing in it one can feel secure in life, one can know what to strive for, and how one can deal most expediently with one's emotions and interests.

If that is the nature of a *Weltanschauung*, the answer as regards psychoanalysis is made easy. As a specialist science, a branch of psychology—a depth-psychology or psychology of the unconscious—it is quite unfit to construct a *Weltanschauung* of its own: it must accept the scientific one. But the *Weltanschauung* of science already departs noticeably from our definition. It is true that it too assumes the *uniformity* of the explanation of the universe; but it does so only as a programme, the fulfilment of which is relegated to the future. Apart from this it is marked by negative characteristics, by its limitation to what is at the moment knowable and by its sharp rejection of certain elements that are alien to it. It asserts that there are no sources of knowledge of the universe other than the intellectual working-over of carefully scrutinized observations—in other words, what we call research—and alongside of it no knowledge derived from revelation, intuition or divination. It seems as though this view came very near to being generally recognized in the course of the last few centuries that have passed; and it has been left to *our* century to discover the presumptuous objection that a *Weltanschauung* like this is alike paltry and cheerless, that it overlooks the claims of the human intellect and the needs of the human mind.

This objection cannot be too energetically repudiated. It is quite without a basis, since the intellect and the mind are objects for scientific research in exactly the same way as any non-human things. Psycho-analysis has a special right to speak for the scientific *Weltanschauung* at this point, since it cannot be reproached with having neglected what is mental in the picture of the universe. Its contribution to science lies precisely in having extended research to the mental field. And, incidentally, without such a psychology science would be very incomplete. If, however, the investigation of the intellectual and emotional functions of men (and of animals) is included in science, then it will be seen that nothing is altered in the attitude of science as a whole, that no new sources of knowledge or methods of research have come into being. Intuition and divination would be such, if they existed; but they may safely be reckoned as illusions, the fulfilments of wishful impulses. It is easy to see, too, that these demands upon a *Weltanschauung* are only based on emotion. Science takes notice of the fact that the human mind produces these demands and is ready to examine their sources; but it has not the slightest reason to regard them as justified. On the contrary it sees this as a warning carefully to separate from knowledge everything that is illusion and an outcome of emotional demands like these.

This does not in the least mean that these wishes are to be pushed contemptuously on one side or their value for human life under-estimated. We are ready to trace out the fulfilments of them which they have created for themselves in the products of art and in the systems of religion and philosophy; but we cannot nevertheless overlook the fact that it would be illegitimate and highly inexpedient to allow these demands to be transferred to the sphere of knowledge. For this would be to lay open the paths which lead to psychosis, whether to individual or group psychosis, and would withdraw valuable amounts of energy from endeavours which are directed towards reality in order, so far as possible, to find satisfaction in it for wishes and needs.

From the standpoint of science one cannot avoid exercising one's critical faculty here and proceeding with rejections and dismissals. It is not permissible to declare that science is one field of human mental activity and that religion and philosophy are others, at least its equal in value, and that science has no business to interfere with the other two: that they all have an equal claim to be true and that everyone is at liberty to choose from which he will draw his convictions and in which he will place his belief. A view of this kind is regarded as particularly superior, tolerant, broad-minded and free from illiberal prejudices. Unfortunately it is not tenable and shares all the pernicious features of an entirely unscientific *Weltanschauung* and is equivalent to one in practice. It is simply a fact that the truth cannot be tolerant, that it admits of no compromises or limitations, that research regards every sphere of human activity as belonging to it and that it must be relentlessly critical if any other power tries to take over any part of it.

Of the three powers which may dispute the basic position of science, religion alone is to be taken seriously as an enemy. Art is almost always harmless and beneficent; it does not seek to be anything but an illusion. Except for a few people who are spoken of as being 'possessed' by art, it makes no attempt at invading the realm of reality. Philosophy is not opposed to science, it behaves like a science and works in part by the same methods; it departs from it, however, by clinging to the illusion of being able to present a picture of the universe which is without gaps and is coherent, though one which is bound to collapse with every fresh advance in our knowledge. It goes astray in its method by over-estimating the epistemological value of our logical operations and by accepting other sources of knowledge such as intuition. And it often seems that the poet's derisive comment is not unjustified when he says of the philosopher:

> Mit seinen Nachtmützen und Schlafrockfetzen
> Stopft er die Lücken des Weltenbaus.[2]

---

[2][Heine, 'Die Heimkehr', LVIII. Literally: 'With his nightcaps and the tatters of his dressing-gown he patches up the gaps in the structure of the universe.' The lines were favourite ones with Freud. He alluded to them in connection with the secondary revision of dreams in Chapter VI (I) of *The Interpretation of Dreams* (1900), and again in a letter to Jung of February 25, 1908. Many years earlier he had quoted them in full in a letter to his future wife, apparently in 1883.]

But philosophy has no direct influence on the great mass of mankind; it is of interest to only a small number even of the top layer of intellectuals and is scarcely intelligible to anyone else. On the other hand, religion is an immense power which has the strongest emotions of human beings at its service. It is well known that at an earlier date it comprised everything that played an intellectual part in men's lives, that it took the place of science when there was scarcely yet such a thing as science, and that it constructed a *Weltanschauung*, consistent and self-contained to an unparalleled degree, which, although it has been profoundly shaken, persists to this day.

If we are to give an account of the grandiose nature of religion, we must bear in mind what it undertakes to do for human beings. It gives them information about the origin and coming into existence of the universe, it assures them of its protection and of ultimate happiness in the ups and downs of life and it directs their thoughts and actions by precepts which it lays down with its whole authority. Thus it fulfils three functions. With the first of them it satisfies the human thirst for knowledge; it does the same thing that science attempts to do with *its* means, and at that point enters into rivalry with it. It is to its second function that it no doubt owes the greatest part of its influence. Science can be no match for it when it soothes the fear that men feel of the dangers and vicissitudes of life, when it assures them of a happy ending and offers them comfort in unhappiness. It is true that science can teach us how to avoid certain dangers and that there are some sufferings which it can successfully combat; it would be most unjust to deny that it is a powerful helper to men; but there are many situations in which it must leave a man to his suffering and can only advise him to submit to it. In its third function, in which it issues precepts and lays down prohibitions and restrictions, religion is furthest away from science. For science is content to investigate and to establish facts, though it is true that from its applications rules and advice are derived on the conduct of life. In some circumstances these are the same as those offered by religion, but, when this is so, the reasons for them are different.

The convergence between these three aspects of religion is not entirely clear. What has an explanation of the origin of the universe to do with the inculcation of certain particular ethical precepts? The assurances of protection and happiness are more intimately linked with the ethical requirements. They are the reward for fulfilling these commands; only those who obey them may count upon these benefits, punishment awaits the disobedient. Incidentally, something similar is true of science. Those who disregard its lessons, so it tells us, expose themselves to injury.

The remarkable combination in religion of instruction, consolation and requirements can only be understood if it is subjected to a genetic analysis. This may be approached from the most striking point of the aggregate, from its instruction on the origin of the universe; for why, we may ask, should a cosmogony be a regular component of religious systems? The doctrine is, then, that the universe was created by a being resembling a man, but magnified in every respect, in power, wisdom, and the strength of his passions—an idealized super-man. Animals as creators of the universe point to the influence of totemism, upon which we shall have a few words at least to say presently. It is an interesting fact that this creator is always only a single being, even when there are believed to be many gods. It is interesting, too, that the creator is usually a man, though there is far from being a lack of indications of female deities; and some mythologies actually make the creation begin with a male god getting rid of a female deity,[3] who is degraded into being a monster. Here the most interesting problems of detail open out; but we must hurry on. Our further path is made easy to recognize, for this god-creator is undisguisedly called 'father'. Psycho-analysis infers that he really is the father, with all the magnificence in which he once appeared to the small child. A religious man pictures the creation of the universe just as he pictures his own origin.

This being so, it is easy to explain how it is that consoling assurances and strict ethical demands are combined with a cosmogony. For the same person to whom the child owed his existence, the father (or more correctly, no doubt, the parental agency compounded of the father and mother), also protected and watched over him in his feeble and helpless state, exposed as he was to all the dangers lying in wait in the external world; under his father's protection he felt safe. When a human being has himself grown up, he knows, to be sure, that he is in possession of greater strength, but his insight into the perils of life has also grown greater, and he rightly concludes that fundamentally he still remains just as helpless and unprotected as he was in his childhood, that faced by the world he is still a child. Even now, therefore, he cannot do without the protection which he enjoyed as a child. But he has long since recognized, too, that his father is a being of narrowly restricted power, and not equipped with every excellence. He therefore harks back to the mnemic image of the father whom in his childhood he so greatly overvalued. He exalts the image into a deity and makes it into something contemporary and real. The effective strength of this mnemic image and the persistence of his need for protection jointly sustain his belief in God.

The third main item in the religious programme, the ethical demand, also fits into this childhood situation with ease. I may remind you of Kant's famous pronouncement in which he names, in a single breath, the starry heavens and the moral law within us. However strange this juxtaposition may sound—for what have the heavenly bodies to do with the question of whether one human creature loves another or kills him?—it nevertheless touches on a great psychological truth. The same father (or parental agency) which gave the child life and guarded him against its perils, taught him as well what he might do and what he must leave undone, instructed him that he must adapt himself to certain restrictions on his instinctual wishes, and made him understand what regard he was expected to have for his parents and brothers and sisters, if he wanted to become a tolerated and welcome member of the family circle and

---

[3][Freud had considerably more to say about female deities in Essay III, Part I, Section D, of *Moses and Monotheism* (1939).]

later on of larger associations. The child is brought up to a knowledge of his social duties by a system of loving rewards and punishments, he is taught that his security in life depends on his parents (and afterwards other people) loving him and on their being able to believe that he loves them. All these relations are afterwards introduced by men unaltered into their religion. Their parents' prohibitions and demands persist within them as a moral conscience. With the help of this same system of rewards and punishments, God rules the world of men. The amount of protection and happy satisfaction assigned to an individual depends on his fulfilment of the ethical demands; his love of God and his consciousness of being loved by God are the foundations of the security with which he is armed against the dangers of the external world and of his human environment. Finally, in prayer he has assured himself a direct influence on the divine will and with it a share in the divine omnipotence.

The scientific spirit, strengthened by the observation of natural processes, has begun, in the course of time, to treat religion as a human affair and to submit it to a critical examination. Religion was not able to stand up to this. What first gave rise to suspicion and scepticism were its tales of miracles, for they contradicted everything that had been taught by sober observation and betrayed too clearly the influence of the activity of the human imagination. After this its doctrines explaining the origin of the universe met with rejection, for they gave evidence of an ignorance which bore the stamp of ancient times and to which, thanks to their increased familiarity with the laws of nature, people knew they were superior. The idea that the universe came into existence through acts of copulation or creation analogous to the origin of individual people had ceased to be the most obvious and self-evident hypothesis since the distinction between animate creatures with a mind and an inanimate Nature had impressed itself on human thought—a distinction which made it impossible to retain belief in the original animism. Nor must we overlook the influence of the comparative study of different religious systems and the impression of their mutual exclusiveness and intolerance.

Strengthened by these preliminary exercises, the scientific spirit gained enough courage at last to venture on an examination of the most important and emotionally valuable elements of the religious *Weltanschauung*. People may always have seen, though it was long before they dared to say so openly, that the pronouncements of religion promising men protection and happiness if they would only fulfil certain ethical requirements had also shown themselves unworthy of belief. It seems not to be the case that there is a Power in the universe which watches over the well-being of individuals with parental care and brings all their affairs to a happy ending. On the contrary, the destinies of mankind can be brought into harmony neither with the hypothesis of a Universal Benevolence nor with the partly contradictory one of a Universal Justice. Earthquakes, tidal waves, conflagrations, make no distinction between the virtuous and pious and the scoundrel or unbeliever. Even where what is in question is not inanimate Nature but where an individual's fate depends on his relations to other people, it is by no means the rule that virtue is rewarded and that evil finds its punishment. Often enough the violent, cunning or ruthless man seizes the envied good things of the world and the pious man goes away empty. Obscure, unfeeling and unloving powers determine men's fate; the system of rewards and punishments which religion ascribes to the government of the universe seems not to exist.

The last contribution to the criticism of the religious *Weltanschauung* was effected by psycho-analysis, by showing how religion originated from the helplessness of children and by tracing its contents to the survival into maturity of the wishes and needs of childhood. This did not precisely mean a contradiction of religion, but it was nevertheless a necessary rounding-off of our knowledge about it, and in one respect at least it was a contradiction, for religion itself lays claim to a divine origin. And, to be sure, it is not wrong in this, provided that our interpretation of God is accepted.

In summary, therefore, the judgement of science on the religious *Weltanschauung* is this. While the different religions wrangle with one another as to which of them is in possession of the truth, our view is that the question of the truth of religious beliefs may be left altogether on one side. Religion is an attempt to master the sensory world in which we are situated by means of the wishful world which we have developed within us as a result of biological and psychological necessities. But religion cannot achieve this. Its doctrines bear the imprint of the times in which they arose, the ignorant times of the childhood of humanity. Its consolations deserve no trust. Experience teaches us that the world is no nursery. The ethical demands on which religion seeks to lay stress need, rather, to be given another basis; for they are indispensable to human society and it is dangerous to link obedience to them with religious faith. If we attempt to assign the place of religion in the evolution of mankind, it appears not as a permanent acquisition but as a counterpart to the neurosis which individual civilized men have to go through in their passage from childhood to maturity.[4]

---

[4][The possibility of society suffering from neuroses analogous to individual ones was mentioned by Freud in Chapter VIII of *The Future of an Illusion* (1927c), and near the end of *Civilization and its Discontents* (1930a). He discussed it at much greater length in Essay III, Part I, Section C of *Moses and Monotheism* (1939a). The analogy between religious practices and obsessive actions had been pointed out much earlier (Freud, 1907b).]

BIBLIOGRAPHY

THE LITERATURE ON psychoanalysis is so vast that a selection of items from it is bound to be somewhat arbitrary and to reflect the views and interests of the bibliographer. This is especially true when the bibliography is like the one given here, in being short and far from all-embracing. It should be noted that some of the references listed here are also mentioned in the Notes to the Introduction.

Freud's work has been brought together in *The Standard Edition* of *The Complete Psychological Works of Sigmund Freud*, edited by James Strachey (London: Hogarth Press, 1953–1974). In references this is usually given as *S.E.* But not all Freud's writings are contained in the *S.E.* Thus, his letters to Wilhelm Fliess are not there, only a selection from them—letters which reveal much about his early thought. These can be found in *The Complete Letters of Sigmund Freud to Wilhelm Fliess*, 1887–1904, translated and edited by J. M. Masson (Cambridge, Mass., and London: Belnap Press of Harvard University Press, 1985). Likewise, Freud's correspondence with Oskar Pfister is not in the *S.E.*

For an account of Freud's life, the obvious source is the biography by Ernest Jones, *Sigmund Freud: Life and Work*, three Volumes (London: Hogarth Press, 1953–1957). Jones was a close early associate of Freud, and casts him in the mold of "a hero" who made "great discoveries." Peter Gay's *Freud—A Life for Our Time* (New York: Norton, 1988) is a more recent comprehensive biography based on many sources not available to Jones. When we put Freud back into his historical context, it is now widely agreed that most of Freud's ideas were not particularly original, and that there were others in the field thinking along similar lines. Freud's originality appears to have lain in the ways he brought current ideas together and elaborated them, in the development of psychoanalytic method, for therapy and research, and in the movement he founded to defend and propagate his ideas. All this is brought out in two fundamental works: H. F. Ellenberger's *The Discovery of the Unconscious* (New York: Basic Books, 1970) and F. J. Sulloway's *Freud: Biologist of the Mind* (New York and London: Basic Books and Burnett Books Ltd., 1979). The movement Freud founded gave rise to the tradition of psychoanalysis with which this book is concerned. Unfortunately, we cannot form a confident and rounded judgment about Freud and his work until the Freud archive is opened to scholarly study.

Freud's work, and that of his associates, also gave rise to a number of other theoretical orientations and methods of psychotherapy of the insight type. The first of these were the traditions associated with the work of Carl Jung and Alfred Adler. For the former see *The Collected Works of C. G. Jung*, twenty volumes, edited by H. Read, M. Fordham, and G. Adler (London: Routledge and Kegan Paul, 1957–1979); *Supplementary Volume A*, edited by W. M. McGuire (London: Routledge and Kegan Paul, 1983); and *Dream Analysis*, edited by W. M. McGuire (London: Routledge and Kegan Paul, 1984). Alfred Adler's chief contributions can be found in the following works: *A Study of Organ Inferiority and its Psychical Compensation* (1907), translated by Smith Ely Jeliffe (New York: Nervous and Mental Disease Publishing Company, 1917); *The Neurotic Constitution* (1912), translated by B. Gluck and J. E. Lind (New York: Kegan Paul, 1917; London: Kegan Paul, 1921); and *Understanding Human Nature* (1921), translated by W. Beran Wolfe (London: Allen and Unwin, 1928).

For an account of the history of psychoanalysis up to Freud's death, see: P. Roazen, *Freud and His Followers* (New York: Alfred A. Knopf, 1975; and London: Allen Lane, 1976).

In recent decades different orientations and methods of psychotherapy have burgeoned vigorously. For example, T. B. Karasu, in "Psychotherapies: An Overview," *The American Journal of Psychiatry* 134:8 (1977), 851–863. This author lists about fifty theoretical orientations and therapies, twenty of which are in the psychodynamic tradition which stems from Freud. For an introductory survey, see S. Bloch, *What Is Psychotherapy?* (Oxford: Oxford University Press, 1982). In view of the development of different orientations and methods, it is understandably difficult, if not impossible, to arrive at a set of criteria that would be generally accepted as defining a psychoanalytic theory or method of treatment.

Freud wrote a very great deal but he did not set out to produce a systematic corpus of writing for the benefit of philosophers. Hence the interpretation of his texts is not infrequently a difficult matter and a task for specialists. This is shown in M. Gill, "Topography and Systems in Psychoanalytic Theory," *Psychological Issues* Monograph 10 (New York: International Universities Press, 1963). The student should be cautioned against jumping to conclusions about what Freud did, or did not, say and believe.

The literature of psychoanalysis is full of technical terms. A dictionary can be of help in understanding them. See C. Rycroft, *A Critical Dictionary of Psychoanalysis* (London: Nelson, 1968).

Some of the papers collected in this volume have brought out that Freud's theory also has a complex and uncertain character logically. A short, overall look at this aspect of the theory can be found in E. Nagel, "Methodological Issues in Psychoanalytic Theory," in *Psychoanalysis, Scientific Method, and Philosophy*, edited by S. Hook (New York: New York University Press, 1959). This volume contains a number of contributions of importance. An "eliminative" view of Freud's theoretical account is given by A. MacIntyre in *The Unconscious* (London: Routledge and Kegan Paul, 1958). A different view of Freud's metapsychology, and an examination of Nagel's argument, is contained in B. A. Farrell, *The Standing of Psychoanalysis* (Oxford: Oxford University Press, 1981). The subject has been recently discussed by P. Kitcher and K. Wilkes in "What Is Freud's Metapsychology?" in *The Aristotelian Society, Supp. Vol. LXII*, The Aristotelian Society, 1988. An "existentialist" account of "self-deception," and of Freud's view of defense and the unconscious, is presented by H. Fingarette in *Self-Deception* (London: Routledge and Kegan Paul, 1969). D. Pears's *Motivated Irrationality* (Oxford: Oxford University Press, 1969) contains an acute examination of Freud's attempt to explain such conduct. I. Dilman's *Freud and the Mind* (Oxford: Blackwell, 1984) contains a sympathetic presentation of Freud's central notions and a discussion of their bearing on the questions of free will and determinism.

Some thinkers have taken the view that Freud was wrong to regard his work as a contribution to psychological medicine, to psychiatry and to psychological science. For, they claim, the analyst is faced by the data of the clinical, therapeutic situation, and these come to him in the language of reasons, intentions (meaning "the patient's wishes"), and so on. It is argued that his discourse is different in kind from the language of Freud's metapsychology and natural science; and it cannot be brought within this language. This general view can be found in the following works among others: J. Habermas, *Knowledge and Human Interests*, translated by J. Shapiro (London: Heinemann, 1972); P. Ricoeur, *Freud and Philosophy*, translated by D. Savage (New Haven and London: Yale University Press, 1970); R. Schafer, *A New Language for Psychoanalysis* (New Haven: Yale University Press, 1976). This view of psychoanalysis is criticized in A. Grünbaum, *The Foundations of Psychoanalysis* (Berkeley: University of California Press, 1984); and in M. Moore, "Mind, Brain and Unconscious," chapter 6 in *Mind, Psychoanalysis and Science*, edited by P. Clark and C. Wrights (Oxford and New York: Blackwell, 1988). This volume contains a number of relevant papers, most of them by philosophers. N. Mackay, in *Motivation and Explanation* (Madison, Conn.: International Universities Press, 1989) presents a robust defense of Freud as offering a causal theory of mind, in which there is no unbridgeable gulf between talking about meaning and about causes.

The issues which are perhaps of chief concern to practicing analysts and psychotherapists at the present time are epistemological; and these issues are closely bound up with the nature of the analytical process. These questions are discussed in the following publications: S. Freud, "Constructions in Analysis" (1937), *The Standard Edition* 23 (London: Hogarth Press, 1964); L. Paul, editor, *Psychoanalytic Clinical Interpretation* (London and New York: Free Press of Glencoe, 1963); H. Ezriel, "Experimentation within the psycho-analytic session," *The British Journal for the Philosophy of Science*, 1956–1957, pp. 29–48; B. A. Farrell, "Criteria for a Psychoanalytic Interpretation," in *The Philosophy of Mind*, edited by J. C. Glover (Oxford: Oxford University Press, 1976); L. H. Levy, *Psychological Interpretation* (New York: Holt, Rinehart and Winston, 1963); M. Eagle, "Psychoanalytic Interpretations: Veridicality and Therapeutic Effectiveness," *Nous* 14:3 (September 1980), 405–425; E. Peterfreund, *The Process of Psychoanalytic Therapy* (Hillsdale, New Jersey, and London: Analytic Press, Lawrence Erlbaum, 1983); H. Thomä and H. Kachele, *Psychoanalytic Practice*, 1, *Principles* (Berlin: Springer-Verlag, 1985); and M. Edelson, *Hypothesis and Evidence in Psychoanalysis* (Chicago and London: University of Chicago Press, 1984).

It is generally agreed that the chief support for psychoanalytic theory and the whole orientation is to be found in the case material, and this has been extensively examined from different points of view: E. Glover, "Research Methods in Psychoanalysis," *International Journal of Psychoanalysis* 33 (1952): 403–409; J. D. Frank, *Persuasion and Healing* (Oxford: Oxford University Press, 1961); R. S. Wallerstein, *Psychotherapy and Psychoanalysis* (New York: International Universities Press, 1975), for a criticism of the method of informal case study; M. Sherwood, *The Logic of Explanation in Psychoanalysis* (New York and London: Academic Press, 1969); B. A. Farrell, *The Standing of Psychoanalysis*, chapter 6 (Oxford: Oxford University Press, 1981); D. Spence, *Narrative Truth and Historical Truth* (New York: Norton, 1982); A. Grünbaum, *The Foundations of Psychoanalysis* (Berkeley: University of California Press, 1984); M. Edelson, *Psychoanalysis: A Theory in Crisis* (London and Chicago: University of Chicago Press, 1988), for a reasonable defense of case studies and a reply to Grünbaum; and K. M. Colby and R. T. Stoller, *Cognitive Science and Psychoanalysis* (Hillsdale, New Jersey, and London: Lawrence Erlbaum, 1988), for the fundamental problem of getting at the data that case studies are supposed to provide. For an example of a scientific way of studying psychoanalytically oriented psychotherapy, see L. Luborsky, *Principles of Psychoanalytic Psychotherapy* (New York: Basic Books, 1984); and in *Understanding Transference: The CCRT Method* (New York: Basic Books, 1990), L. Luborsky and P. Crits-Cristoph present an admirable example of how objective methods can be used to explore transference, and to investigate Freud's main suggestions about it.

The weakness of the evidence provided by the case material stimulated interest in the scientific investigation of psychoanalytic claims. This issue is discussed in S. Fisher and R. P. Greenberg, *The Scientific Credibility of*

Freud's Theories and Therapy (New York: Basic Books, 1977); S. Fisher and R. P. Greenberg, editors, *The Scientific Evaluation of Freud's Theories and Therapy* (New York: Basic Books, 1978); P. Kline, *Fact and Fantasy in Freudian Theory*, second edition (London and New York: Methuen, 1981); and H. J. Eysenck and G. D. Wilson, editors, *The Experimental Study of Freudian Theories* (London: Methuen, 1973). The student would be well advised to interpret the results of these studies with caution. For objective psychological methods of inquiry are apt to be weak and crude, when considered in relation to the psychological subtleties that psychoanalytic theory and generalizations purport to be about. Psychoanalysis has also stimulated some social anthropologists to take a fresh look at some of the material in their field: W. N. Stephens, *The Oedipus Complex Hypothesis: Cross-cultural Evidence* (New York: Free Press of Glencoe, 1962); M. E. Spiro, *Oedipus in the Trobriands* (Chicago: University of Chicago Press, 1982). The latter contains an examination of the classic critique by a social anthropologist of the hypothesis of the Oedipus complex namely, B. Malinowski, *Sex and Repression in Savage Society* (London: Routledge and Kegan Paul, 1927).

Psychoanalysts are also troubled by another question which is closely related to the epistemological problem of evidence and justification. How do they explain, and deal with, the proliferation of psychoanalytic traditions and ways of talking? See R. L. Munroe, *Schools of Psychoanalytic Thought* (London: Hutchinson Medical Publications, 1957). For recent attempts to deal with the problem of proliferation, see M. N. Eagle, *Recent Developments in Psychoanalysis: A Critical Evaluation* (New York: McGraw-Hill, 1984); and Stephen A. Mitchell, *Relational Concepts in Psychoanalysis: An Integration* (Cambridge, Mass., and London: Harvard University Press, 1988). For some implications of psychotherapeutic work and its different traditions, see R. J. Lifton, "Advocacy and Corruption in the Healing Professions," *International Review of Psychoanalysis* 3 (1976):385–398.

The therapeutic efficacy of psychoanalysis has been the subject of considerable inquiry and discussion in recent decades. This discussion, however, has taken place in the context of the wider discussion about the efficacy of psychotherapy in general. I choose a mere handful of readings from the hundreds of references available on this subject: H. J. Eysenck, "The Effects of Psychotherapy: An Evaluation," *J. Consulting Psychol.* 16:5 (1952), 319–324; M. J. Lambert, David A. Schapiro, and Allen E. Bergin, "The Effectiveness of Psychotherapy," chapter 5 in *Handbook of Psychotherapy and Behaviour Change*, third Edition, edited by S. L. Garfield and A. E. Bergin (New York: Wiley, 1986); R. B. Sloane et al., *Psychotherapy versus Behaviour Therapy* (Cambridge, Mass., and London: Harvard University Press, 1975); M. Shepherd, "What Price Psychotherapy?" *British Medical Journal* 288:6420 (1984), 809–810; S. Bloch and M. J. Lambert, "What Price Psychotherapy? A Rejoinder," *British Journal of Psychiatry* 146 (1955), 96–98.

Some idea of the attitude of psychiatrists in the United States to psychoanalysis can be obtained from: S. Arieti, editor, *American Handbook of Psychi-*

atry, second edition, volumes 1–6 (New York: Basic Books, 1976). This work is strongly colored by the notions of psychoanalysis. Perhaps a more accurate picture is presented in H. I. Kaplan and B. J. Sadock, editor, *Comprehensive Textbook of Psychiatry*, fourth edition (Baltimore: Williams and Wilkins, 1985). For Great Britain, see M. Shepherd, editor, *Handbook of Psychiatry*, volumes 1–5 (Cambridge: Cambridge University Press, 1982–1985); and also M. Gelder, D. Gath, and R. Mayou, *Oxford Textbook of Psychiatry*, Second Edition (Oxford: Oxford University Press, 1989). The latter is a work in which, in my view, the authors give a very fair account of the place that psychoanalysis occupies at the present time in psychiatric thought and practice in Great Britain.

It hardly needs to be said that Freud's work and psychoanalysis have had an enormous influence on difference aspects of our culture. Freud's influence is discussed in the following works: I. D. MacCrone, *Race Attitudes in Southern Africa* (London: Oxford University Press, 1937); J. C. Flugel, *Man, Morals and Society* (London: Duckworth, 1945); E. Fromm, *Psychoanalysis and Religion* (London: Gollanez, 1951); P. Rieff, *Freud, the Mind of a Moralist* (New York: Doubleday, 1961); A. Storr, *The Dynamics of Creation* (New York: Atheneum, 1972); D. Z. Phillips, *Religion without Explanation* (Oxford: Blackwell, 1976); P. Horden, editor, *Freud and the Humanities* (London: Duckworth, 1985); B. A. Farrell, *Introduction to Leonardo* by S. Freud, pp. 11–88 (London: Pelican Books, 1963), reprinted in *Leonardo da Vinci: Aspects of the Renaissance Genius*, edited by Morris Philpson (New York: George Braziller, 1966); D. E. Stannard, *Shrinking History* (New York and Oxford: Oxford University Press, 1980); P. Gay, *Freud for Historians* (New York and Oxford: Oxford University Press, 1985); B. A. Farrell, "Psychoanalytic Explanation, with special reference to Historical Material," in *Mindwaves*, edited by C. Blakemore and S. Greenfield (Oxford: Blackwell, 1987).

It is well known that students of psychoanalysis are apt to adopt firmly, and even strongly, held opposing views on the subject, which they also tend to present in an eristic way. For a sympathetic view, see R. Wollheim, *Sigmund Freud* (London: 1971); for distinctly unfavorable, F. Cioffi, "Freud and the Idea of a Pseudo-Science," in *Explanation in the Behaviour Sciences*, edited by F. Cioffi and R. Borger (Cambridge: Cambridge University Press, 1970); H. J. Eysenck, *The Decline and Fall of the Freudian Empire* (Harmondsworth and New York: Viking, 1985); and E. Gellner, *The Psychoanalytic Movement* (London: Paladin Books, 1985).